The Time-Life Gardener's Guide

GREENHOUSE GARDENING

A
REDEFINITION
BOOK

Other Publications:

AMERICAN COUNTRY
VOYAGE THROUGH THE UNIVERSE
THE THIRD REICH
MYSTERIES OF THE UNKNOWN
TIME FRAME
FIX IT YOURSELF
FITNESS, HEALTH & NUTRITION
SUCCESSFUL PARENTING
HEALTHY HOME COOKING
UNDERSTANDING COMPUTERS
LIBRARY OF NATIONS
THE ENCHANTED WORLD
THE KODAK LIBRARY OF CREATIVE PHOTOGRAPHY
GREAT MEALS IN MINUTES
THE CIVIL WAR
PLANET EARTH
COLLECTOR'S LIBRARY OF THE CIVIL WAR
THE EPIC OF FLIGHT
THE GOOD COOK
WORLD WAR II
HOME REPAIR AND IMPROVEMENT
THE OLD WEST

For information on and a full description of any of
the Time-Life Books series listed above, please call 1-800-621-7026
or write:

    Reader Information
    Time-Life Customer Service
    P.O. Box C-32068
    Richmond, Virginia 23261-2068

This book is one of a series of guides to good gardening.

The Time-Life Gardener's Guide

GREENHOUSE GARDENING

TIME-LIFE BOOKS, ALEXANDRIA, VIRGINIA

CONTENTS

There is something magical about a greenhouse. Within this glass-skinned, climate-controlled environment, gardeners can turn winter into summer and bring a breath of the tropics to the chilliest reaches of North America. Once the prerogative of professional nurseries and wealthy amateurs, greenhouses are now available in a wide range of shapes and sizes, designed to fit any home and budget.

The following pages provide a complete guide to the pleasures of indoor gardening. You'll learn how to pick the greenhouse that's right for you and how to arrange the interior to make the most of the limited space. You'll also find instructions on what kinds of plants to grow and how to give them the care and attention they deserve.

A troubleshooting section explains the special challenges that face greenhouse plants and the steps you can take to diagnose and correct any problems. There's a detailed chart that will show you how to force your favorite plants to bloom in time for a particular holiday or family celebration. Finally, there's an informative Dictionary of Plants with more than 150 cross-referenced entries.

4

MAKING
THE GARDEN GROW

5

CHECKS
AND BALANCES

6

DICTIONARY
OF PLANTS

1
A HOUSE WITHIN A HOUSE

A nurseryman walking the paths of a professional greenhouse cannot offer plants more specialized care than an amateur gardener lucky enough to own a modern window greenhouse. Prepackaged and architect-designed to fit windows of almost any dimensions and to satisfy most building codes, these small but exotic settings for plants offer every sort of environmental control—double- or triple-glazed windows, built-in heating devices, vents for air circulation and solar screens that in some models come with thermostatic controls that operate the screens automatically.

Possessed of such ideal growing conditions, the indoor gardener has the broadest imaginable choice of plants, keeping in mind that all the plants in the greenhouse should have compatible needs. The greenhouse can be a kitchen garden filled with culinary herbs, or a purely decorative display of luxuriant tropical plants or contorted cacti. A greenhouse set into a bathroom window provides an ideal environment for ferns, which thrive on warm moisture, and a window greenhouse in a workroom can become a forcing bed for starting young plants from seed that will, when spring comes, be moved outdoors. At the opposite extreme, it can even house a forest-in-miniature, filled with carefully tended bonsai.

For all these potential uses the one important element is the growing medium. For safety's sake, it should be a sterile soilless medium, since the greenhouse will lack earthworms to keep the soil aerated, and such natural predators as birds and praying mantises to eliminate plant-devouring insects. In the section that follows are recipes for such a medium, and instructions for planting seeds and transplanting seedlings in this rarefied atmosphere. There are also instructions for turning familiar plants such as azaleas, gardenias and small-leafed citrus into the subjects for bonsai.

A WINDOW
FOR GREENHOUSE GARDENING

Several potted plants—a hanging geranium, a fern, a pink hibiscus, a yellow chrysanthemum and an ivy—luxuriate on a sunlit shelf in a window greenhouse. Almost any window can be converted into such a greenhouse.

The main benefits of greenhouse gardening—year-round control of humidity and temperature—are within reach of any gardener. Without investing a lot of money or time, you can mount a high-quality, custom-fitted greenhouse in a window of your home—provided local building codes permit and provided you follow the manufacturer's instructions carefully. To find one, look through gardening magazines for the names of companies that manufacture window greenhouses, or consult the telephone yellow pages under "Greenhouse."

Before settling on a particular make and model, give some thought to choosing your site. A south-facing window, which provides maximum daily exposure to the sun, is best; but if you have no southern exposure, southeast or southwest will do. Window greenhouses can be affixed to any kind of wall surface: aluminum or wood siding, stone or brick. Installation usually requires removal of the window, but there are units designed to fit over existing windows; these are ideal for town-house and apartment dwellers. To ensure a tight fit, arrange to have a manufacturer's representative visit your home to measure the window.

The frame of a window greenhouse may be constructed of aluminum or of treated wood. Glass that is double- or triple-layered offers superior insulation. Most units come with interior shelves (you can usually add more if you want), a tray on the floor to hold pebbles and water to maintain humidity, and removable shade screens on the outside. Screens are necessary because temperatures in windows that get direct sun can rise as much as 20° F during the day. Good air circulation is also a must, for temperature control; the greenhouse vents should be conveniently located and easy to operate. To supply extra warmth in the winter, a small heater may be necessary.

You will need as least three other people to help you get started with installing a window greenhouse. For safety's sake, wear goggles when hammering.

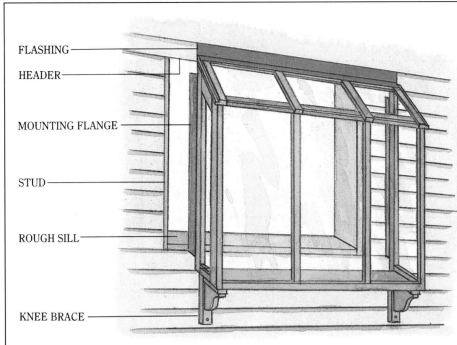

FLASHING

HEADER

MOUNTING FLANGE

STUD

ROUGH SILL

KNEE BRACE

THE STRUCTURE OF A WINDOW GREENHOUSE

Step-by-step procedures for mounting custom-made window greenhouses vary from manufacturer to manufacturer. But a typical unit (shown at left in an exploded diagram) is installed by slipping the mounting flange inside the studs (the sideboards that encase the rough window opening). Make sure that the bottom of the unit is level and flush with the rough sill (the bottom board of the opening) and the header (the top board). All sides of the unit should be flush with the walls. The flashing (fastened after the unit is in place) seals the seam where the unit joins the wall; the knee braces (also added later) support the weight of the unit.

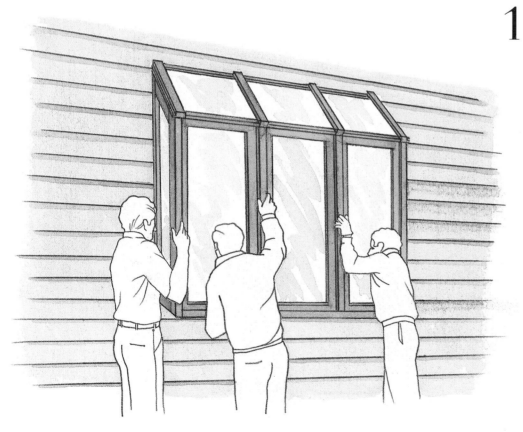

1 To prepare your site for a window greenhouse, remove the old window, leaving the studs and rough sill intact. Together with two or three other people, lift up the greenhouse unit and push it against the wall of the house (left); the mounting flange should be level and flush with the existing frame.

2 While your helpers continue to support the unit from the outside, enter the house and approach the window greenhouse from the inside. To secure the top and sides of the flange to the existing frame, hammer in galvanized nails at 10- to 12-inch intervals. Before hammering, place a piece of wood or a ruler against the base of each nail; this will guard against damaging the interior finish.

3 Cover the exterior seam where the top of the unit meets the outside wall with a strip of flashing *(below)*. This will prevent moisture and air from leaking indoors. On siding that is aluminum or wood, slip the flashing under the siding and screw it in place. On walls of brick and stone, procedures differ; follow the instructions provided by the greenhouse manufacturer.

4 With a standard caulking gun, caulk all edges of the flashing and all seams around the sides and bottom of the unit *(left);* the tighter the seal around a window greenhouse, the better for your own comfort and for the comfort of your plants.

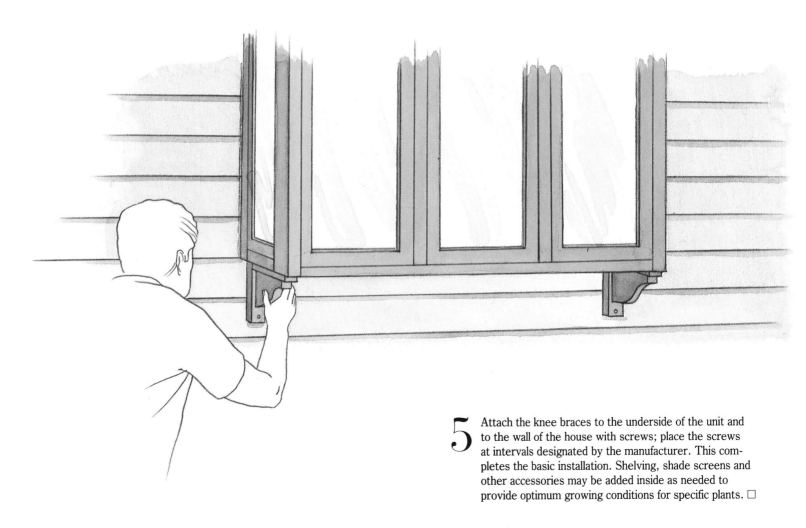

5 Attach the knee braces to the underside of the unit and to the wall of the house with screws; place the screws at intervals designated by the manufacturer. This completes the basic installation. Shelving, shade screens and other accessories may be added inside as needed to provide optimum growing conditions for specific plants. ☐

A SOILLESS MEDIUM
FOR HEALTHY PLANTS

Virtually all plants do best in a loose, well-drained growing medium that is free of diseases and harmful insects. Outdoors, earthworms act to aerate and loosen compacted soil, while bacteria, fungi and insects detrimental to plants are kept in check by animals and benevolent insects that feed on the harmful organisms. But in the closed environment of a greenhouse, neither worms nor insects nor animals are present, so it is best to use a sterile, soilless potting mix. You can make such a mix yourself. To do so, combine equal parts of ground peat moss, vermiculite, perlite and builder's sand. Avoid beach sand because of its high salt content. Use the horticultural coarse grade of perlite and vermiculite.

Each ingredient plays an important role in nurturing your plants. Peat moss aerates the mix, holds moisture and aids drainage. Vermiculite is porous and therefore retains nutrients as well as moisture. Perlite and builder's sand are both nonporous and shed water; and because their particles are of different sizes, they create air pockets that help drainage.

Most plants in a greenhouse prefer a pH of 6.5, meaning that it is slightly acid; pH measures acidity on a scale of 0 to 14, and the lower the number the greater the acidity. Since the soilless mix described above has a pH of 5.5, you should correct the acidity before planting by adding ground dolomitic lime.

The consistently warm temperatures in a greenhouse tend to lower the pH level, so test every eight to 12 weeks and correct as necessary. And since the soilless mix lacks adequate nutrients, add fertilizer that contains equal parts of nitrogen, phosphorus and potassium—a blend labeled "14-14-14" is ideal—plus trace amounts of sulfur, calcium, magnesium, iron and other elements. You can use ground or liquid fertilizer or slow-release pellets. If you buy pellets, get the kind that remain active for a few months.

On a sun-filled greenhouse workbench, an array of onion, marigold and parsley seedlings stands ready for transplanting into peat pots and a soilless growing medium. The growing medium is easy to mix in the greenhouse.

1 To make a large supply of potting mixture, combine in a wheelbarrow equal parts—2 to 2½ gallons—of each of the following ingredients: sterile ground peat moss, coarse-grade vermiculite, coarse-grade perlite and builder's sand. Then mix in ¼ cup each of ground dolomitic lime and slow-release fertilizer pellets.

2 With a watering can, add enough water to moisten the mixture so that the ingredients hold together. Mix thoroughly with a hoe or a trowel. Store the mixture in a clean garbage can. Cover to keep moisture in and harmful organisms out. Use as needed. □

STARTING PLANTS
FROM SEED

M ost gardeners agree that there is joy in nurturing a tiny seed and watching as it grows into a robust plant. And window greenhouses, with their controllable climates, are ideally suited for starting plants such as annuals, perennials, vegetables and herbs from seeds.

Success with seeds requires attention to details. Before sowing, the gardener should follow the instructions on the seed packet that indicate whether any presowing preparations, such as soaking seeds in water to soften the seed coat, are required. The instructions will also include spacing and depth recommendations for sowing, light requirements, optimum growing-medium temperature and the rate of germination.

For sowing, a shallow plastic pot or a plastic tray (called a seed flat) is best, since plastic enables the soil to retain more moisture than clay. Similarly, a soilless growing medium is a good choice because it retains moisture and is sterile. Seeds will sprout only if they are shallowly embedded in a growing medium that is kept moist and warm—65° F for most plants, 80° F for tropical varieties.

Any change in conditions, such as lower or higher temperatures, too much or too little light, or a dried-out growing medium, will terminate the germination process. A thermostatically controlled heating pad underneath the pot or seed flat guarantees an even temperature. Only pads designed for propagation should be used.

The growing medium can be kept moist by covering the pot or flat with plastic or glass, creating, in effect, a minigreenhouse within the window greenhouse. For seeds requiring partial light, place the pot or flat on a lower shelf where it will be shaded by plants above. If darkness is required, cover the seeds with a sheet of black plastic or a plate. When the seedlings have sprouted, remove the cover and keep them moist with a regular misting of water.

Vibrant pepper seedlings prosper on a sun-drenched shelf of a window greenhouse. With their easily controlled climates, greenhouses are ideal for germinating seeds.

1 Fill a shallow pot to within an inch or so of the top with a soilless growing medium. If the seeds are fine, sprinkle them over the surface; if they are large, space them at least ⅛ inch apart and top them with a loose covering such as perlite, vermiculite or peat moss.

2 Place the pot in a tray of water until water beads appear on the surface of the growing medium—an indication that the medium is saturated. Then remove the pot from the water tray and let it drain for one hour.

3 Place the pot in the window greenhouse and cover it with a sheet or a dome of plastic or glass. For seeds requiring darkness, cover the pot with a black plastic sheet or a plate. If necessary, use a specially designed heating pad to ensure a constant temperature. Keep the medium moist and remove the cover as soon as the seeds have sprouted. □

OUT OF THE SEED FLAT AND INTO A POT

Given enough light, moisture, warmth and nutrients, delicate seedlings can blossom into healthy, mature plants in a window greenhouse. However, to get them off to the right start, it is important to know when and how to transplant the young seedlings. Seedlings should not be transplanted until they have developed their second, or "true," pair of leaves. (A seedling's first growth is known as its "seed" leaf since it emerges from within the seed.)

Transplanting seedlings *(opposite)* is fairly straightforward. You will need several small pots filled with a well-drained, soilless growing medium. The seedlings are delicate and need to be handled with care. Never touch the fragile stems; instead, lift the seedlings by one of their leaves— preferably a seed leaf.

After transplanting, seedlings can be cared for in a window greenhouse. A south-facing window will provide adequate light, but seedlings should be protected from direct light immediately after transplanting, so place them on a bottom shelf for several days. Regular misting will keep the growing medium and foliage moist, and a liquid fertilizer added to the water every two weeks will supply adequate nutrients.

For optimum results, keep the temperature in the greenhouse at 70° F. To ensure constant heat in a cold climate, it may be necessary to install a thermostatically controlled miniheater in the greenhouse.

Seedlings are very susceptible to damping-off, a fungus disease that develops on the growing medium's surface and causes seedlings to wilt and rot. Too much moisture and poor air circulation can spread the disease, so it is best to open the greenhouse vents periodically. Also, water the seedlings in the morning so the surface of the soil is dry before night. A fungicide added to the water will also help prevent damping-off.

A young pocketbook plant thrives in the partial shade of a greenhouse. Pocketbook plants (so called because of their pocket-shaped blooms) are started from seed in late spring and transplanted to individual pots once they develop true leaves.

1 When the true leaves (the second pair) have appeared and the seedlings are ready to be transplanted, invert the pot and carefully remove the seedlings and the growing medium. To loosen the growing medium, it may be necessary to tap the bottom and sides of the pot.

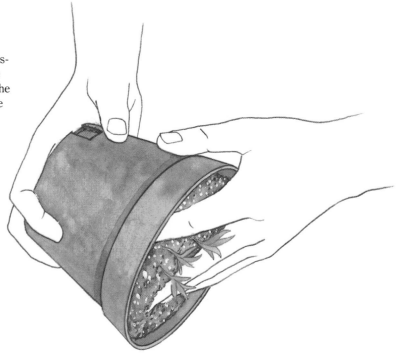

2 Gently separate one seedling at a time from the clump of growing medium and make sure the root system of each is intact.

3 Use a pencil or a stick to poke a hole in a small pot that has been filled up to within 1 inch of the top with fresh soilless growing medium. Holding the seedling by its leaves, lower the roots into the hole—taking care not to bend them—and gently tamp down the growing medium around the transplanted seedling. Make sure that the lower leaves are not buried and mist each seedling with a diluted fungicide solution. Water whenever the growing medium feels dry, and supplement with liquid fertilizer every two weeks. □

BONSAI: AN IDEAL OCCUPANT FOR AN IN-HOUSE GREENHOUSE

The dwarfed and carefully shaped trees and shrubs that the Japanese call bonsai are wonderfully adapted to window greenhouses—and vice versa. An azalea or a camellia trained as a bonsai can be the dramatic focal point in a sun-filled window, especially when the plant puts on its yearly show of blooms. A window greenhouse, for its part, provides precisely the environment a bonsai needs: lots of sunlight and warmth during the day and cool temperatures at night.

To start a bonsai, visit a good nursery and select a woody flowering plant with small leaves and a thick, strong main stem that will, when the plant is trained, look like the trunk of a tiny but mature tree. Good candidates besides azaleas and camellias include gardenias, star jasmines and small citrus trees. Watch for a specimen with a short trunk and irregular branching that will give the plant an unusual shape.

The next step is to decide what contour your bonsai should have when trained. The Japanese favor the five traditional contours shown opposite. After settling on one of these shapes, buy a pot that best enhances the chosen design.

Then place the plant in the container. As a general rule, slanting and cascading plants should be placed off-center; an upright plant should be centered if the container is round, square or hexagonal, but off-center if the container is rectangular or oval. Once the plant is established there, trim and guide it into the desired shape. This process, perfected by the Japanese centuries ago, is explained in detail on the following pages. Transplanting should be done in fall or winter, when the plant is dormant, to reduce the shock of being moved. Later, a bonsai made from a hardy plant like an azalea will need to be taken from its cozy greenhouse each winter and placed in a chilly but protected area where temperatures approach freezing. Hardy plants must go dormant to rebloom in the spring.

A handsome bonsai azalea, blooming lavishly, stands on a shelf in a window greenhouse. Following the Japanese ideal of subtle asymmetry, the bonsai is planted slightly off-center in its container and has an odd number of trunks—seven—that are of varying heights and thicknesses.

CONTOURS COPIED FROM NATURE

Japanese gardeners were inspired to begin making bonsai about 700 years ago by the windblown little trees they saw clinging to rocky coastal and mountain outcrops. Thus the traditional shapes shown below, all emulating trees stunted by their struggle to survive in stony, stormy environments. Which shape you choose is a matter of taste, but it makes sense to select one that is close to the natural contour of the plant you intend to train. All the bonsai below are azaleas, but the same training techniques *(pages 20-21)* apply to any number of woody plants.

CHOKKAN (UPRIGHT FORMAL)
A straight trunk and a symmetrical arrangement of horizontal branches. By tradition, this and other upright bonsai are planted in shallow containers.

MOYOGI (UPRIGHT INFORMAL)
A slightly crooked trunk with branches massed toward the top. For balance, this and other leaning bonsai should be planted a bit off-center in the container.

SHAKAN (SLANTED)
The trunk, growing straight for a few inches, then slants at a 45° angle, as if pushed by steady winds. Irregular branching adds to the illusion of wildness, and the plant is usually placed off-center.

HAN-KENGAI (SEMICASCADING)
With trunk and foliage bent outside the container, this bonsai appears even more storm-lashed than slanted ones. The container is high-sided and square, to help balance the leaning plant.

KENGAI (CASCADING)
The plant bends dramatically downward over one side of a tall, round container like a wild dwarf tree clinging to a rock and seeking shelter behind it.

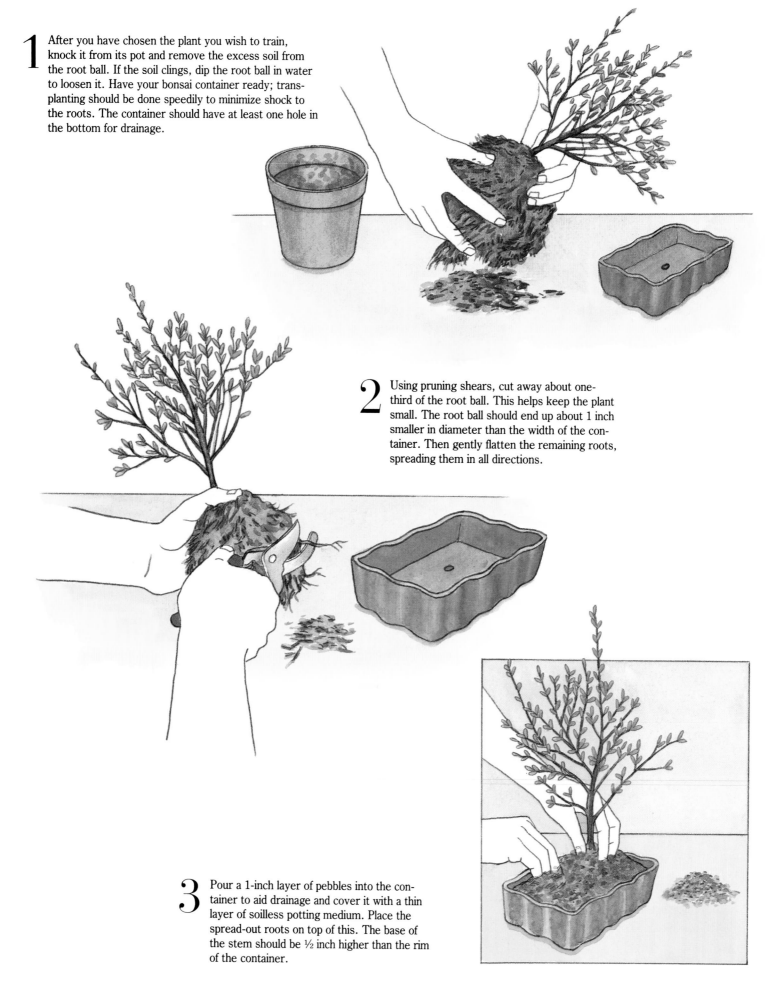

1 After you have chosen the plant you wish to train, knock it from its pot and remove the excess soil from the root ball. If the soil clings, dip the root ball in water to loosen it. Have your bonsai container ready; transplanting should be done speedily to minimize shock to the roots. The container should have at least one hole in the bottom for drainage.

2 Using pruning shears, cut away about one-third of the root ball. This helps keep the plant small. The root ball should end up about 1 inch smaller in diameter than the width of the container. Then gently flatten the remaining roots, spreading them in all directions.

3 Pour a 1-inch layer of pebbles into the container to aid drainage and cover it with a thin layer of soilless potting medium. Place the spread-out roots on top of this. The base of the stem should be ½ inch higher than the rim of the container.

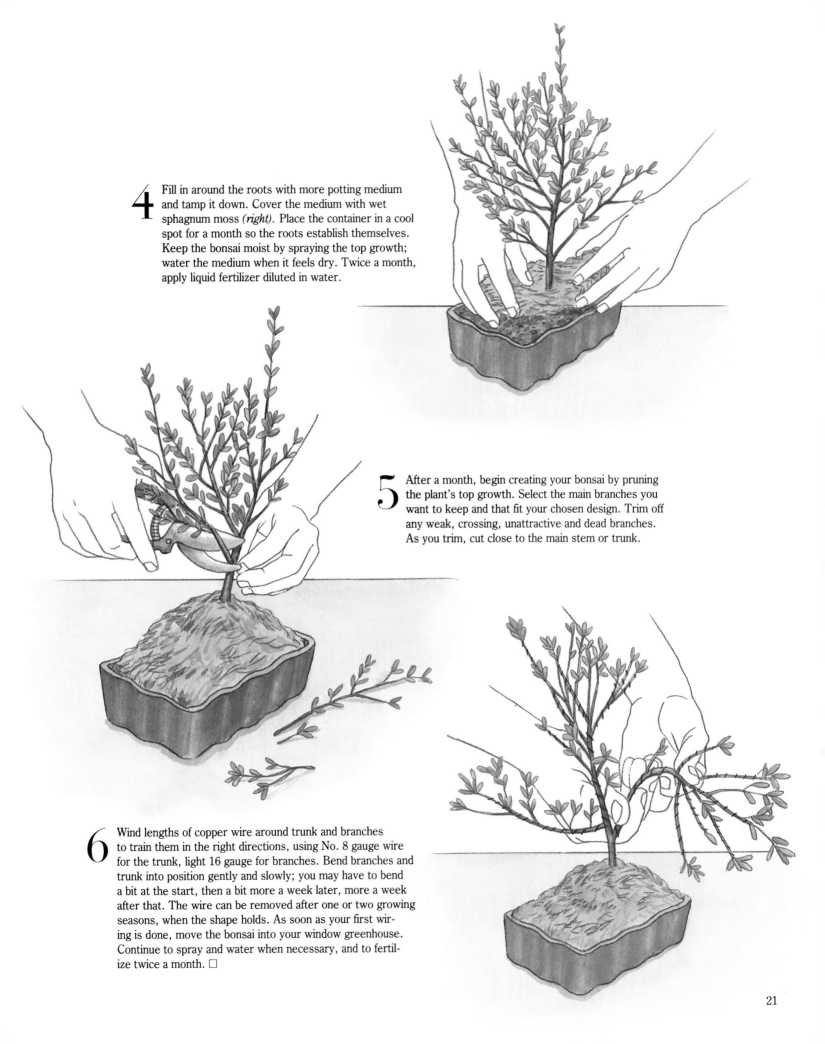

4 Fill in around the roots with more potting medium and tamp it down. Cover the medium with wet sphagnum moss *(right)*. Place the container in a cool spot for a month so the roots establish themselves. Keep the bonsai moist by spraying the top growth; water the medium when it feels dry. Twice a month, apply liquid fertilizer diluted in water.

5 After a month, begin creating your bonsai by pruning the plant's top growth. Select the main branches you want to keep and that fit your chosen design. Trim off any weak, crossing, unattractive and dead branches. As you trim, cut close to the main stem or trunk.

6 Wind lengths of copper wire around trunk and branches to train them in the right directions, using No. 8 gauge wire for the trunk, light 16 gauge for branches. Bend branches and trunk into position gently and slowly; you may have to bend a bit at the start, then a bit more a week later, more a week after that. The wire can be removed after one or two growing seasons, when the shape holds. As soon as your first wiring is done, move the bonsai into your window greenhouse. Continue to spray and water when necessary, and to fertilize twice a month. □

2
GLASS HOUSES FOR GARDENING

Greenhouses are almost as old as civilization. They were found among the ruins of first-century Pompeii. The Roman emperor Tiberius built one to guarantee himself a year-round supply of cucumbers. In the 17th century they spread throughout Europe, and in the 1800s they became something of a craze among the rich and the well-born of Victorian England. Happily, greenhouses are no longer the sole preserve of the fabulously rich, since they are available in a wide variety of shapes and sizes to suit nearly every pocketbook. The modern greenhouse is more versatile and more efficient than ever, and offers its owners the chance to nurse orchids in the dead of winter and to propagate delicate seedlings all year long.

For the gardener who wishes to start modestly, a window greenhouse or perhaps a lean-to model—so called because it literally "leans" against a house or other structure—may be the best choice; such a greenhouse draws on the heating, cooling and water systems of the house and then returns some of its own heat back to the house. Freestanding models are more expensive and require the installation of independent heating and cooling systems, but they provide more space and design alternatives.

After you have chosen the style of greenhouse that best suits your needs and means, you will want to turn your attention to designing its interior, for the secret of successful greenhouse gardening is maintaining just the right environment for plant growth. On the following pages are techniques for insulating and heating a greenhouse, do-it-yourself plans for building a handy workbench, and details on installing a self-watering system and how to use it.

SELECTING AND OUTFITTING
A MODEST MODERN GREENHOUSE

Once exotic luxuries that only royalty could afford, greenhouses today are within the reach of any gardener with a bit of extra outdoor space and a modest amount of money to spend on growing plants year round. And greenhouses are readily available —some by mail order—in a variety of sizes and shapes, from fairly roomy ones to small A-frames *(pages 26-27)*. One or another of them will fit almost any plot of land, or any budget.

These modern greenhouses come virtually ready-made, shipped by their manufacturers in prefabricated sections that can be assembled with relative ease. A dedicated do-it-yourselfer should be able to put together one of the smaller prefabs over a long weekend. A local builder can swiftly erect the largest of them.

The best of these mail-order glass houses are durable as well, and simple to maintain. The framing is usually of non-corroding aluminum or rot-resistant redwood. Some have sides of regular glass with roofs of shatterproof glass or clear fiberglass; the least expensive are covered with polyethylene sheets. The flooring can be simple or sophisticated—as long as it drains well. Gravel spread over dirt works well; paving of brick or flagstone is more elegant. As for the foundation, see the manufacturer's instructions, or consult the nearest agricultural extension office for suggestions.

After the greenhouse is built, it will need workbenches, a water system, and some means of heating, cooling and ventilating. The best ways to heat, cool, ventilate and manage water are shown in detail in the subsequent sections of this volume. The schematic drawing opposite shows the equipment any small greenhouse should have to make it able to accommodate plants in any season. How the heating system works is shown in detail on pages 28-29; how the cooling system works is shown in detail on pages 30-31.

Fitting snugly in an urban backyard, a neat aluminum-frame greenhouse shelters dozens of brightly blooming plants through an otherwise dreary, leafless season. The furnishings inside are simple but functional: a gravel floor, roof vents for fresh air and lots of counter space.

EQUIPMENT TO MAKE PLANT CARE EASY

The key to having a successful greenhouse is to control the environment inside, by maintaining the right temperatures, humidity and air quality for the plants. In winter, of course, cold seeps through the glass walls and roof, so some means of heating is needed. In summer (and on sunny days even in winter) excess heat builds up, requiring vents in the glass sheathing. The floor, the back wall and the water-filled containers standing under the workbench absorb and radiate solar heat. An evaporative cooling system having an exhaust fan on one outside wall to draw in cool air and drive out hot air also helps, as do sunshades that unroll and ceiling fans to keep the air circulating. It makes everything easier if some of these systems are automatically turned on and off as needed by thermostats. Then for nurturing the plants, and especially for propagating new ones, it helps to have water readily available—here a capillary system fed by irrigation tubes—as well as a misting device to spray seedlings and artificial lighting to spur the growth of young plants.

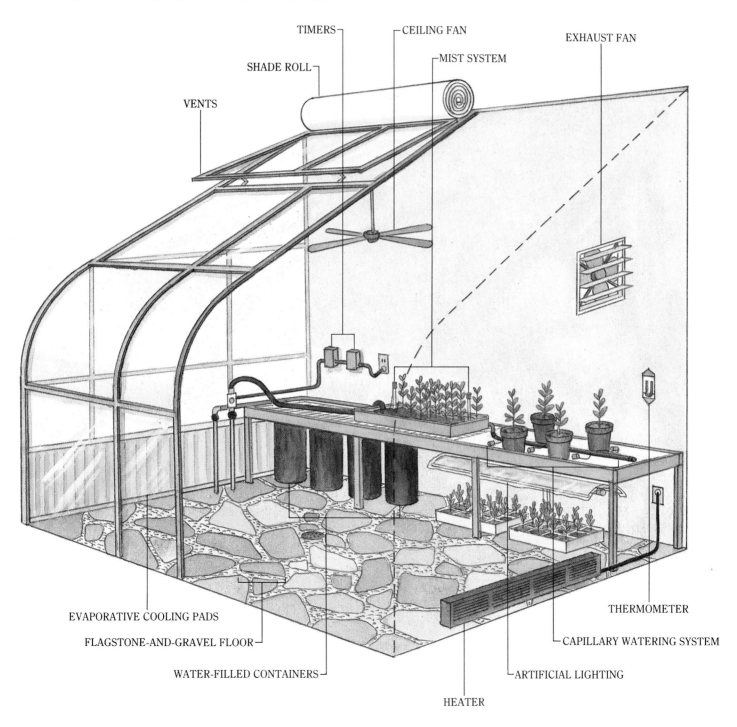

A WEALTH OF STYLES

The greenhouse models available from manufacturers run the gamut from space-age geodesic domes to box-like, peak-roofed models called even-spans. Most are freestanding structures, but you can also buy lean-tos—that is, glassed-in rooms that attach to your house. These in effect become bright sun-rooms as well as greenhouses, adding some welcome living space as well as providing a fine place for plants to flourish. □

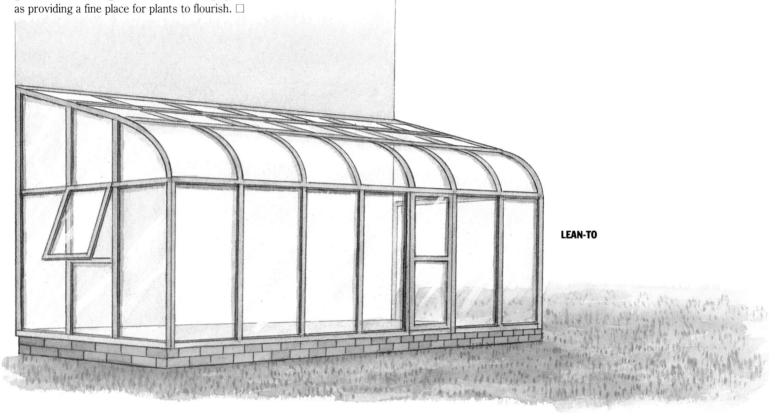

LEAN-TO

EVEN-SPAN

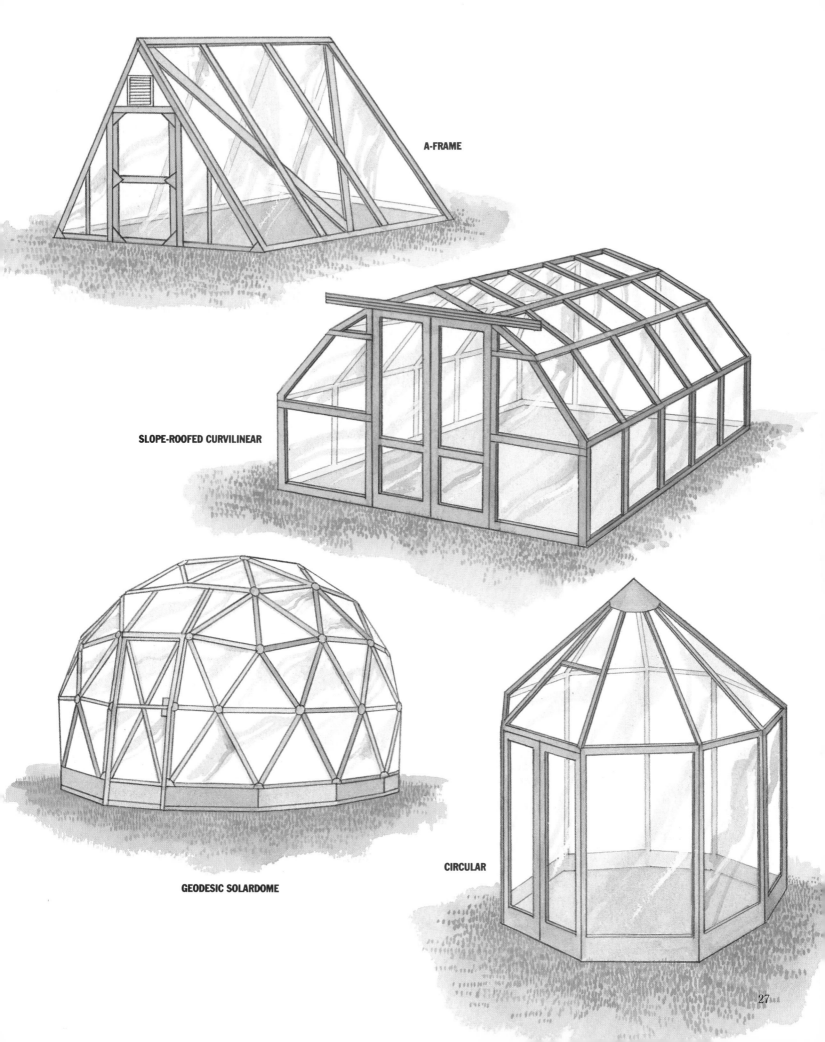

A-FRAME

SLOPE-ROOFED CURVILINEAR

GEODESIC SOLARDOME

CIRCULAR

27

EXPLOITING THE SUN
TO WARM A GLASS HOUSE

Rugged, corrosion-resistant drums of a sort used by industry simultaneously help support a greenhouse bench and hold water warmed by the sun. Water containers that radiate stored heat at night form a vital part of the heating system in a home greenhouse.

The least expensive and most efficient way to maintain needed warmth inside a greenhouse is to let the sun help out—with what is called a passive solar heating system. Such a system collects and stores the sun's heat, then radiates it when nighttime temperatures drop. Solar heating can provide up to 60 percent of the warmth plants need even when the weather is wintry.

Getting the optimum benefit from the sun calls for some planning. First, the greenhouse should be built so that it faces south—or at least southeast or southwest—to get maximum sunlight through the day. On its north side it should have one solid wall, as in the lean-to-style greenhouse diagrammed on the facing page. Made of insulated brick, stucco or concrete and painted a dark color, the wall will absorb solar heat. So will an insulated floor of dark gravel, brick or slate. Then, to collect still more solar heat, place some water-filled drums of dark-painted metal or plastic along the floor under the workbenches. The warmth stored in the water, walls and floor when the sun shines during the day will flow outward when the temperature drops.

Insulation is important, too. In areas where winters are cold, the glass surfaces of the greenhouse should be double- or even triple-glazed—there should be two or three layers of glass with insulating air space between them. The glass should be tightly caulked to prevent air from leaking in or out, and outside doors need weather stripping. For more insulation, there are curtains of quilted fabric, available from greenhouse equipment firms, that roll down the inside of the glass at night *(not shown)*.

Even with all this, a greenhouse will require some sort of heater that can be thermostatically controlled. How big the heater should be depends on the climate and the dimensions of the greenhouse. Consult a heating engineer or a county extension office for recommendations.

HOW SOLAR HEATING WORKS

The black arrows in the drawing below represent the sun's rays
shining through the glass of a lean-to greenhouse and striking the
slate-and-gravel floor, a stuccoed north wall and four water-filled
containers under a workbench. The wide red arrows show the cur-
rents of warm air radiating upward from the water tubs, wall and
floor and then being recirculated by a ceiling fan. The thermostatically controlled heater, located on the floor by one side wall, will turn
on when built-up solar heat has begun to dissipate. A thermometer
on the north wall, recording highs and lows within the greenhouse,
will help the gardener be sure the solar heating system and automatic
heater are working together to provide enough warmth, and to make
adjustments if necessary. □

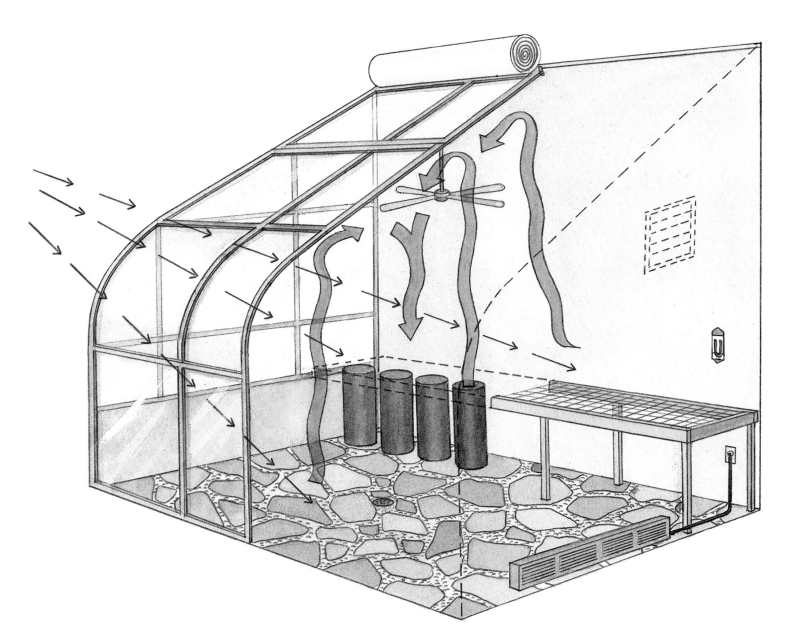

COOLING THE GREENHOUSE WHEN THE WEATHER HEATS UP

There are three primary ways to cool a greenhouse whenever the temperature builds up inside: vents in the glass roof, various shading devices and an evaporative cooling system. Simplest are the vents— movable glass panels (hidden under a shade in the illustration opposite) that open to draw hot air, which rises naturally, up and out. They also freshen the atmosphere in a greenhouse by drawing off excess humidity. Vents can be operated manually or hooked to devices that will open and close them automatically in response to temperature changes.

Shades that deflect or diffuse the sun's hot, direct rays come in several forms. Some are rolls made of cloth, or of thin wooden or plastic slats. Most such shades are installed on the outside of the glass and roll up or down as needed. There are also liquid shading compounds that can be sprayed or painted on the glass itself. Most versatile of these is a material that is sensitive to humidity levels. It becomes opaque, providing shade, when hot sunlight causes the humidity inside the greenhouse to drop, but turns clear and lets in needed sun when the temperature falls and the humidity rebounds.

In addition to shades and vents, most greenhouses should have an evaporative cooling system. One such system consists of thick padding of corrugated cardboard or pressed wood that is installed along the lower portion of one side wall, replacing the glass. Water drips from a perforated pipe above and runs down the face of the padding. A pump keeps the water recirculating. When the exhaust fan on the opposite side wall starts up, it will pull air through the wet padding. The moisture cools the air, lowering the temperature inside the greenhouse. There are only two drawbacks: the rest of the greenhouse glazing must be airtight for this system to work effectively, and in winter, the padding must be covered with wooden panels or plastic sheeting to keep out the cold air.

Three green-tinted shade rolls protect the southern side of a greenhouse—which is attached lengthwise to a shingled country home—from the intense rays of a summer afternoon sun. Together with vents and a fan or two, shades are vital to keeping a greenhouse cool during hot summer days.

DEFLECTING SUN, PUMPING AIR

A shade roll partially drawn down deflects the slanting rays of a summer afternoon sun *(black arrows)* in the drawing of a small greenhouse below. Shades like these can be drawn down farther on especially hot days, preventing even sharply angled morning light from striking delicate plants and beginning the day's heat-up. The larger arrows show the evaporative cooling system in action. Warm air drawn from outdoors *(red arrows)* by the exhaust fan on the opposite wall is cooled as it passes through the water-soaked padding in the lower wall; the fan continues to pull the cooled air *(blue arrows)* across the length of the greenhouse and drives it out as warm air. This sort of system is effective because evaporating water absorbs heat. Firms that sell greenhouse supplies offer ready-made and easily installed evaporative coolers. □

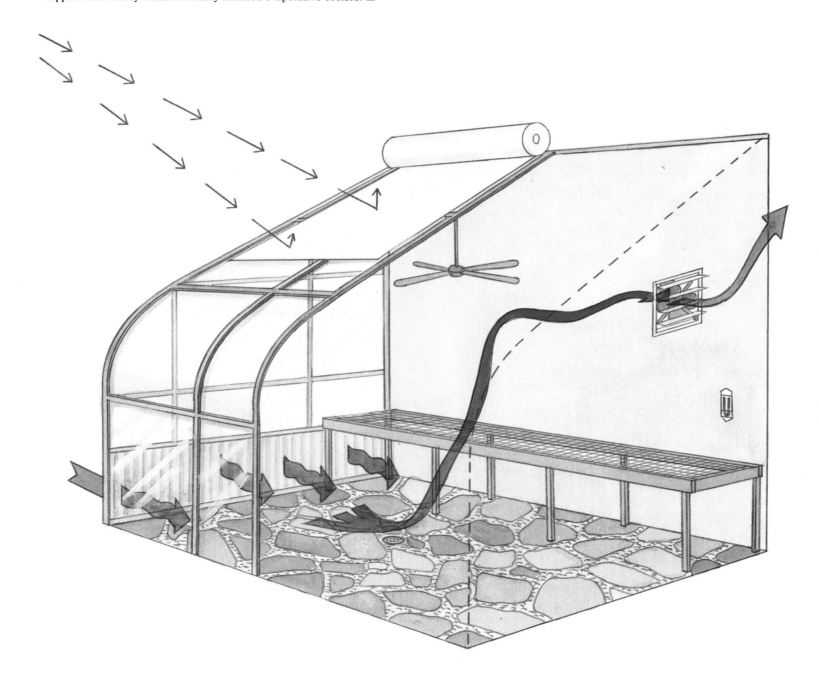

A DO-IT-YOURSELF BENCH
FOR WORK SPACE AND DISPLAY

A greenhouse is a place for working on plants and displaying the results of your labors. To make the work easier and the displays more effective, a good greenhouse bench is a necessity. You can buy such a bench—made from aluminum or treated wood with a slatted or mesh top to promote quick drainage—at a garden supply center. Or you can build your own with a few simple materials, some standard tools and one helper.

For the frame you will need five 2-inch-by-4-inch boards of treated wood—two to extend the length and three to form the width. To cover the frame, use wire mesh (1 inch by 2 inches or 2 inches by 2 inches) cut into a long rectangle. Support the frame with eight cinder blocks stacked two to a corner.

The dimensions of a homemade bench can be tailored to your specific needs. The mesh top should be about 3 feet high—or whatever height is right to prevent back strain. Since most people prefer work surfaces within easy reach, no area should be more than an arm's length from the edge. This means a maximum width of 3 feet if the bench is to stand against a wall; you can double that width for a freestanding bench that will be accessible from both sides. If the bench stands against the wall, be sure to leave a few inches between it and the bench to allow the air to circulate.

If your greenhouse is large enough, you may want more than one bench. Plan the layout ahead of time. Locate benches near a water supply but don't block windows or utility fixtures. For freedom of movement, make the aisles between benches at least 2 feet wide—3 feet if you expect to use a wheelbarrow or a cart.

While displaying plants on top of the bench, you can store empty pots and other supplies underneath. When you need a solid surface to work on, simply lay an extra board across the top, or suspend a board over an aisle between the ends or sides of two benches.

Pots of delicate begonias and vibrant geraniums stand on the wire mesh top of a homemade greenhouse workbench that doubles as display table.

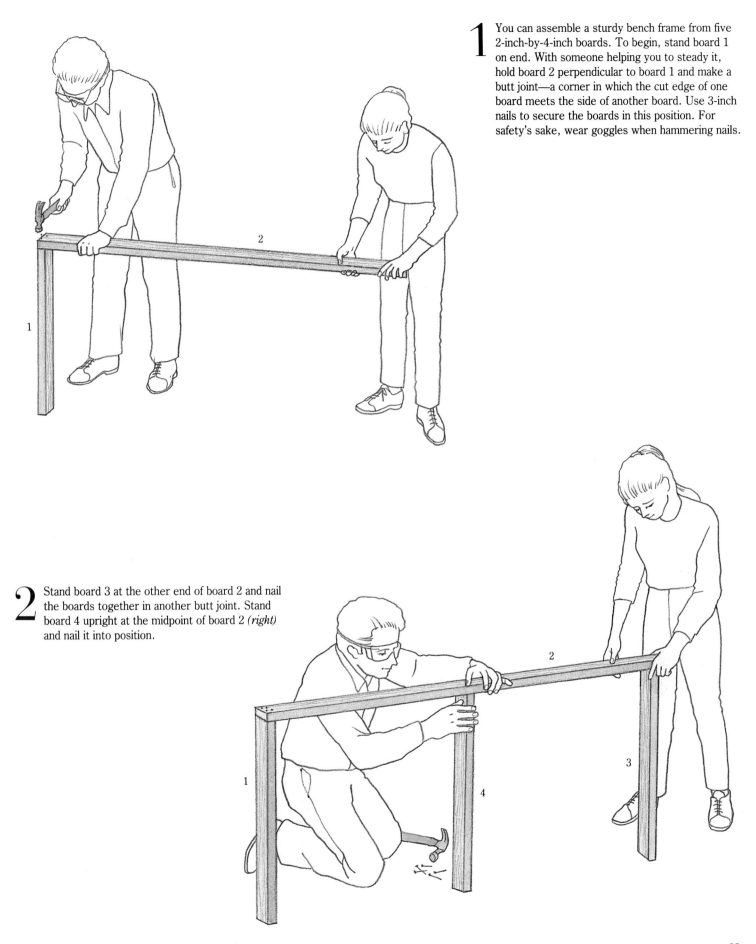

1 You can assemble a sturdy bench frame from five 2-inch-by-4-inch boards. To begin, stand board 1 on end. With someone helping you to steady it, hold board 2 perpendicular to board 1 and make a butt joint—a corner in which the cut edge of one board meets the side of another board. Use 3-inch nails to secure the boards in this position. For safety's sake, wear goggles when hammering nails.

2 Stand board 3 at the other end of board 2 and nail the boards together in another butt joint. Stand board 4 upright at the midpoint of board 2 *(right)* and nail it into position.

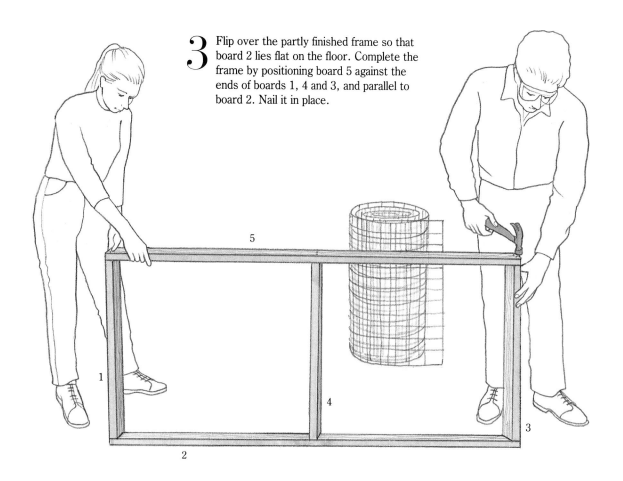

3 Flip over the partly finished frame so that board 2 lies flat on the floor. Complete the frame by positioning board 5 against the ends of boards 1, 4 and 3, and parallel to board 2. Nail it in place.

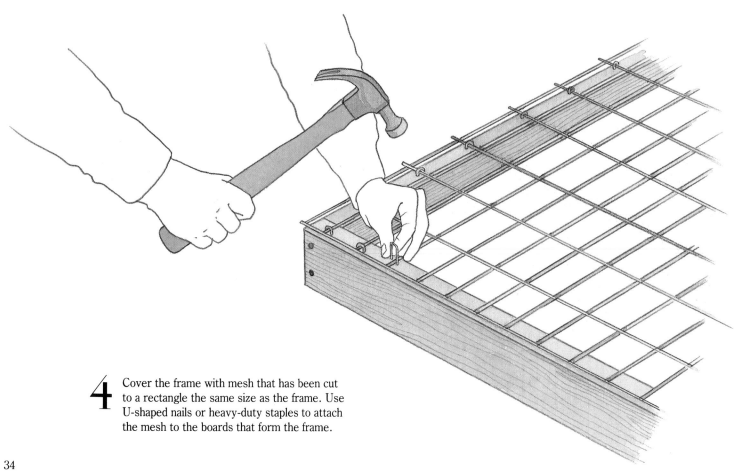

4 Cover the frame with mesh that has been cut to a rectangle the same size as the frame. Use U-shaped nails or heavy-duty staples to attach the mesh to the boards that form the frame.

5 To support the frame, stack four pairs of cinder blocks, each pair in the shape of an inverted T, underneath each corner of the frame. Balance the frame on the blocks, and the structure is ready to serve as a bench. ☐

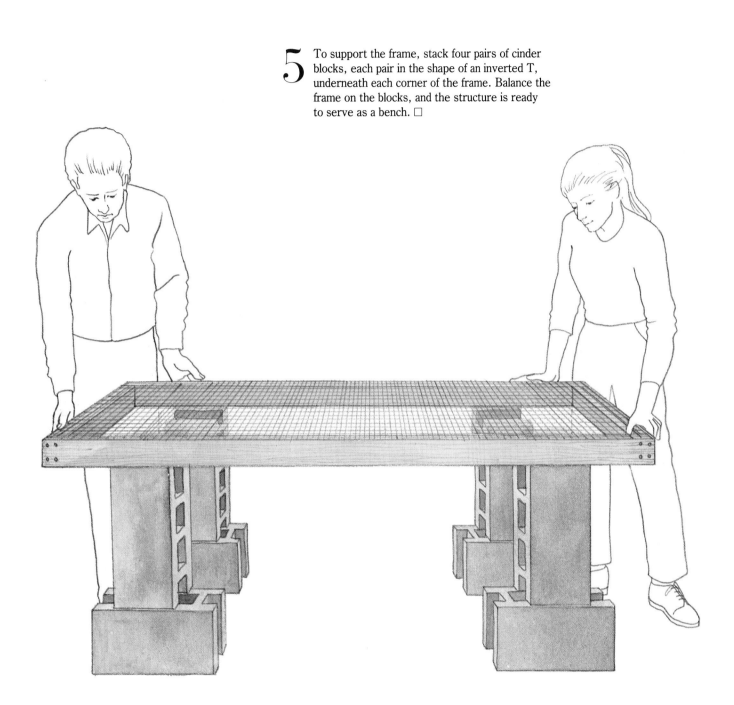

A WATERING SYSTEM THAT DOES IT ALL AT ONCE

All plants need water, but their needs vary widely. Most are thirsty and in sunny summer weather may require watering as often as every day; a few exceptions, such as cacti and other succulents, retain moisture and can go from two to four weeks without being watered at all. Whatever the plant, too little water will eventually cause browning and withering; too much can rot the roots. Supplying the proper amounts to individual plants by hand with a watering can would be a time-consuming and mind-boggling job that most gardeners lack the patience to do.

In the greenhouse, a practical solution to the problem is to install a system that can water dozens of plants simultaneously and safely, even in the gardener's absence. There are a number of systems capable of providing this service. One of the simplest and most reliable is a capillary system like that illustrated opposite.

Capillary watering provides moisture at the bottom of a plant, where the roots can absorb whatever amount of moisture the plant may require, instead of at the top, as is the case when watering with a can or a hose. In the greenhouse, capillary watering can be accomplished by covering an entire bench with a mat of absorbent material available in garden supply stores. When potted plants are placed on the wet surface, they draw up moisture through the drainage holes at the bottom of the pots. As the excess moisture from the surface material evaporates, it supplies beneficial humidity to foliage and flowers.

Capillary watering can be further simplified and made more efficient by adding a drip irrigation system. This is a length of pipe or hose fitted with a series of thin, spaghetti-like tubes that allow water to trickle from the main hose at intervals. The rate of flow is controlled by the amount of water released from the outlet valve. The system can be fully automated by adding a timer to turn the water on and off at set intervals.

The thin black tubes of a simple drip irrigation system provide a steady supply of water to a variety of potted greenhouse plants that stand on a capillary mat—a sheet of absorbent material that holds moisture for the plants and adds humidity to the atmosphere.

1 To install a capillary watering system, cover a bench with a plastic sheet to protect the surface and then cut a length of absorbent matting to the dimensions of the bench top. Place the matting over the plastic so that it lies flat and does not extend over the edges of the bench.

2 Place a drip irrigation pipe in the center of the bench so that it runs the entire length of the matting. Space the tubes on the matting at 12-inch intervals on both sides of the pipe. Connect the pipe to a hose attached to a water faucet.

3 Place potted plants alongside the irrigation tubes on either side of the pipe. Turn on the water and let it flow until the matting is wet to the touch; then turn off the water and let the plants remain until the soil in the pots has begun to dry. Or attach an automatic timer to the faucet so that the plants will be watered regularly at specified times. □

FERTILIZING WHILE YOU WATER
WITH A SIPHON PROPORTIONER

A hose attached to a siphon proportioner (located out of sight) showers a benchful of bright-leaved coleus plants, fertilizing and watering in one operation. The blue color of the water indicates the presence of the fertilizer.

Greenhouse plants should be started in a growing medium that supplies all the nutrients necessary for good health. But a few weeks of fast growth and frequent watering will deplete many of these nutrients, and you will have to begin fertilizing on a regular basis.

The three principal minerals that plants cannot do without are nitrogen, phosphorus and potassium. Nitrogen helps build healthy leaves, phosphorus enables plants to make new cells out of stored carbohydrates, and potassium is crucial to the manufacture of chlorophyll for photosynthesis. Also required, but in much smaller amounts, are calcium, magnesium, iron, sulfur, chlorine, boron, copper, zinc, molybdenum and manganese.

Fertilizers labeled "complete" contain all the necessary nutrients. Each blend is identified by a number giving the percentages of the three principal minerals in a fixed order; for example, a bag labeled "10-15-10" contains 10 percent nitrogen, 15 percent phosphorus and 10 percent potassium.

Either granular fertilizer or powdered fertilizer that is dissolved in water works well for greenhouse plants. Granular fertilizer, spread on the surface of the growing medium, is absorbed gradually; absorption of water-soluble powdered fertilizer begins almost immediately on application.

The easier of the two to use is the water-soluble powder, which is colored blue. Dissolve it in water according to the manufacturer's instructions. If you have a number of plants with similar nutritional requirements, an inexpensive device known as a siphon proportioner will allow you to fertilize automatically while you water, as shown opposite. A siphon proportioner automatically adds 1 part of fertilizer solution to 16 parts of water, so the original solution needs to be 16 times stronger than the manufacturer's instructions for a solution that is to be applied by hand.

1 To adapt the manufacturer's instructions for hand-fertilizing to a siphon proportioner, multiply by 16: for example, if the label calls for 3 tablespoons of fertilizer to 1 gallon of water, place 3 cups (which equal 48 tablespoons) of fertilizer in a 1-gallon bucket. Add a gallon of water and mix thoroughly.

2 Insert the proportioner siphoning tube in the bucket of fertilizer solution. Attach one end of the siphon proportioner to the faucet; connect a hose to the other end *(left)*.

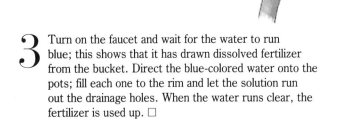

3 Turn on the faucet and wait for the water to run blue; this shows that it has drawn dissolved fertilizer from the bucket. Direct the blue-colored water onto the pots; fill each one to the rim and let the solution run out the drainage holes. When the water runs clear, the fertilizer is used up. □

A MOIST MICROCLIMATE
FOR PLANTS THAT LIKE HUMIDITY

Two maidenhair ferns sit in pots placed upon upended pots that stand in a tray filled with water. The roots are safely elevated above the water to guard against rotting. As the water evaporates, it humidifies the warm air around the ferns, providing them with the moisture they need.

Plants absorb moisture through their roots and release it through pores (known as stomata) in their leaves. Very dry air can act like a sponge, drawing too much moisture from leaves; if this excessive water loss goes uncorrected, plants may wilt and die. To keep the air around your plants properly moist, you must maintain a sufficiently high relative humidity in the greenhouse.

Relative humidity (RH) measures the relationship between the moisture-holding capacity of air at a given temperature and the actual moisture present in the air. When the RH is 100 percent, the air is saturated; if you try to add more moisture, it will condense out. Temperature plays a major role in determining relative humidity. The warmer the air, the more moisture it can hold. So if the temperature goes up but no moisture is added to the atmosphere, the RH goes down—and plants will start to lose more moisture to the air.

Most plants do best when the relative humidity is in the 50 to 70 percent range. In the consistently warm environment of a greenhouse, it is usually necessary to add extra moisture to the air. You will need an accurate hygrometer to measure RH and a humidifier to supply the moisture needed.

But some plants from the tropics thrive in a relative humidity of 80 percent. Since you don't want to keep your entire greenhouse at such a high RH, you can create small areas, or microclimates, of high humidity. One simple way to do this is to place a moisture-loving plant on a pebble-filled water tray; another is to place it atop an empty pot that has been inverted in a water tray. As the water in the tray evaporates, the RH around the plant goes up. And because the plant itself does not sit in water, there is no danger that its roots will rot. Both of these methods will also benefit plants growing in a window greenhouse or near a heater, where RH levels tend to be low.

MOISTURE FROM A BED OF PEBBLES

Use a shallow tray made of some nonporous material, such as metal, glass or glazed ceramic. Cover the bottom with a layer of clean pebbles or gravel. Pour in water to a level just below the tops of the pebbles. Place a potted plant on top of the pebbles. Water the plant as usual. As the water in the tray evaporates, replace it to the original level.

MOISTURE THROUGH AN INVERTED POT

Use a nonporous tray. Add 1 to 2 inches of water. Place a clean, empty pot upside down in the water tray. Balance a potted plant on the inverted pot. Water the plant as usual; excess water will drain out into the tray. As the water in the tray evaporates, add more to maintain the original level. □

SIMULATING NIGHT AND DAY
TO FORCE PLANTS INTO BLOOM

Once the heating and cooling equipment are in place, a greenhouse owner can use the glassed-in, temperature-regulated growing space to do some horticultural experimentation. One possible project is forcing plants to bloom. This sounds vaguely sinister, but it only means encouraging a few favorite species to flower out of season by manipulating light and dark. With a lamp or two and a shaded, lightproof area, it is easy to persuade fall-blossoming flowers to bloom in the spring, or to have fresh spring blossoms to cheer up the darkening days of autumn.

Forcing works because a majority of plants are biologically programmed to bud and bloom only when they get a specific amount of daylight and a set number of hours of darkness each night. Lilies and hibiscus are spring bloomers because their flowers respond to the short nights and long days of springtime. Poinsettias and other fall blossomers normally flower when the days have shortened and the world is dark for 12 hours or more out of the 24.

There are some mavericks, including roses and carnations, that bloom any time their buds are ready. But most species blossom only at preordained seasons—and therefore can be forced, if the seasons are simulated, to flower when the grower wants them to. The illustrations at right and opposite show how to install a shade table that will make nights longer as well as two sorts of lighting fixtures to lengthen the periods of daylight.

Several poinsettias put forth delicately colored pinky red bracts, the leaflike structures that "bloom" around the plants' actual, small, yellow-green flowers. Normally late-fall bloomers, poinsettias need at least 14 hours of darkness per day for 40 days to produce their bracts.

1 To begin setting up an area in your greenhouse that will provide darkness for plants requiring long nights to flower, attach upright posts at the corners of a workbench. The posts should be at least 1 foot taller than the plants you will be putting on the bench and covering.

2 Affix two lengths of wire between the upright posts, running them along the bench's two longer sides. The easiest way is simply to twist the ends of the wires around the posts. For greater neatness and permanence, drill holes in the tops of the posts and thread the wire through them.

3 Drape a lightproof black cloth over the wires so that it reaches across the top and encloses all four sides of the bench—with some extra hanging below to make sure no light leaks in. Heavy black cotton sateen is best for the purpose. Do not use what is called shade cloth; it is not thick enough. To determine how many hours the cloth should be in place each day to promote blooming of any given plant, consult the production schedule on pages 82-83 and the Dictionary of Plants at the back of this volume. □

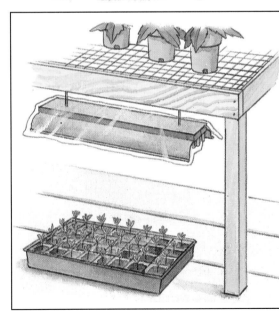

LONGER DAYS WITH ARTIFICIAL LIGHT

Plants that normally bloom during the long days of spring and summer can be forced to bloom at other, darker times of year by means of lamps using ordinary incandescent bulbs, such as the fixture at right shining on some potted lilies. The light emitted by incandescent bulbs includes the entire red wavelength, which promotes flowering. The bulbs get hot, though, and must be kept at least 1 foot from the plants to avoid scorching the foliage.

For nurturing plants during fall and winter, and in poorly lit areas of the greenhouse—such as underneath benches—fluorescent tubes can be used since they emit a far wider, more sunlike spectrum of light: they contain both the red and blue wavelengths necessary for plant growth. Be sure a fluorescent lamp has a shield to protect it from dripping water if it is used under a bench (left).

GIVING PLANTS A HEAD START
IN A PROPAGATION BED

Their young roots warmed by a buried heating cable, seedlings and cuttings thrive in a humid microclimate maintained by a three-nozzle misting system controlled by automatic timers.

The best way to raise large numbers of plants from seeds or stem cuttings is in an automated propagation bed that allows complete control of the environment and makes it possible to speed seed germination and root development.

To make such a bed, start by constructing a simple wooden frame. Use rot-resistant boards that are 6 inches wide and 1 inch or 2 inches thick. Place them on a greenhouse bench topped with slats or wire mesh to allow excess water to drain away. If the openings are large enough to let pieces of gravel fall through, first cover the bench with a plywood sheet in which you have drilled many small holes; then place the frame on top of the plywood. Add a layer of gravel and a layer of builder's sand.

To maintain warmth at about 72° F, lay an insulated, thermostatically controlled heating cable on top of the sand, then cover it with more sand and a layer of loose growing medium, such as a mix of half perlite, half vermiculite. By heating the bed from the bottom instead of through the air, you will save both energy and money; the air around seedlings and cuttings can be safely kept 10 to 15 degrees cooler than the growing medium itself.

An automated misting system—with spray nozzles connected to a buried plastic hose—will keep young leaves moist so young roots can grow strong. The delivery of water is controlled by two timers; one turns the entire system on by day and off at night, and the other triggers a gentle, even spray at intervals throughout the day. Have a plumber and an electrician install the misting system.

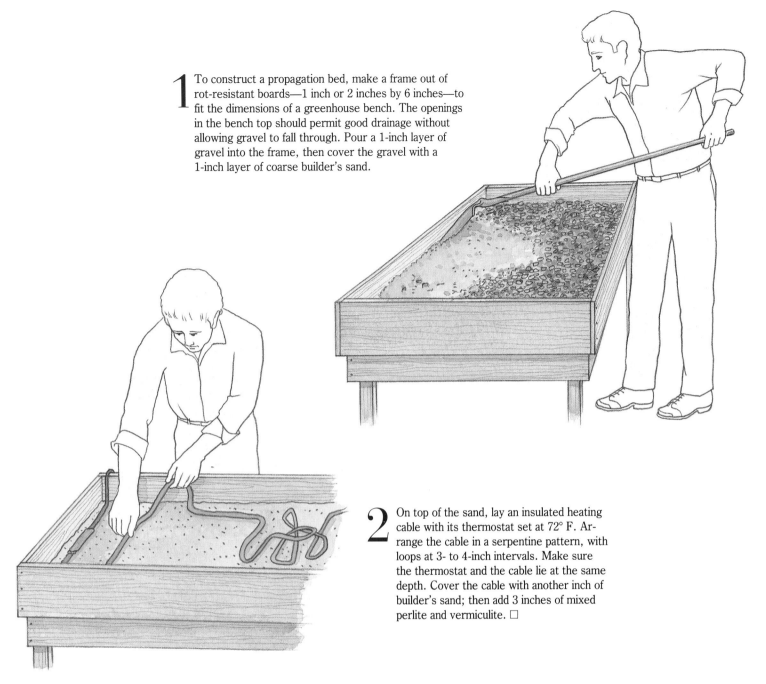

1 To construct a propagation bed, make a frame out of rot-resistant boards—1 inch or 2 inches by 6 inches—to fit the dimensions of a greenhouse bench. The openings in the bench top should permit good drainage without allowing gravel to fall through. Pour a 1-inch layer of gravel into the frame, then cover the gravel with a 1-inch layer of coarse builder's sand.

2 On top of the sand, lay an insulated heating cable with its thermostat set at 72° F. Arrange the cable in a serpentine pattern, with loops at 3- to 4-inch intervals. Make sure the thermostat and the cable lie at the same depth. Cover the cable with another inch of builder's sand; then add 3 inches of mixed perlite and vermiculite. □

ON/OFF MISTING

An automated system can be installed to give young plants precisely the moisture they need. In a typical misting system, a length of ¾-inch black plastic hose *(dotted line)* is buried in the growing medium. One end is plugged, the other end is connected to a solenoid valve that regulates water flow from an outside source. At intervals specified by the manufacturer, tiny tubes are attached to the hose and to fine-mist nozzles that rise 18 inches above the bed. Separate timers turn the entire system on and off, and deliver brief bursts of spray at predetermined intervals throughout the day. For safety's sake, the installation should be done by licensed professionals—a plumber and an electrician.

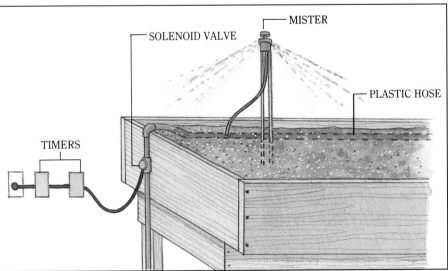

MISTER

SOLENOID VALVE

PLASTIC HOSE

TIMERS

3
EXPANDING YOUR COLLECTION

Greenhouse gardeners have an advantage over outdoor gardeners; they do not have to be slaves to nature's whims. The controlled climate of the greenhouse allows the luxury of reproducing plants with ease.

Soft-stemmed plants, such as wax begonias and dahlias, can be easily reproduced all year round in a greenhouse propagation bed. A stem cut from a healthy parent plant will soon root and reward the greenhouse gardener with a robust addition to his collection. Cactus plants, the mainstays of many greenhouses, can be propagated by grafting, a technique especially suited to them because all cacti are varieties of the same family and are therefore compatible. Another greenhouse favorite, the hardy tropical bromeliad, such as the sword plant and the urn plant, can easily be reproduced by transplanting its offshoots, or "pups."

Although many gardeners have devoted their lives to growing orchids, most greenhouse owners will admit that—given the right conditions—there is no great secret to propagating these beauties. Their rhizomes make them ideal choices for greenhouse propagation. Woody-stemmed plants, such as bougainvilleas, rubber plants and camellias, can be replicated by air layering (wounding a stem and then binding the wound in growing medium until it grows roots), a simple technique that is described on the following pages along with guidelines on propagating ferns from the microscopic organisms called spores they produce.

All of these propagation techniques—cutting, grafting, dividing, air layering and germinating spores—enable you to fill your greenhouse with exotica you couldn't grow anywhere else. More important, they allow you to explore the joys and conveniences of gardening throughout the year.

MULTIPLYING PLANTS
WITH SOFT-STEMMED CUTTINGS

A majority of greenhouse plants belong to species having soft, fleshy stems—that is, stems that are the opposite of tough and woody. This is a big plus when it comes to propagating new, young plants from older, established ones. The soft stems are easy to slice off and plant in a propagation bed; once there, given some care, they will produce fresh roots and turn themselves into fledgling plants. And this process has a built-in bonus: the offspring, when grown, will be exact copies of their parents. So using stem cuttings is an ideal way to create stocks of choice, favorite specimens.

To make stems grow roots properly, simply cut off sections measuring 2 to 4 inches with a small, sharp knife, as shown at the top of the facing page. The cut should always be just below a leaf node—the point where a leaf stalk meets the stem. Leaf nodes are natural growth spots; it is from them that the new roots will emerge.

To channel the cuttings' energy into making the roots, snip off any flowers and buds, and trim any leaves growing from the bottom 1½ inches of the stems. Then, after a dusting with rooting hormone powder *(opposite, middle),* plant the cuttings in a tray containing a soilless growing medium. The planting mixture should be kept moist and warm as the roots form; it is easiest to do this in a special propagation bed *(pages 44-45).*

The speed with which the roots grow will differ from one plant species to another. To test for root formation, tug lightly on the tops of the cuttings. If they feel anchored, the roots are probably large enough for transplanting. A second way of checking is to dig around carefully with a spoon, lifting up sets of roots. If they are an inch long, move the cuttings into individual pots. There, given normal care, they will grow into mature plants.

Blooming in dense clusters, wax begonias show their mottled red-pink-white blooms and their small, shiny, deep green leaves. Having soft stems, all species of begonia can be propagated from stem cuttings as well as from seed.

1 To reproduce soft-stemmed plants such as this begonia, slice off portions of stem at least 2 inches long, cutting just below the leaf stalks so as to include the node. To avoid spreading plant diseases, use a sterilized knife.

2 Trimming with the knife, remove flowers, buds and bottom leaves. Then sprinkle some rooting hormone powder on a piece of paper and dip the cuttings in it. The powder will encourage root formation.

3 Make holes slightly less than 1 inch deep in the growing medium with a small stick or a pencil. Insert the cuttings and firm the medium around them. When planting a number of stems, space them so that their top leaves do not touch. Label the tray with the name of the parent plant. Cuttings can be transplanted when their roots are 1 inch long. □

GRAFTING CACTUS PLANTS FOR LIVING SCULPTURES

This dramatic cactus is a creation formed by grafting a brightly colored top portion (a scion) of a plaid cactus to a green understock of a Peruvian apple cactus for strength—as well as a pleasing color contrast.

S ince all cacti belong to the same family and all varieties are therefore compatible, cacti are among the easiest of all plants to propagate by grafting—that is, joining the top growth of one plant (called the scion) to the understock of another. Cacti are grafted for a number of reasons. You might want to propagate a favorite variety that does not establish roots easily; you might want to preserve a cactus with a damaged or dying root system; or you might want to experiment with exotic sculptural effects, creating new combinations of colors and spine patterns.

For a graft to be successful, the two plants must be of the same size so that they can be joined at the layers of cambium—the tissue that lies just beneath the outer skin and manufactures cells necessary for new growth. The graft must be held tightly together until union is achieved.

In one kind of grafting, as shown opposite, a V-shaped indentation is cut into the understock and a matching V-shaped wedge is made in the scion. The two pieces are then fitted together and secured in place with rubber bands. While you work, the cut surfaces of the graft should be kept clean and moist; have all your tools and materials ready and work quickly to prevent undue exposure to drying air. After a few weeks you can test to see whether the graft has taken. Nudge the scion gently with your finger; if it does not move, union is under way.

The best time to graft cacti is during the growing season—spring and summer— when the transfer of life-giving sap through the cambium is most forceful. As with all cacti, water the new plant once every two weeks in the growing season, once a month the rest of the year.

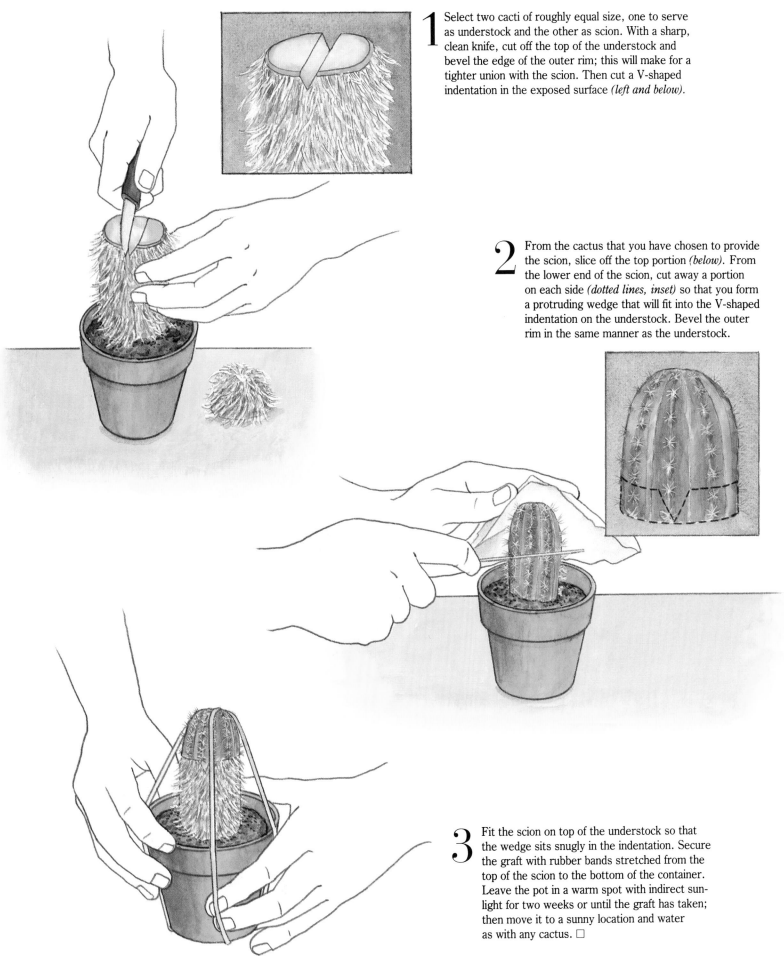

1 Select two cacti of roughly equal size, one to serve as understock and the other as scion. With a sharp, clean knife, cut off the top of the understock and bevel the edge of the outer rim; this will make for a tighter union with the scion. Then cut a V-shaped indentation in the exposed surface *(left and below)*.

2 From the cactus that you have chosen to provide the scion, slice off the top portion *(below)*. From the lower end of the scion, cut away a portion on each side *(dotted lines, inset)* so that you form a protruding wedge that will fit into the V-shaped indentation on the understock. Bevel the outer rim in the same manner as the understock.

3 Fit the scion on top of the understock so that the wedge sits snugly in the indentation. Secure the graft with rubber bands stretched from the top of the scion to the bottom of the container. Leave the pot in a warm spot with indirect sunlight for two weeks or until the graft has taken; then move it to a sunny location and water as with any cactus. □

HELPING BROMELIADS REPRODUCE AS THEY DO IN NATURE

The complex, many-petaled pink flower of an urn plant pokes up from the cup formed by some of the plant's broad, fleshy leaves. Like other bromeliads, urn plants give birth to the little models of themselves called pups, which can be split off and used to propagate new plants.

Sword plants, urn plants and other members of the exotic bromeliad family that are often grown as houseplants do especially well in greenhouse conditions. Being natives of the tropics and subtropics, they thrive in year-round warmth. And they particularly like the high humidity greenhouses offer, since their leaves—although often appearing tough and leathery—can absorb much of the moisture the plants need from the air. Given warm and humid surroundings, bromeliads require minimum care, and they produce handsome, often mottled, foliage and dramatic tropical blooms.

They are also easy to propagate because of the way they naturally do the job on their own. Bromeliads die a year or two after flowering, but before expiring they send out little copies of themselves called suckers or offsets or pups. These offspring appear at the base of the parent plant, often nestling in among the lower leaves.

When a pup has reached 2 to 4 inches in length, it can be separated from the parent. Pups that have not yet developed roots will need a bit of special treatment before being put in pots of their own. Those that already have small root systems can be planted right away in small pots. The planting mixture can be of any sort that drains readily and does not pack down. A ready-mixed potting soil will do if loosened up with some perlite and coarse, nonpacking sand. A fibrous material like fine-ground tree bark adds substance and some nutrients.

After potting, put the pup in a bright spot but not one that gets blazing sun all day. Water moderately but fairly often; the potting mixture should remain moist but not soaked. About every other week, fertilize with a liquid solution about one-fourth normal strength. It can be sprayed right onto the foliage; those absorbent leaves will quickly soak up the nutrients.

1 To propagate an urn plant *(right)* or other bromeliad that has produced an offset or pup, start by removing the parent plant from its pot. Isolate the pup with your fingers and wiggle it back and forth until it breaks off at the base. If it resists coming off, use a knife and slice the pup off cleanly and as near its bottom as possible.

2 If the pup has no roots of its own, set it aside for a couple of days to dry in the air and heal the wound where it was separated from the parent plant. Then pour some rooting hormone powder on a piece of paper and dust the base of the pup in it.

3 Fill a pot that has a drainage hole in the bottom with a light planting medium. Make a hole in the soil about ¾ inch deep and put the base of the pup in it. The surface of the medium should just reach the bottom of the leaves. Tamp down the medium so that the pup is firmly settled. Water the medium until it is moist; lightly spray some water on the leaves as well. □

MULTIPLE OFFSPRING FROM A SINGLE ORCHID

Thanks to their rhizomes—the specialized stems that grow horizontally on or just below the soil's surface—orchids are ideal plants for propagation by division. Rhizomes are an orchid's lifelines. When cut and transplanted properly, they will develop into new plants.

An orchid can be divided as long as it contains a rhizome, roots, a few pseudobulbs, leaves, and an emerging shoot, or lead, that develops from a bud at the base of a rhizome *(box, opposite)*. It is a good idea to soak a plant overnight before attempting to remove it from its pot—overgrown orchid roots tend to attach themselves to their containers. When dividing the plant, be sure to select a section of the rhizome that has three or four young pseudobulbs (to nourish the new plant) and at least one lead. The young pseudobulbs usually face front and lean forward, and should be allowed room to grow in their new pot. Therefore, when planting the new orchid, place the rhizome with its oldest pseudobulb against the side of the pot.

For potting, clay is a better choice than plastic because it is porous and allows for good air circulation around the roots. Whatever the container, it should be sterile and layered with pebbles to aid drainage. Orchids thrive in a loosely packed fibrous growing medium such as fir bark. However, they need to be treated with a high-nitrogen liquid fertilizer such as 30-10-10 every two weeks.

It is important not to divide orchids too frequently, or the mother plant's capacity for growth may be hindered. However, an orchid does benefit from division whenever it has grown too large for its pot. If its roots and pseudobulbs have grown over the pot, it is time to divide, as shown opposite and on the following two pages.

An elegant cattleya orchid shows the mature pseudobulbs (the swollen green stems in the center) that store the nutrients on which the plant grows and reproduces. When new shoots develop at the base of one or more pseudobulbs, the plant is ready to be divided.

ANATOMY OF AN ORCHID

Rhizomes are an orchid's source of new growth. The new growth begins with a bud that sends out roots at the base of last year's growth. As the bud develops, it becomes a "lead" that extends the length of the rhizome, turns upward and thickens into a shoot called a pseudobulb.

As the name implies, a pseudobulb is not a real bulb but a swollen stem that stores nutrients and water. One or two folded leaves emerge from the tip of this pseudobulb, and as a leaf unfolds, a flower sheath *(not shown)* appears and encases the flower buds, which blossom in about two months. After flowering, the sheath withers and the plant becomes dormant. During dormancy the pseudobulb ripens and the cycle reoccurs. The appearance of a new lead signals the time for division.

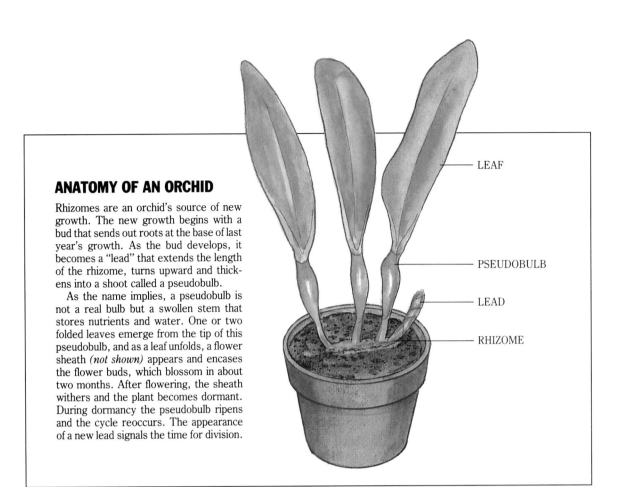

LEAF

PSEUDOBULB

LEAD

RHIZOME

1 To divide an orchid, choose a time when it has finished blooming and a new lead has appeared. Place the plant on its side atop a flat surface and gently tap the pot to loosen the orchid. It may be necessary to break the pot, but be careful to disturb the roots as little as possible.

2 Examine the orchid's rhizomes. For best results, choose a section of the rhizome that contains three or four pseudobulbs, at least one new shoot (the lead) and a good root system. Using a clean, sharp tool—shears *(above, left)* or a knife—cut through the root ball and the rhizome. Then, holding the orchid with both hands *(above, right)*, gently separate the new division from the mother plant.

3 To prevent the spread of disease, cut off any dead, mangled or broken roots and trim back healthy roots by one-third. Also trim any brown portions of the leaves and the outer skins of the pseudobulbs.

4 After trimming, wash the division with mild soap and water, and with a toothbrush gently scrub the top growth and undersides of the leaves to remove any insects, diseases or deposits that may have collected. Rinse with water.

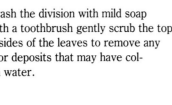

5 For potting, select a sterile, shallow container that will be large enough to accommodate two years' growth. If you use a clay pot, dip it in water first to saturate it with moisture. To aid drainage, add a 1-inch layer of pebbles to the bottom of the pot. Holding the orchid with one hand, position the oldest pseudobulb (the one farthest away from the lead) against the side of the pot and the top of the rhizome ½ inch below the rim. Fill the pot with fir tree bark, working it around the roots, and leave the top of the rhizome exposed.

6 If the plant does not have a good root system, it may be necessary to secure it with a U-shaped pin until its roots are established *(right)*. Water the orchid thoroughly and place it in a sunny location. Water it again whenever the fir bark feels almost dry, and give it a solution of 30-10-10 fertilizer every two weeks. □

WOUNDING WOODY STEMS TO ENCOURAGE NEW GROWTH

The stiff, woody stems of dracaenas, camellias, bougainvilleas and rubber plants are best propagated by air layering, a technique borrowed from nature's bag of reproductive tricks. In the wild, when trailing branches are forcibly bent to the ground by strong winds or the weight of snow and ice, the plant's circulatory system is obstructed and nutrients unable to get past the blockage build up in the stem. As blocked nutrients accumulate, the plant is stimulated to grow a second set of roots near the obstruction. If you wound a segment of a stem, you will cause an obstruction; if you place the wounded part in a moist medium, roots will develop. Then you can remove the entire top of the plant, together with the newly formed roots, and you will have another plant. This procedure does no harm to the parent plant, which grows a new top in time. The same technique can rejuvenate mature plants that have lost their lower leaves and become unattractively "leggy."

The easiest way to air-layer a plant is to score the stem with two horizontal knife cuts and peel away a section of the bark. Since roots will develop only in a moist environment, the wound should be wrapped in moist sphagnum moss and sealed in plastic.

The time required for air layering varies from plant to plant; some develop a new set of roots in a few weeks, others may take an entire growing season.

Framed by its glossy, dark green leaves, this dazzling camellia blossom testifies to the vigor of a shrub propagated by air layering.

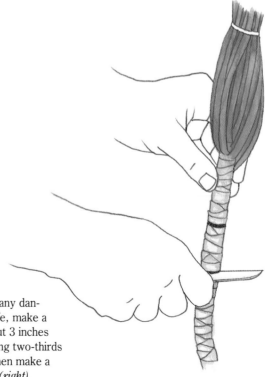

1 To prepare a plant for air layering, tie up any dangling top growth. With a sharp sterile knife, make a horizontal cut, just through the bark, about 3 inches below the lowest healthy leaf and extending two-thirds around the circumference of the stem. Then make a similar cut 1½ to 2 inches below the first *(right)*.

2 Starting at the lower cut, lift a strip of bark with the edge of the knife blade and peel it off *(right)*. Remove all bark between the two cuts. Brush the entire exposed area with rooting hormone powder.

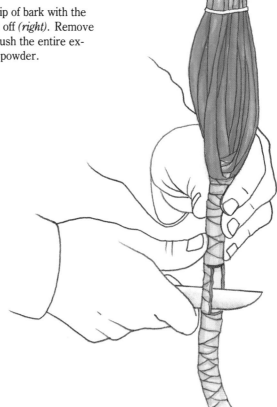

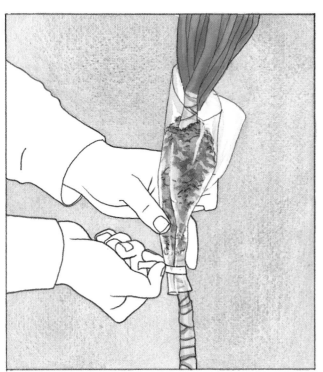

3 Moisten a handful of sphagnum moss and pack it around the wound. Then wrap the moss in clear plastic wrap, leaving no exposed strands. Seal both ends of this plastic "bandage" with water-resistant tape *(left)*.

4 After a few weeks (or longer, depending on the plant) you will see roots growing through the moss. Remove the plastic and discard it. Use pruning shears to cut off the stem just below the new roots. Plant the rooted stem in a container about 2 inches larger than the root ball. Water thoroughly. □

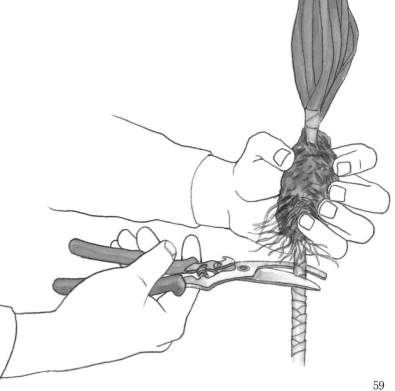

COLLECTING SPORES
TO PROPAGATE NEW FERNS

Four graceful baby maidenhair ferns, called sporophytes, rise above a low-growing cluster of leafy prothallia—tiny plants that reproduce ferns. The baby ferns, only four months old, will grow into mature plants within two years.

Equal doses of patience and understanding are the prerequisites for the successful propagation of ferns. Unlike other plants, ferns typically take up to two years—from germination to transplanting—before you can reap what you have sown. And to do so, you will need to understand the unique way in which ferns reproduce.

Ferns produce no seeds; instead they reproduce from clusters of sporangia that appear as small, round, rusty capsules on the undersides of fronds. Sporangia contain thousands of microscopic spores that, when released, fall to the ground and may germinate to become prothallia—tiny, heart-shaped, mosslike plants that contain both male and female reproductive organs. After fertilization, the prothallia's eggs develop into sporophytes—the fern's equivalent of seedlings. It takes approximately two years for these sporophytes to develop enough to be recognized as ferns.

To propagate ferns *(right)* it is necessary to simulate the conditions found in nature. After gathering fronds (from garden ferns in the autumn or anytime from greenhouse ferns), wrap them in paper and store them in a dry place. Within four or five days, the spores will fall out of their cases and be ready for germination.

The spores should then be planted in a flat container between two layers of a moist medium—preferably a lower layer of peat moss and vermiculite and an upper layer of sphagnum moss. The medium should be kept moist and be treated with a fungicide. The container should be covered with glass and placed in a warm location in filtered sunlight. In about two weeks, the prothallia will appear as a green moss.

After two years or so, when the miniature ferns—the sporophytes—have grown tall enough to touch the container's glass cover, they can be transplanted into individual pots.

1 After you have gathered fern fronds that have ripe sporangia—recognizable by the miniature brown, black or gold capsules on the undersides of the fronds—wrap them in paper (the sporangia side down) to dry. After four or five days, unwrap the fronds and collect the spores; they will have fallen from the sporangia and will look like fine dust.

2 Spread the spores evenly over a 1½-inch moistened layer of peat moss and vermiculite. Crumple sphagnum moss between your hands and sprinkle a thin layer of it over the spores to help retain moisture. Then mist the medium with a diluted fungicide.

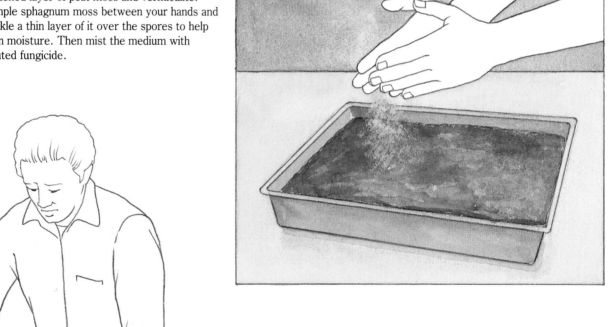

3 Cover the container with glass to keep the medium moist and place it in diffused light. Remove the glass and mist the plants with water periodically. In about two weeks a green mosslike growth (pro-thallia) will appear and begin to spread. If a whitish gold mold develops, spray it with fungicide. In two or three years, when the tiny ferns (sporophytes) have grown tall enough to reach the glass cover, they can be transplanted into individual pots. □

4
MAKING THE GARDEN GROW

1 To make a plant grow full and compact, remove the terminal leaf bud from each stem completely with your fingers. You can begin pinching off the terminal buds of several greenhouse plants—a chrysanthemum is shown here—when they are quite young, but not before the stems have developed several sets of leaves on each of their stems. As the plants grow and put out side branches, continue to pinch the terminal buds again when they develop, in a few weeks.

2 When flower buds begin to appear, you can encourage a chrysanthemum plant to put out especially large blooms. Use your thumb and forefinger to remove all the extra flower buds around the terminal flower bud *(above, left)*. The buds should roll off easily with a little pressure. Be sure to leave the terminal bud intact. Also remove the axillary flower buds *(above, right)* below the terminal bud. □

A BOUGAINVILLEA CANOPY FOR DAPPLED LIGHT

Climbing plants like bougainvillea, roses and passionflower fit beautifully into a greenhouse environment. They allow you to take full advantage of unused space overhead while affording natural shade to other plants that need to be shielded from the direct sun, such as camellias, African violets and most ferns.

Any vigorous plant with a long pliable stem can be trained to grow up a wire support that has been anchored to a glazing frame, a trellis or a brick wall. Some climbing plants, like passionflower, come complete with little tendrils that curl around a support and cling; all you have to do is guide the plant along the supports in the desired direction.

Bougainvillea, which has no tendrils, must be tied to its supports. But this fast-growing, colorful vine can be readily trained to arch across a wall or curve above a doorway or form a canopy parallel to the ceiling. Always keep the supports several inches away from the glazing, since contact with hot or cold glass can damage plants.

Start training bougainvillea early—as soon as the young stem droops under its own weight. Stretch a vertical wire support from a plastic container to the glazing frame. Wind the stem around the wire and tie it loosely with ribbons. As the plant grows, add new wire supports to guide the plant in whatever direction you choose.

When lateral shoots, or side branches, emerge, prune them back; this will encourage more flowering along the main stem. Or, if you prefer, you can allow some lateral stems to continue growing, and then treat them in the same fashion as the main stem— supporting their growth with wire. But take care not to overdo it. You don't want your bougainvillea canopy to become so dense that it cuts off all sunlight from the lower levels of the greenhouse.

The showy fuchsia bracts of a bougainvillea bring a welcome touch of the tropics to a greenhouse. Trained to form a canopy along the ceiling, it helps to filter and soften sunlight reaching other plants below.

1 Begin training a bougainvillea as soon
as its main stem starts to lean over.
Drill a hole in the top of a plastic container containing the plant. Through the
hole, thread one end of a length of wire
that is long enough to reach the ceiling.
Twist the wire around itself several
times to secure it. Drill a second hole
(or insert an eye hook) into the glazing
frame at the ceiling, and tie the other
end of the wire to it.

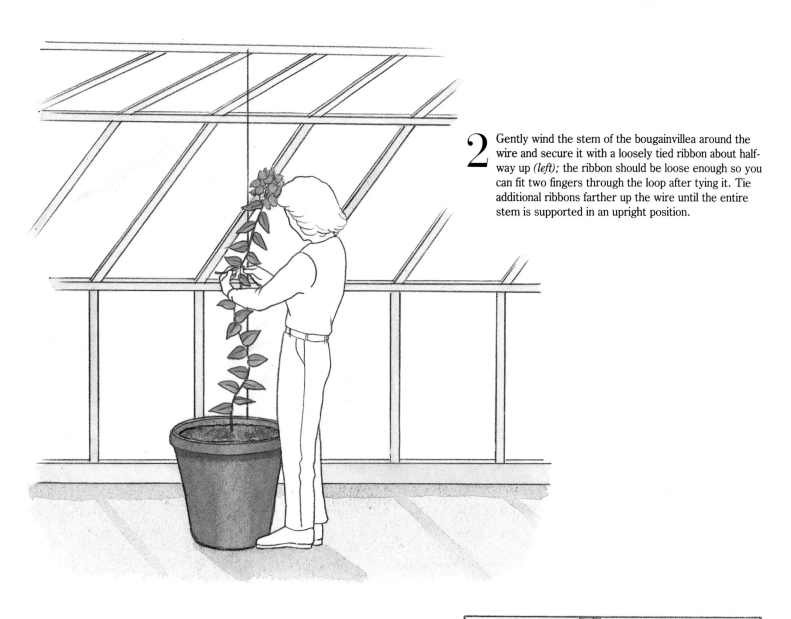

2 Gently wind the stem of the bougainvillea around the wire and secure it with a loosely tied ribbon about halfway up *(left);* the ribbon should be loose enough so you can fit two fingers through the loop after tying it. Tie additional ribbons farther up the wire until the entire stem is supported in an upright position.

3 The growing stem will put out lateral shoots, or side branches. If you want these to develop into long stems, add wire supports and train as with the main stem. Otherwise, prune the lateral shoots back to 1-inch stubs *(right)* to encourage the flower buds along the main stem to blossom.

4 When the main stem or side branches grow to the top of the greenhouse, you can attach more wire supports to the glazing frame and train the vine to make a decorative arch along one wall. Or you can hang wires horizontally just beneath the ceiling to coax the bougainvillea into forming a shady canopy *(above)*. □

BUILDING A HYDROPONIC GARDEN FOR MORE PLANTS IN LESS SPACE

The roots of these snapdragons drink deep of nutrient solution in a hydroponic system constructed in a lean-to greenhouse. Before being filled with white gravel, the wooden box was lined with sheets of black plastic.

Hydroponics is a modern word that means "working with water." It describes a type of gardening that delivers nutrients to plants in solution instead of relying on soil or some other standard growing medium. The basic concept is not new. The Hanging Gardens of Babylon incorporated hydroponic techniques. Modern variants have won a place in many a commercial nursery. But only recently have home gardeners been able to enjoy the benefits of "working with water."

Hydroponic gardening saves greenhouse space because roots fed directly by a nutrient solution don't have to spread out as much as they would in soil. And you have more precise control over growing conditions, since you determine exactly what nutrients your plants receive.

A hydroponic system is easy to build *(opposite)*. A basic system consists of a waterproof container, granular aggregate (such as pea-sized gravel) to support the plants as they grow, a water pump, an electric timer and a pair of rubber tubes—one to deliver the nutrient solution to the plants and the other to prevent the container from overflowing.

The aggregate will help retain nutrient-rich moisture around the roots; it also promotes drainage and allows air to reach the roots when the solution is drained from the system. Drainage is essential, since roots will drown if kept in water for more than 30 minutes at a time. Flood the bed with nutrient solution at least twice a day—more often during a hot summer—and let it drain completely. Set the timer to turn the pump on and off as required.

Many different nutrient formulas designed to be dissolved in water are available. Check the pH of the solution every few days and maintain it around 6.5. To lower pH, add white vinegar; to raise pH, add baking soda. Replace the old solution with a fresh batch every week or so. Flush the bed with clean water every two weeks to prevent a buildup of mineral salts that could damage plant roots.

1 To construct a simple hydroponic system, start by building a wooden box 12 to 24 inches wide, 8 inches deep and any convenient length up to the length of your bench. With a power drill, make two holes side by side in the bottom of the box near one end *(left)*. The holes must be large enough to allow you to insert the rubber tubes you have selected.

2 Line the box with 4- to 6-millimeter plastic. Using a staple gun, attach the plastic to the top rim of the box; trim any excess plastic from the edges. Cut an X in the plastic above each hole.

3 Through one hole insert a rubber tube until its top is 1 inch below the rim of the box; this will act to drain away overflow. To secure it, pull the corners of the X-cut plastic tightly around the tube and fasten them together with a hose clamp *(left)*.

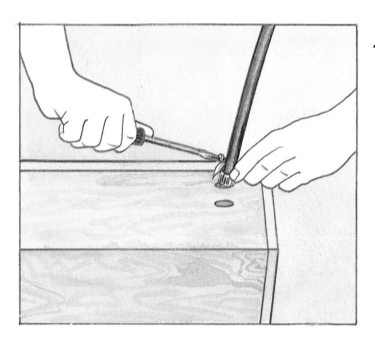

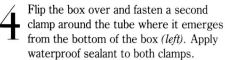

4 Flip the box over and fasten a second clamp around the tube where it emerges from the bottom of the box *(left)*. Apply waterproof sealant to both clamps.

5 To prepare to deliver nutrient solution to the system, drill several ¼-inch holes in the top 6 inches of a second rubber tube. Slide the tube through the second hole in the box, so that the top of the tube is 2 inches below the top of the box. Clamp and seal this tube inside and out, as you did the first. Close off one end with a tube stopper.

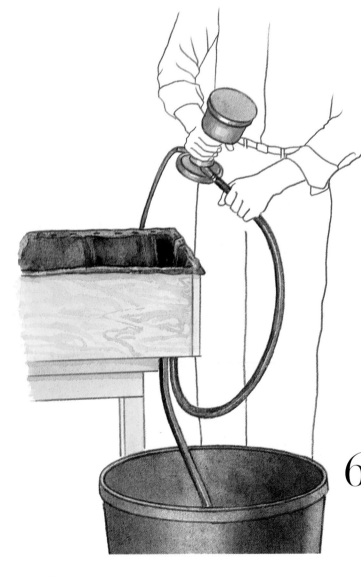

6 Connect the bottom end of the delivery tube to a small water pump *(left);* then set the pump inside a plastic trash can. Place the end of the overflow tube in the trash can as well. Plug the pump into an electric timer that will turn the pump on and off according to a preset schedule.

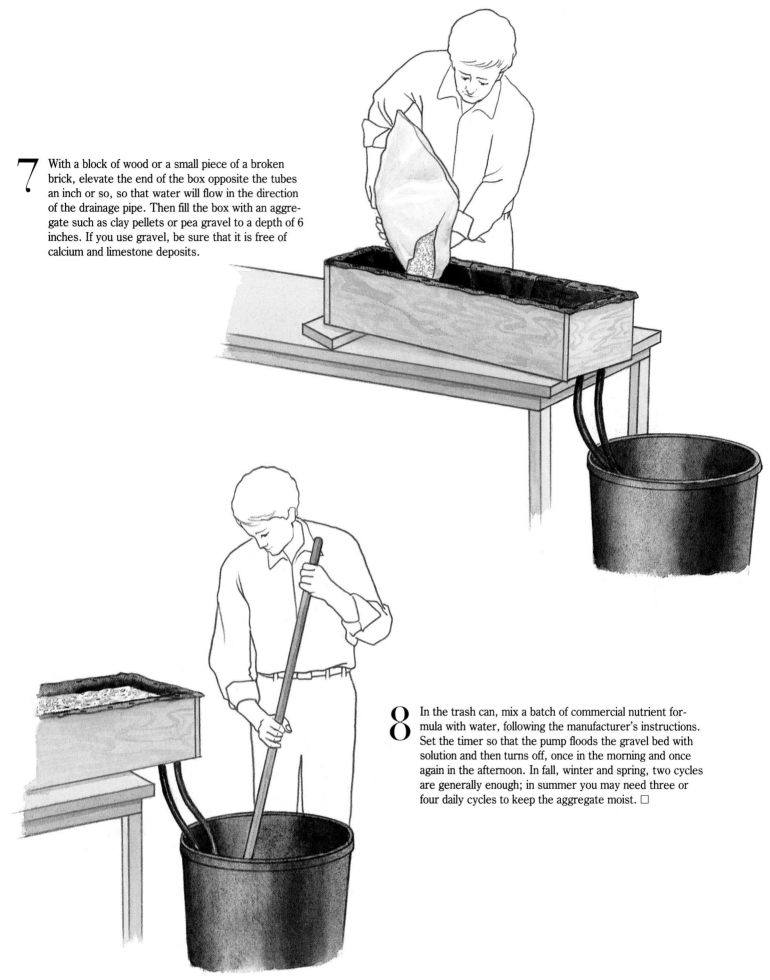

7 With a block of wood or a small piece of a broken brick, elevate the end of the box opposite the tubes an inch or so, so that water will flow in the direction of the drainage pipe. Then fill the box with an aggregate such as clay pellets or pea gravel to a depth of 6 inches. If you use gravel, be sure that it is free of calcium and limestone deposits.

8 In the trash can, mix a batch of commercial nutrient formula with water, following the manufacturer's instructions. Set the timer so that the pump floods the gravel bed with solution and then turns off, once in the morning and once again in the afternoon. In fall, winter and spring, two cycles are generally enough; in summer you may need three or four daily cycles to keep the aggregate moist. □

GROWING HYDROPONICALLY FOR FASTER AND BIGGER YIELDS

Standing in front of water-filled black drums that absorb and later give off the warmth of the sun, vining tomato and bean plants grow up out of a hydroponic bed, taking full advantage of available space by climbing up vertical support strings.

Almost any plant can be grown hydroponically. Vining plants are good because they can climb vertically, and tomatoes *(opposite)* are the most popular because when raised hydroponically they take up half the space of tomatoes grown in soil or in a standard soilless medium. They also produce more fruit and ripen as much as eight weeks earlier.

No matter what plants you intend to grow in a hydroponic unit, it's best to start from seed in a sterile medium. That way you won't have to clean soil from delicate roots or worry about soilborne diseases. For starting seeds, hydroponic foam cubes are ideal because they are made of a resin that retains moisture but drains well. After sowing the seeds, place the cubes in a tray of water to keep them moist. When the seeds have sprouted and roots are just visible, move the cubes to the aggregate bed; since you handle the cubes and not the plants themselves, damage to tender young roots is kept to a minimum.

Vining tomato plants that grow upright will produce more fruit if you cut off all but the strongest stem after the plant has had several weeks to grow in the aggregate bed. Also snap off any side shoots (known as suckers) when they are a few inches long.

Some varieties can reach a height of 25 feet, and as the main stem grows it will need to be supported. Run a length of string from the container to the greenhouse ceiling. When the stem gets long enough, tie it loosely to the string support with another piece of string. Then, when the plant reaches the top of its string support, coil the bare lower portion of the stem outside the hydroponic container and retie the fruiting portion to the string. Don't worry if the lower leaves drop off while the upper portion of the stem produces healthy foliage and fruit; this is quite normal. When the plant ceases to produce fruit, remove it from the aggregate bed and discard it.

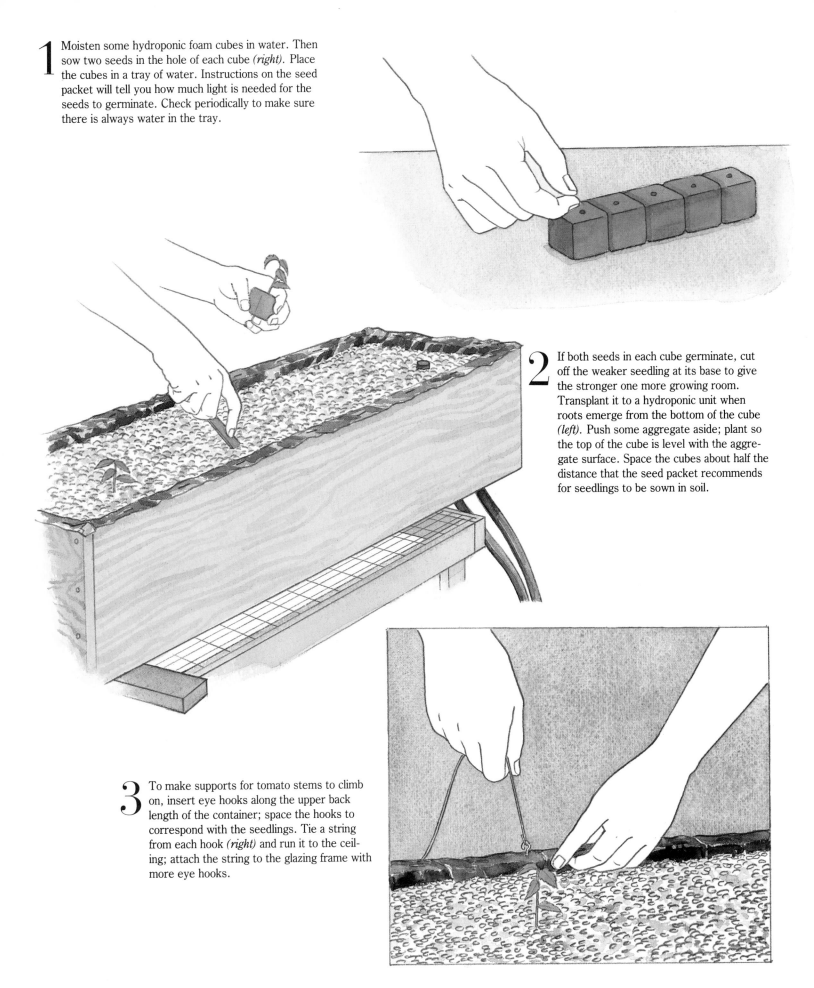

1 Moisten some hydroponic foam cubes in water. Then sow two seeds in the hole of each cube *(right)*. Place the cubes in a tray of water. Instructions on the seed packet will tell you how much light is needed for the seeds to germinate. Check periodically to make sure there is always water in the tray.

2 If both seeds in each cube germinate, cut off the weaker seedling at its base to give the stronger one more growing room. Transplant it to a hydroponic unit when roots emerge from the bottom of the cube *(left)*. Push some aggregate aside; plant so the top of the cube is level with the aggregate surface. Space the cubes about half the distance that the seed packet recommends for seedlings to be sown in soil.

3 To make supports for tomato stems to climb on, insert eye hooks along the upper back length of the container; space the hooks to correspond with the seedlings. Tie a string from each hook *(right)* and run it to the ceiling; attach the string to the glazing frame with more eye hooks.

4 After the seedlings have been growing in the hydroponic unit for several weeks, use a sharp clean knife to cut off all stems but the main one from each plant. Limiting a tomato plant to a single stem will actually stimulate it to produce more fruit.

5 When the main stem of each tomato plant has grown long enough to require support, train it to grow up the string; loosely tie it to the string support with another length of string *(left)*.

6 As the tomato plant grows and produces small side shoots that will sap the plant's energy, snap them off with your fingers when they are a few inches long *(right)*.

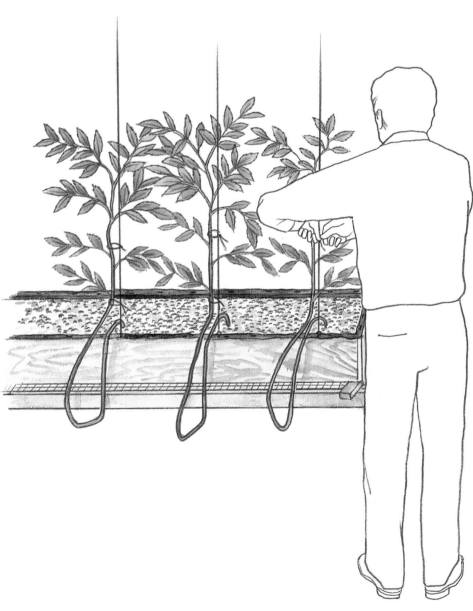

7 Pluck off fruit as it ripens. Then, as the plant grows taller and as the lower part of the stem loses its leaves, untie the growing tip from the top of the string support, lower the leafless bottom portion of the stem and drape it over the outside of the hydroponic container. Retie the fruit-producing portion of the stem to the string support *(left)*. Once the plant stops producing fruit, remove it from the container and discard it. □

5

CHECKS AND BALANCES

Gardening in a greenhouse is a heady experience. With so much of nature under control—heat, light, air, humidity—seasons and climates no longer seem to matter. Orchids and bromeliads can flourish while a blizzard rages outside, a rain forest of ferns can live in a desert, tulips can flower long before the green tips of their outdoor cousins have pushed through the ground and it is possible to have fresh-plucked tomatoes in February.

But in spite of all these botanical marvels, there are limits. Plants grown in a greenhouse must progress through their normal life cycle, even if on a stepped-up schedule. Thus, if nature decrees that they need a period of cold or darkness in order to fruit or flower, such a period must still be provided, artificially if necessary. And unfortunately greenhouse plants are prey to many of the same insects and diseases that attack them outdoors. Aphids, spider mites, mealybugs and mildew inhabit greenhouses, too. Indeed, they can often be more damaging, partly because the cosseted plants are less able to withstand them, partly because it is not always wise to use pesticides and fungicides in a closed environment.

In the following section are suggestions for dealing with some of these problems. There is, for example, a chart for timing the forcing procedures needed for various plants, a recipe for a bug trap that is a simple substitute for chemicals, and instructions for how to introduce natural predators, such as ladybugs and lizards, into the greenhouse environment. Among other helpful items are several on the production, care and treatment of flowers grown expressly for cutting—including information on growth hormones, instructions for constructing a stake-and-wire grid to keep flower stems upright, and advice on how to prolong the life of flowers once they have been cut.

BLOOMS ON DEMAND

Some flowering plants are traditionally associated with holidays: red poinsettias with Christmas and white lilies with Easter. But in nature, poinsettias flower in December only in their native tropical habitat, and Easter lilies don't begin blooming until midsummer. Florists are able to make these plants bloom for a holiday by controlling light and temperature levels to re-create the environment a plant needs in order to blossom. With a little planning, you too can control the life cycle of these and other plants in the greenhouse and force them to bloom earlier than they would in nature.

The chart below lists several plants that can be made to flower at a desired time by following this schedule, which lists the type of treatment and the amount of time needed for forcing. Some plants do best at certain times of year. Azaleas, for example, should be brought to bloom between mid-December and mid-May because they need the cool temperatures and short day length that winter and early spring provide. Although they can be made to bloom indoors at another time of year, making them do so requires extensive adjustments for day length and temperature. Other plants, such as carnations, can be made to bloom at any time of year because they do not depend on particular combinations of light and temperature to blossom; carnations flower as soon as they are old enough to produce blooms. With these plants, you can simply choose the date you want flowers, then count back the recommended 12 weeks to determine when you should begin.

The schedule is based on the time required for treatment in the greenhouse. Many plants can be purchased when they are ready for forcing. But some plants, such as bulbs like tulips, need to be chilled for several weeks before they are brought into the greenhouse. Detailed growing conditions for each plant are given in the Dictionary of Plants.

PLANT	TOTAL TIME REQUIRED	SELECTED BLOOM DATE	START DATE	TYPE OF TREATMENT
AMARYLLIS *Hippeastrum*	4 to 5 weeks	Mid-November through mid-May	Mid-October through April	Cool nights: 60° to 70° F for 3 weeks until flower buds form; then lower to 55° to 60° F.
AZALEA *Rhododendron*	8 to 12 weeks	Mid-December through mid-May	Mid-May through mid-August	Chilling period: 35° to 50° F for 4 to 8 weeks, then 60° to 65° F for 4 weeks.
CARNATION *Dianthus*	12 weeks	Any time, year round	12 weeks before desired bloom date	Cool nights: 50° to 55° F for 12 weeks.
CHRISTMAS CACTUS *Schlumbergera bridgesii*	12 weeks	December 15	May 1	Short days: shade cloth for 16 hours per night for 4 weeks from mid-September to mid-October.
CHRYSANTHEMUM	12 to 15 weeks	Any time, year round	12 to 15 weeks before desired bloom date, depending on the variety	Short days in summer: shade cloth for 12 hours per night for 5 weeks. Long days in winter: provide lighting for 3 hours per night for 4 weeks.

PLANT	TOTAL TIME REQUIRED	SELECTED BLOOM DATE	START DATE	TYPE OF TREATMENT
CROCUS	2 weeks	Mid-December through April	Early December through mid-April	Cool period: 50° to 55° F for 2 weeks.
EASTER LILY *Lilium longiflorum eximium*	17 weeks	Mid-March through late April	Mid-November through late December	Cool period: 63° to 65° F for 17 weeks.
FREESIA	10 to 12 weeks	Mid-January through April	Mid-January through April	Cool nights: 40° to 50° F for 12 weeks.
GRAPE HYACINTH *Muscari*	3 to 4 weeks	January through April	December through March	Cool period: 45° to 55° F for 3 to 4 weeks.
HYACINTH *Hyacinthus*	3 to 4 weeks	Late November through February	Late October through January	Cool period: 60° F for 3 to 4 weeks.
IRIS	10 to 11 weeks	Mid-December through mid-June	Early October through March	Cool period: 60° F for 10 to 11 weeks.
KALANCHOE *Kalanchoe blossfeldiana*	20 weeks	September through December	April through July	Cool period and short days: 60° F for 20 weeks; after 12 weeks, use a shade cloth for 14 hours per night until plants bloom.
NARCISSUS	4 weeks	Late December through mid-May	Late November through mid-April	Cool period: 60° F for 4 weeks.
POCKETBOOK PLANT *Calceolaria*	28 to 32 weeks	Mid-February through May	Mid-July through August	Cool period and long days: 50° to 58° F once seedlings are established. After 12 to 16 weeks, provide lighting for 4 hours a night until plants bloom.
POINSETTIA *Euphorbia pulcherrima*	16 weeks	Mid-December	Late August	Cool period and short days: 60° F for 16 weeks. Shade cloth for 15 hours per night for 5 weeks, from late September through early November.
THANKSGIVING CACTUS *Schlumbergera truncata*	12 weeks	Mid-November	Early April	Short days: shade cloth for 16 hours per night for 4 weeks, from mid-August to mid-September.
TULIP *Tulipa*	4 to 6 weeks	Late December through May	Mid-November through early April	Cool period: 55° F for 10 days, then 60° F for 5 to 6 weeks until plants bloom.

WHAT TO DO
WHEN THINGS GO WRONG

T he chemical insecticides, miticides and fungicides that are widely used to control pests and diseases are toxic substances and should be used with caution in any location. In the greenhouse, they call for strict attention to safety measures because the chemicals may enter heating and cooling systems, leave a residue on surfaces and remain in the air for a long time. The best control is vigilance. Inspect your plants regularly for early signs of pests or diseases, and spot-treat problems as soon as they arise—if possible by using non-poisonous remedies such as soapy water made with liquid detergent or insecticidal soap made from plant and animal fats; by sponging instead of spraying when you must use chemicals; and, when a chemical spray is the only remedy, by spraying sparingly on an infected leaf or plant instead of into the air at random. When the infestation is so severe that there is no recourse but to spray the entire greenhouse, shut all vents, close the greenhouse tightly and spray as quickly as possible. Wear gloves and a mask while spraying and leave as soon as you finish. Do not reenter the greenhouse until the spray has had time to dry, the greenhouse has been ventilated and there is no lingering odor of chemicals in the air. This may take from several hours to one full day, depending on the chemical; consult the label and follow the manufacturer's instructions.

PROBLEM	CAUSE	SOLUTION
Plants fail to grow. Foliage at the base of the plant turns yellow, wilts and dies. Stems and crowns are brown and soft at the soil line. Roots are brown or black, and may be either soft and wet or hard and dry.	Crown rot, root rot and stem rot, diseases caused by fungi or bacteria that thrive in wet soil.	There are no chemical controls. Damaged plants should be discarded. Water remaining plants sparingly. To prevent the disease from occurring, pot plants in fast-draining, soilless medium.
Seedlings develop brown areas on their stems, and suddenly topple over and die.	Damping-off, a disease caused by fungi that live in the growing medium and feed on the roots of young plants.	There are no controls for damping-off. To prevent the disease from occurring, drench pots and flats with a fungicide before sowing seeds and use only sterile soilless growing media. Do not overwater seedlings.
Stems, buds, leaves and flowers are covered with a fuzzy gray or brown growth. Flowers may not open or may be distorted. Leaves develop gray or brown spots and eventually turn yellow and die.	Botrytis blight, sometimes called gray mold, a fungus disease. It is most prevalent when humidity is high, night temperatures are low and light is low during the day.	Prune off and destroy infected flowers and foliage. In severe cases, spray plants with a fungicide. Decrease humidity and raise temperature. Give plants adequate spacing and keep the greenhouse well ventilated. Do not splash water on plants; botrytis blight spreads in water.

PROBLEM	CAUSE	SOLUTION
A fine, white powder appears on upper leaf surfaces, stems and flower buds. Foliage becomes distorted, turns yellow and dies.	Powdery mildew, a fungus disease. It is most prevalent when night temperatures are low and humidity is high.	Mildew may be washed off leaves with warm, soapy water. In severe cases, spray plants with a fungicide. Decrease humidity and raise the temperature at night. Give plants adequate spacing and keep the greenhouse well ventilated.
Citrus leaves develop small, semi-translucent spots that evolve into corklike bumps, and the fruits develop white or tan wartlike growths. Avocado leaves develop small red spots, and brown corklike bumps develop on the fruit. Cucumber leaves develop water-soaked spots and wilt. Fruits develop gray sunken spots that darken and enlarge with age.	Scab, a fungus disease that is especially active in high humidity.	Prune off and discard infected plant parts. In severe cases, spray plants with a fungicide approved for edible crops. Keep the greenhouse free of weeds and debris, where the scab fungus breeds. If cucumber plants are infected, do not plant cucumbers again for two years; they are susceptible to airborne spores that may remain in the greenhouse up to two years.
Leaves turn yellow, starting at the margins and progressing inward. Leaves eventually wilt, turn brown and die. Symptoms appear first at the bottom of the plant and progress upward. Growth stops and eventually the plant dies.	Wilt diseases caused by bacteria or fungi that live in soil and are especially active in wet soil.	There are no chemical cures. Prune off and destroy infected plant parts. Allow soil to dry slightly between waterings. To help prevent wilt diseases, use only sterile, soilless growing medium for planting. Purchase plants and cuttings that are certified free of wilt diseases.
Red, brown or black spots appear on leaves; each spot may be surrounded by a yellow halo. The spots enlarge and increase in number until they cover the leaves, which eventually die and fall from the plant.	Leaf spot diseases, caused by fungi and bacteria that are active in high humidity.	Prune off and destroy infected leaves. Increase ventilation and decrease humidity. Do not splash water on foliage; leaf spot spreads in water.
An orange powdery growth appears on the undersides of leaves. Leaves turn yellow and wilt. Plants cease to grow.	Rust, a fungus disease that is most prevalent in cool, humid conditions.	Remove and destroy infected foliage. In severe cases, spray plants with a fungicide. Keep the temperature above 70° F. Do not splash water on plants; rust spreads in water.
Leaves become mottled or streaked with yellow, light green, white or brown. Leaf edges may pucker or curl. Flowers may be deformed or streaked, or they may turn green. Plant growth is stunted.	Virus diseases.	There are no chemical controls. Isolate infected plants from healthy ones; if the condition persists, discard the plants and disinfect the containers before reusing them. The symptoms may disappear on their own. Viruses are spread by insects, which should be controlled. Purchase plants that are certified to be virus-free.

PROBLEM	CAUSE	SOLUTION
Leaves turn yellow and may be distorted in shape. Flowers may be deformed. Foliage may be covered with a clear shiny substance.	Aphids, 1/8-inch semitransparent yellow, green, pink, brown or black insects. Aphids suck sap from foliage and flower buds and secrete the shiny substance. They also spread diseases.	Aphids may be knocked off plants with a strong stream of water or they may be sponged off with household detergent and lukewarm water. Spray the plants with an insecticidal soap or, if the infestation is severe, an insecticide.
White streaks appear on foliage. Flower buds may not open; if they do open, the petals will have brown or pale margins, spots or streaks. Eventually, flowers and foliage turn brown, dry up and die.	Thrips, which are barely visible flying insects that hide and feed in buds, flowers and leaf axils. To confirm their presence, tap buds or flowers over a sheet of white paper. Thrips will fall onto the paper and can be seen. They may be yellow, brown or black.	Prune off and destroy infested buds, flowers and leaves. Install yellow insect traps (page 89). If the infestation is severe, spray plants and the surrounding growing medium with an insecticide. Keep the area around the greenhouse free of weeds and tall grass, which is where thrips breed.
When a plant is disturbed or moved, a cloud of white insects appears around the leaves. Eventually, foliage becomes mottled with yellow and plants cease to grow.	Whiteflies, tiny insects that cluster on the undersides of leaves and suck sap from the plants.	Install yellow insect traps (page 89). Spray plants with an insecticidal soap or, if the infestation is severe, an insecticide. Repeat applications are usually necessary for complete control.
Plants cease growing, turn yellow and wilt. Small flying insects are evident in the greenhouse.	Fungus gnats, 1/8-inch-long black flies. The gnats feed on organic matter in the growing medium, thus depriving plants of nutrients. The flies also spread diseases. The larval form, a 1/4-inch white worm with a black head, hatches in the growing medium and may feed on roots, bulbs and seedlings.	Install yellow insect traps (page 89). Spray affected plants with an insecticidal soap, and drench the soil with a liquid insecticide.
White or light green serpentine trails appear on leaves. Eventually the trails turn brown or black. Leaves lose color, dry up and die.	Leaf miners, 1/10-inch larvae of a fly. The miners create the trails by tunneling between layers of leaf tissue.	Prune off damaged foliage. If the infestation is severe, drench the growing medium with a liquid systemic insecticide.

PROBLEM	CAUSE	SOLUTION
Leaves curl, flowers dry up and turn brown. Small black spots appear on the undersides of leaves. Eventually, thin webbing will appear on the leaves or flowers.	Spider mites, nearly microscopic pests that may be green, yellow, red or black. Mites thrive in hot, dry environments.	Mist the undersides of the leaves regularly to help prevent and control infestation. Raise the humidity to above 50 percent. Spray the plants with an insecticidal soap or, if the infestation is severe, a miticide.
Jagged holes appear in foliage. Young seedlings may be completely consumed. Shiny silver streaks appear on plants, greenhouse benches and the floor.	Snails and slugs. They feed at night. During the day, they hide under pots and benches, especially in dark, moist places.	Inspect the greenhouse at night; slugs and snails may be removed by hand. Poisonous bait is available; it may be scattered on benches or on the floor. Keep the area around the greenhouse clear of vegetation and debris, which attract snails and slugs.
Small round or oval bumps appear along the stems and on the undersides of the leaves. Foliage may be covered with a waxy film or a shiny, sticky substance. Eventually, leaves turn yellow, wilt and die.	Scales, 1/8- to 1/4-inch insects that have round or oval shells. The shells may be green, gray or brown. Scales suck sap from the foliage and stems. Some secrete a waxy substance; others secrete a shiny, sticky substance on which diseases may breed.	Scales may be removed from plants with tweezers or with a brush. Wash the leaves with soapy water and rinse well. Spray the plants with an insecticidal soap or, in severe infestations, an insecticide.
Plants are stunted and foliage wilts and may turn yellow. Plant roots are abnormally short and thick and have knots or swellings.	Root knot nematodes, also called eelworms, which are nearly microscopic worms that live in the soil and burrow into plant roots.	There are no chemical controls. Discard infested plants. To prevent infestation, use only soilless potting medium.
Small white fuzzy growths appear on the undersides of leaves and at the points where leaves join the stems. Leaves may be covered with a clear shiny substance. Eventually, leaves turn yellow.	Mealybugs, 1/4-inch insects that have oval bodies covered with waxy white filaments. They suck sap from the leaves and stems, and may inject a toxic substance into the plant. They secrete the shiny substance.	Moisten a cotton swab with rubbing alcohol and dab it on the mealybugs to kill them. Wash plants with ordinary soap and lukewarm water, and rinse them. Spray the plants with an insecticidal soap or, if the infestation is severe, an insecticide.
Leaves curl inward and may be deformed and develop bronze or gray blotches. Flower buds may not open; if they do, the flowers are deformed.	Cyclamen mites, microscopic pests that feed on the crowns of plants and in flower buds. They proliferate in cool temperatures and high humidity.	Prune out and destroy damaged plant parts. Keep the humidity level below 80 percent. In severe cases, spray the plants with a miticide.

TIPS AND TECHNIQUES

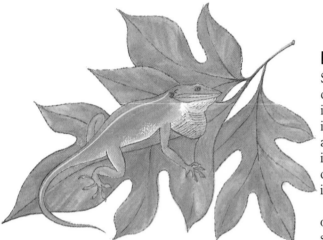

LIVE INSECT CONTROLS

Some destructive plant pests can be controlled with beneficial insects and lizards. Certain insects and lizards do not damage plants, but prey on the insects that do. These helpful creatures can easily be brought into a greenhouse.

Some insects feed on only one or two types of troublesome pests, so select the right type of predator for the insects you need to control. Ladybugs feed on aphids; lacewings feed on aphids as well as mealybugs, spider mites, scales, thrips and whiteflies. Parasitic nematodes feed on fungus gnats and predatory mites feed on spider mites. Some greenhouse-supply and specialized mail-order firms sell predatory insects.

Lizards feed on a variety of insects, and they can be brought into the greenhouse to help keep insect populations under control. The most commonly available lizard is the chameleon *(above),* which can be purchased at pet stores. For the average-sized greenhouse, three or four chameleons should suffice.

Insecticides should not be used in combination with lizards and beneficial insects.

WINTER'S GROWTH

In winter, when the greenhouse is tightly shut, the level of carbon dioxide drops and many flowering plants and vegetables stop growing. You can keep your plants growing, flowering and producing fruit through the winter by opening windows and vents during the day to admit outside air—and with it, carbon dioxide. To compensate for the cold, you may need to raise the temperature by turning on the heater. Alternatively, you can purchase from a greenhouse-supply firm small, specially designed gas burners that produce carbon dioxide. To be useful, they should be operated only during daylight hours, since plants photosynthesize only in daylight. Before starting the burner, turn fans off and close vents to keep the carbon dioxide inside the greenhouse.

SUPPORTING LONG-STEMMED FLOWERS

Part of the beauty of cut flowers is the burst of color they provide atop long, straight stems. Long-stemmed flowers grown for cutting, such as carnations, chrysanthemums, roses and snapdragons, need to have their stems supported to keep them growing straight. Individual stems can be staked, but this is a time-consuming process. Instead, you can make a simple grid system of stakes, wire and string to guide and support the stems of all your plants in planting benches.

Attach a stake or a board to each corner of the bench. Run a length of sturdy wire around the four stakes about 6 inches above the bench. To make a grid system *(right),* tie a piece of string to the wire on one side of the bench, then stretch it straight across the width of the bench and tie it to the wire on the opposite side. Repeat the procedure, tying parallel strings to the lengths of wire at 6-inch intervals. Then tie more strings across the length of the bench so they are perpendicular to those you just attached.

As the plants grow, each is supported by a square of string so the stems will remain erect and straight. When the plants are about 9 inches tall, add another tier of wire and string supports 6 inches above the first. Continue adding tiers as needed.

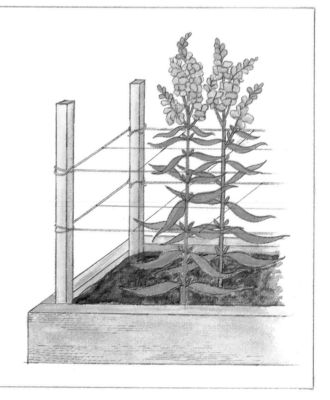

IT'S IN THE BAG

One of the simplest ways to grow vegetables and annuals is to plant them in the plastic bags that prepared soilless growing medium comes in. The medium is commonly available in 2-quart, 4-quart, 8-quart and 16-quart bags. A 4-quart bag can hold two tomato plants, eight lettuce plants, 10 wax begonias, six geraniums or four nasturtiums (above).

There are several advantages to planting in such bags. You don't need to prepare any soil mix for planting, the bags are easy to move and they can be kept almost anywhere there's space—on greenhouse benches or on the floor. Prepared medium needs little maintenance, since it is sterile and free of insects, diseases and weed seeds. The medium will retain moisture longer than it would in pots since it is enclosed and there is little evaporation. And once you harvest your flowers and vegetables, you can simply toss the bags away.

To plant, first cut crosses in the top of a bag where you want to place the plants; use the same spacing as you would in the garden. Punch a few small holes in the sides of the bag for drainage and then moisten the medium thoroughly. Some packaged growing media already contain fertilizer, which will be indicated on the label. If the mix you are using does not contain fertilizer, add some according to the directions on the label. Put the plants in the crosses and firm them in place.

COMPACT PLANTS

Even in the ideal greenhouse environment, some flowering plants, such as chrysanthemums, geraniums and poinsettias, tend to become tall and lanky. The usual way to keep such plants compact and full is by regular pruning or pinching of stems. An alternative is to use plant hormones, which are called growth regulators. There are several types of growth regulators; some are made from organic plant hormones and others are made from synthetically produced compounds. They can have several effects on a plant. Some inhibit the growth of plant stems. Some induce early flowering and profuse side branching. Some also cause the plant to produce a larger number of flower buds.

Some growth regulators can be sprayed directly onto plants; others are liquids meant to be poured onto the soil or growing medium after plants have been watered. Not all growth regulators work on every plant; check the label to see if a regulator is recommended for the plant you wish to treat. One treatment is usually sufficient, and should be made at the start of a plant's annual growth cycle, when it begins to produce new shoots.

A LONG LIFE FOR CUT FLOWERS

You can extend the life of your cut flowers by following a few simple guidelines for treatment before and after you cut the flowers from the plant.

Before you cut, fill a bucket with warm water—about 100° F —and add a floral preservative to the water. Cut the flowers in the afternoon, when their sugar content is highest. Place the stems in the bucket immediately after cutting. Before you arrange the flowers, recut all of the stems under water so they can absorb the maximum amount of water. Then place the flowers in a cool, dark area for several hours to condition them. They may be kept in a refrigerator, provided there are no fruits or vegetables stored there —fruits and vegetables release ethylene gas, which can damage flowers.

Whenever you arrange cut flowers, place them in a clean container and add a floral preservative to the water. Change the water every few days, recutting the stems underwater each time the water is changed. Keep cut flowers out of direct sun and away from heat and drafts.

MAKING YOUR OWN INSECT TRAPS

To help keep flying insects under control in the greenhouse without the use of chemicals, you can buy ready-made traps— or you can make your own. Most traps are nothing more than yellow cardboard or paper covered with glue. Several insects, including winged aphids, fungus gnats, thrips and whiteflies, are attracted to the color yellow. The hue draws the insects to the cards, where they become trapped in the sticky material.

To make your own traps, cut yellow poster board into 1½-by-8-inch strips and coat the strips with a thin layer of honey. Hang several cards from the roof or from overhead pipes. The traps should be changed when they have become coated with insects or when the honey crystallizes on the cards.

6
DICTIONARY OF PLANTS

A greenhouse can foster a profusion of plants. Vines, annuals, bulbs, perennials, vegetables, ferns, orchids, herbs, cacti, succulents, foliage plants, even shrubs and trees pruned regularly to limit their size—all these are subjects for the garden under glass. Many of the plants in this dictionary are tender tropicals that, in temperate regions, must have a carefully regulated environment in order to thrive or even survive. A greenhouse provides just such an environment. Other plants such as iris, crocus and cucumber can be grown out of doors, but the greenhouse makes it possible to benefit from their blooms and fruit out of season.

The nearly 150 dictionary entries, which are arranged alphabetically by genus and cross-referenced under their common names, describe the requirements of each plant, including growing medium, fertilizer, watering regimen, humidity, night temperature and light. The illumination a plant needs is measured in footcandles—technically, the amount of light received on 1 square foot of surface located 1 foot away from a burning candle. On a bright day, sunlight hitting the ground ordinarily registers 8,000 to 10,000 on a footcandle meter; on an unusually brilliant summer day the reading can climb to 14,000. By contrast, a combination of dense clouds and the sun's low angle on a winter day may limit illumination to only 500 footcandles. Humidity in the atmosphere and air pollution can also lower light intensity at ground level, since those conditions scatter the sun's rays in all directions.

Most greenhouse plants require from 3,000 to 4,000 footcandles for good growth, but there are of course wide variations. The leaves of ferns are at their best and African violets bloom most heavily in the soft light of their native forest habitats—which the greenhouse can re-create at 1,000 to 2,000 footcandles; roses, which grow best in bright sun, require 8,000 to 10,000. To determine how much light is present in one location or another in your greenhouse, use a footcandle meter (available at garden supply centers) and place your plants accordingly—manipulating the light, if necessary, with fluorescent lights or shading devices.

ACHIMENES LONGIFLORA

ADIANTUM CAPILLUS-VENERIS

AECHMEA FASCIATA

Achimenes (a-KIM-e-neez)
Magic flower

Flowering plant in the gesneriad family that has erect or trailing stems and is suitable for hanging baskets. Flowers are tubular and five-lobed.

Selected species and varieties. *A. longiflora* has 12-inch stems and oval to lance-shaped, 3½-inch, shiny, often hairy, toothed leaves. Flowers are satiny, 2½ inches wide, and blue, white, pink, yellow, red or purple. Blooms appear during the summer.

Growing conditions. Grow magic flower at 2,000 footcandles. Leaf burn results when light is too bright. Night temperature should be 65° F. Grow in well-drained, soilless medium. Fertilize weekly during the growing and flowering period with quarter-strength 20-20-20. Water with 60° F water and do not allow the water to touch the foliage, which will cause spotting. Keep the medium evenly moist but do not overwater, which can cause crown rot. Magic flower is susceptible to aphids, mealybugs and thrips.

Propagation. Divide rhizomes in late winter or early spring and plant them 1 inch deep. Keep the medium evenly moist. After the plant has flowered, gradually withhold water until the plant fades; then remove the rhizomes from the medium and store over the winter at 45° F in dry sand or vermiculite. Magic flower may also be propagated by stem cuttings and from seeds.

—

Adiantum (ad-ee-AN-tum)
Maidenhair fern

Foliage plant in the fern family that has dainty, thin, fan- or wedge-shaped, pea green foliage and wiry, shiny black stems.

Selected species and varieties. *A. capillus-veneris,* southern maidenhair fern, has 18- to 24-inch fronds and 1-inch finely lobed or toothed leaves.

Growing conditions. Grow maidenhair fern at 1,000 to 2,000 footcandles. Night temperature should be 55° to 60° F. Grow in very rich, well-drained, soilless medium to which lime, bone meal or other source of calcium has been added. Fertilize with half-strength 20-20-20 in early spring and again in early summer. Water to keep the medium constantly moist during the growing period; in the winter, water only

to keep the fronds from wilting. Provide humidity of at least 70 percent to prevent brown leaf tips. Maidenhair fern is susceptible to scales, mealybugs, aphids and whiteflies, and to botrytis blight.

Propagation. Divide maidenhair fern in late winter or early spring by cutting the fronds to soil level and dividing the wiry roots. Maidenhair fern may also be propagated from spores.

—

Aechmea (EEK-mee-a)
Air pine, living-vase

Flowering plant in the bromeliad family that has long, stiff leaves that appear in basal rosettes. Showy flowers appear in spikes.

Selected species and varieties. *A. fasciata,* urn plant, has leaves that are 2 feet long, toothed, and streaked or banded with a silver or white powder. Flower spikes are up to 2 feet long and have tiny blue or purple flowers appearing amid pink to red bracts.

Growing conditions. Grow urn plant at 3,000 to 5,000 footcandles, and shade from direct sun during the summer. Night temperature should be 60° to 65° F. Grow in well-drained, loose, soilless medium with coarse perlite, bark chips or osmunda fiber added. Keep the medium evenly moist but not overly wet, and keep the cup at the base of the plant filled with water. Fertilize monthly with half-strength 20-20-20 by adding the fertilizer solution to the water in the cup. There are commercial products available to induce flowering. Bromeliads are generally free of insects and diseases, but they are susceptible to scales and crown rot.

Propagation. Propagate urn plant by removing and planting side shoots that grow at the base of the plant after it flowers. Urn plant may also be propagated from seeds or by division of large plants.

—

African lily see *Agapanthus*
African violet see *Saintpaulia*

—

Agapanthus (ag-a-PAN-thus)
African lily, lily-of-the-Nile

Flowering plant in the amaryllis family that has linear to strap-shaped leaves and large, round clusters of tubular to bell-shaped flowers that bloom on top of leafless stems.

Selected species and varieties. *A. africanus* has leaves that are 2 feet long and ½ inch wide. Flowers are blue-violet, 1½ inches in length and bloom during summer in 6-inch clusters of 12 to 30 individual blooms. Flowering stems grow 24 inches high.

Growing conditions. Grow African lily at 3,000 to 5,000 footcandles, and shade from direct sun during the summer. Night temperature should be 50° to 55° F. Grow in average, well-drained, soilless medium. Keep the medium evenly moist and fertilize with 20-20-20 every two weeks during the growing and flowering period. During the winter, keep the medium moist enough only to prevent the foliage from wilting. African lily blooms best if it is pot-bound. It is generally pest- and disease-free.

Propagation. Divide the rhizomes of African lily after the plant has flowered or when growth starts in spring. African lily may also be grown from seeds.

—

Agave (a-GAH-vee)
Century plant

Succulent plant usually grown for its foliage. Leaves are stiff and appear in basal rosettes; most leaves have a sharp spine at the tip. Although century plant flowers, it takes 20 years or more for it to reach flowering age. After it flowers, it dies.

Selected species and varieties. *A. victoriae-reginae,* Queen Victoria century plant, has a rounded mound of tightly spaced, upright leaves that are 6 inches long and 2 inches wide. The leaves are dark green and have white lines and edges. Flowers are pale green, 2 inches long and appear in spikes.

Growing conditions. Grow century plant at 3,000 to 5,000 footcandles. Night temperature should be 50° to 55° F. Grow in soilless medium that has extra perlite or sharp sand added to ensure excellent drainage. Water when the medium surface has dried out to keep the medium barely moist and reduce the chance of rotting. In winter, water enough only to keep the foliage from shriveling. Do not feed newly potted plants for one year; fertilize established plants once in spring with 20-20-20. Humidity should be less than 50 percent. Insects that attack century plant include mealybugs, spider mites and scales.

Propagation. Queen Victoria century plant is propagated from seeds.

—

Air pine see *Aechmea*

—

Aloe (AL-o)

Succulent plant usually grown as a foliage plant although it occasionally produces spikes of red or yellow flowers. Leaves are thick, hard, sharply pointed and spiny, and grow in compact rosettes.

Selected species and varieties. *A. barbadensis,* formerly designated *A. vera,* Barbados aloe, burn plant, has leaves that are 1 to 2 feet long and have red or white teeth on their margins. This plant is the major source of the drug aloe used for burns. *A. nobilis,* golden-tooth aloe, has 6- to 10-inch pale green leaves with gold prickly teeth along the edges. *A. variegata,* tiger aloe, has 12-inch dark green leaves banded horizontally in white or gray.

Growing conditions. Grow aloe at 3,000 to 5,000 footcandles if you are growing it for its foliage only; high light intensity of up to 8,000 footcandles is necessary to produce flowers. Night temperature should be 50° to 55° F. Grow in soilless medium that has extra perlite or sharp sand added to ensure excellent drainage. Water when the medium surface has dried out to keep the medium barely moist and reduce the chance of rotting. In winter, water enough only to keep the foliage from shriveling. Do not feed newly potted plants for one year; fertilize established plants once in spring with 20-20-20. Humidity should be less than 50 percent. Aloe is susceptible to mealybugs, spider mites and scales.

Propagation. Aloes are propagated by offshoots, division and leaf cuttings, and from seeds.

—

Alternanthera
(al-ter-NAN-the-ra)
Joseph's coat, copperleaf

Plant in the amaranth family usually grown for its colorful foliage; it will produce inconspicuous heads of white or beige flowers when mature.

Selected species and varieties. *A. ficoidea* is a bushy plant that grows 6 to 12 inches tall. Leaves are 1

AGAPANTHUS AFRICANUS

AGAVE VICTORIAE-REGINAE

ALOE NOBILIS

ALTERNANTHERA FICOIDEA

ANANAS COMOSUS 'VARIEGATUS'

ANTHURIUM ANDRAEANUM

to 1½ inches long; round, oval or pointed; and a bright mixture of green, red, orange, yellow, rose or purple.

Growing conditions. Grow Joseph's coat at 5,000 to 8,000 footcandles. Night temperature should be 65° F. Grow in average, well-drained potting medium that is kept evenly moist. Fertilize monthly with 20-20-20 during spring and summer. Joseph's coat is susceptible to scales.

Propagation. Joseph's coat is propagated by division or by stem cuttings taken in the fall.

—

Aluminum plant see *Pilea*
Amaryllis see *Hippeastrum*

—

Ananas (a-NAN-us)
Pineapple

A member of the bromeliad family grown commercially to produce pineapples and as an ornamental plant in the greenhouse. Leaves are stiff, long, narrow and spiny, and form in basal rosettes.

Selected species and varieties. *A. comosus* has upright or slightly arching leaves that are 3 feet long and 1½ inches wide. Violet or red flowers are produced on a 2- to 4-foot stem and are followed by the fruit. 'Variegatus' has ivory-colored margins on its leaves.

Growing conditions. Grow pineapple at 5,000 to 8,000 footcandles. Night temperature should be 60° to 65° F. Grow in well-drained, loose, soilless medium with additional coarse perlite, bark chips or osmunda fiber added. Keep the medium evenly moist but not overly wet and keep the cup at the base of the plant filled with water. Fertilize monthly with half-strength 20-20-20 by adding the fertilizer solution to the water in the cup. There are commercial products available to induce flowering. Pineapples are generally insect- and disease-free, but they are susceptible to scales and crown rot.

Propagation. To grow your own pineapple from a purchased plant, cut off the top with the foliage intact, allow it to dry for several days and plant it in potting medium. It may take two years or more for the plant to flower and fruit. Pineapples may also be propagated by removing and planting the offshoots that develop at the base of the plant after it flowers.

Anthurium (an-THUR-ee-um)
Tailflower

Flowering plant in the arum family that has thick, firm, prominently veined leaves. The tiny flowers are found along a tail-like structure called a spadix and are surrounded by colorful bracts called spathes.

Selected species and varieties. *A. andraeanum,* flamingo flower, grows 1 to 3 feet tall. Leaves are heart- or lance-shaped, dark green, shiny, 8 to 10 inches long and 4 to 5 inches wide. The spathe is puckered, 3 to 5 inches long and as shiny as patent leather. The species is salmon-red, and hybrids are dark red, bright red, salmon, pink or white. The spadix is 2¼ inches long and golden to ivory. Flamingo flower may bloom all year but the heaviest flowering occurs from late winter through midsummer. Individual blooms last for one month.

Growing conditions. Grow flamingo flower at 1,500 to 2,500 footcandles. Night temperature should be 65° F. Grow in well-drained, soilless medium with additional bark chips or osmunda fiber added. Keep the medium evenly moist but not overly wet. Fertilize monthly with 20-20-20. Keep humidity above 70 percent to ensure flowering. There are no insects that bother flamingo flower; but it is susceptible to leaf spot disease.

Propagation. Propagate flamingo flower by offshoots, by division or by leaf cuttings. Flamingo flower may also be grown from seeds, but the seeds are short-lived and must be sown immediately.

—

Antirrhinum (an-te-RY-num)
Snapdragon

Perennial member of the figwort family grown in the greenhouse for cutting flowers. Leaves are lance-shaped and up to 3 inches long. Flowers are tubular and two-lipped and bloom in erect spikes.

Selected species and varieties. *A. majus* grows up to 6 feet tall in the greenhouse and has 1½- to 2-inch flowers of rose, bronze, crimson, magenta, lavender, pink, white, yellow or red. Varieties grown in the garden generally do not grow well in the greenhouse. Greenhouse varieties are divided into four groups based on their flowering response to light and temperature. Group 1 varieties flower during the winter in the North. Group 2 varieties flower from midwinter to midspring and from midfall to early winter in the North, and from early winter to midspring in the South. Group 3 varieties flower from midspring to midsummer and from early fall to midfall in the North, and from midspring to early summer and from midfall to early winter in the South. Group 4 varieties flower from early summer to midfall in both North and South. Seeds should be purchased according to your growing schedule.

Growing conditions. Snapdragons grow and flower best at 4,000 to 8,000 footcandles, but will grow and flower under lower light conditions if the proper variety group is selected. It will take anywhere from 11 weeks during the summer to 26 weeks during the winter to produce flowers from seed. Night temperature should be 50° F during the winter and may be raised as high as 65° F during the summer. Grow in neutral, soilless medium with excellent drainage. Plants may be grown in pots or directly in the greenhouse bench. Allow the medium to dry out slightly between waterings in the fall, winter and spring, and keep evenly moist in the summer. Fertilize weekly with quarter-strength 20-20-20; stop fertilizing when flower buds start to show color. Humidity should not be over 50 percent. Apply shading to the greenhouse during the summer if it is not cooled. Plants may be pinched to produce more flowering stems, but this will delay flowering from two to five weeks. Tall plants need to be staked. Cut spikes when the bottom flowers are open and the top flowers are still in tight bud. It is best to discard the plants after they have flowered and start again, because succeeding blooms are significantly smaller, but it is possible to produce a second or third crop. Snapdragons may be attacked by aphids, cyclamen mites and spider mites. They are also susceptible to damping-off, root rot, wilt diseases, rust and powdery mildew.

Propagation. Snapdragons are propagated from seed; the seed is fine and should not be covered during germination. Snapdragons may also be propagated by stem cuttings.

——

Aralia ivy see *Fatshedera*
Areca palm see *Chrysalidocarpus*
Artillery plant see *Pilea*

Asparagus (a-SPA-ra-gus)
Asparagus fern

Plant in the lily family that is grown for its foliage. Stems may be erect or trailing and are covered with flat, needlelike or fernlike leaves. Flowers are small; white, yellow or green; and unreliably produced. Red berries follow the blooms.

Selected species and varieties. *A. densiflorus* 'Myers', foxtail asparagus fern, has stiff, 2-foot stems and dense, fluffy plumes of foliage that are 2½ inches wide. *A. densiflorus* 'Sprengeri', Sprenger asparagus, emerald fern, has 2- to 3-foot arching branches covered with airy, soft, needlelike bright green foliage. *A. setaceus,* formerly designated *A. plumosus,* has sprays of lacy foliage that are triangular in shape and arranged on a flat plane. This is the "fern" most often used in flower arrangements.

Growing conditions. Grow asparagus fern at 3,000 to 4,500 footcandles. Too much light will cause the foliage to turn yellow. Night temperature should be 60° F. Grow in soilless, well-drained potting medium kept evenly moist in spring, summer and fall. Allow the medium to dry out slightly between waterings in winter. Fertilize every two weeks with 20-20-20 during the summer months. Keep the humidity level above 60 percent. Aphids and spider mites may attack asparagus fern; it is not susceptible to diseases.

Propagation. Asparagus fern may be propagated by division whenever the roots become crowded. It may also be propagated from seeds soaked in warm water for 24 hours before sowing.

——

Asplenium (as-PLEE-nee-um)

Foliage plant in the fern family that may have either divided or undivided leaves.

Selected species and varieties. *A. bulbiferum,* mother fern, has feathery foliage with slightly scalloped leaflets. Leaves grow to 24 inches long. Small bulblets or plantlets form on the upper surface of the leaves. *A. nidus,* bird's nest fern, has stiff, shiny, erect leaves that grow in rosettes. Leaves grow to 24 inches long and have slightly wavy edges. Unlike most ferns, bird's nest fern has foliage that is undivided.

Growing conditions. Grow asplenium at 1,000 to 2,000 foot-

ANTIRRHINUM MAJUS

ASPARAGUS DENSIFLORUS 'MYERS'

ASPLENIUM NIDUS

BEGONIA × SEMPERFLORENS-CULTORUM

BOUGAINVILLEA GLABRA

candles. Night temperature should be 50° to 55° F. Grow in very rich, well-drained, soilless medium to which lime, bone meal or other source of calcium has been added. Fertilize with half-strength 20-20-20 in early spring and again in early summer. Do not fertilize newly potted plants for six months. Water to keep the medium constantly moist during the growing period; in the winter, water only to keep the fronds from wilting. Maintain humidity of at least 70 percent to prevent brown leaf tips. Asplenium can be damaged by scales, mealybugs, aphids and whiteflies. It is also susceptible to botrytis blight.

Propagation. Asplenium may be propagated by division in late winter or early spring, or from spores. Mother fern may also be propagated from the small bulblets or plantlets that form on the leaf surface.

Australian umbrella tree
see *Brassaia*

Avocado see *Persea*

Azalea see *Rhododendron*

Baby's tears see *Soleirolia*

Ball cactus see *Notocactus*

Banana see *Musa*

Barrel cactus see *Echinocactus*

Basil see *Ocimum*

Begonia (be-GO-nee-a)

Plant in the begonia family. Some species are fibrous-rooted and are grown for their flowers. Others are rhizomatous-rooted and are grown for their brightly colored and marked foliage. Flowers are single or double, and white, red, pink, orange or yellow.

Selected species and varieties. *B. × erythrophylla,* beefsteak begonia, is rhizomatous and grows 12 inches high. The leaves are round, 2½ to 3 inches across, thick, with white hair on the margins and with red undersides. Flowers are light pink and sometimes drooping, and bloom primarily in winter and spring. *B. × rex-cultorum,* rex begonia, is rhizomatous and grows 12 inches tall. The leaves are shaped like an elephant's ear and are strikingly marked, zoned, marbled or spotted in green, purple, red, bronze, pink,

gray or silver. Inconspicuous white or pink flowers appear in spring. *B. × semperflorens-cultorum,* wax begonia, has fibrous roots and grows 6 to 8 inches tall. Foliage is shiny, round, 1 inch across, and may be either green or dark bronze. Flowers of white, pink or red bloom continually throughout the year.

Growing conditions. Grow begonias at 3,000 to 4,000 footcandles. The rex begonia prefers less light than other begonias. Night temperature should be 65° F for rex and beefsteak begonias and 60° F for wax begonias. Grow in rich, well-drained, soilless medium. Water to keep soil evenly wet but not soggy; in winter, allow soil to dry out slightly between waterings. Fertilize wax begonias monthly during the growing and flowering period with 20-20-20; fertilize rex and beefsteak begonias every other month during the growing and flowering period with 20-20-20. Wax begonias grow best when slightly pot-bound and may be pinched to keep them shapely and compact. Begonias are subject to attack by whiteflies, aphids, mealybugs, spider mites and nematodes. They are also susceptible to damping-off, powdery mildew, botrytis blight and leaf spot diseases.

Propagation. All begonias may be propagated by stem cuttings or from seeds. Rex begonias may also be propagated by leaf cuttings. Rex and beefsteak begonias may be increased by dividing the rhizomes in spring or fall.

Belgian evergreen see *Dracaena*

Bird-of-paradise see *Strelitzia*

Bird's nest fern see *Asplenium*

Black-eyed Susan vine
see *Thunbergia*

Boston fern see *Nephrolepis*

Bougainvillea
(boo-gan-VIL-ee-a)

Woody vine in the four-o'clock family grown for the showy, papery bracts of white, yellow, copper, pink, red or purple that surround the insignificant flowers.

Selected species and varieties. *B. × buttiana* has oval leaves and crisp bracts of crimson or orange that fade to purple or mauve. Hybrids have bracts of yellow, orange and crimson. *B. glabra,* paper flower, has oblong foliage and bracts of purple or magenta. It may bloom all year in the greenhouse if conditions are right, but the chief blooming period is from late winter through summer.

Growing conditions. Grow bougainvillea at 4,000 to 8,000 footcandles. Night temperature should be 50° F during the winter and may go up to 60° F during the summer. Grow in average, well-drained, soilless medium. Water very sparingly in winter, and at other times of year only after the growing medium starts to dry out. Fertilize monthly with 20-20-20 from early spring through late summer. Bougainvillea needs to be trained to a support. It can be pruned into a bush form after it flowers, but this will delay future flowering. Bougainvillea is susceptible to few if any insects or diseases.

Propagation. Bougainvillea may be grown from seeds or propagated by stem cuttings taken in middle to late spring.

—

Brake fern see *Pteris*

—

Brassaia (BRASS-ee-a)

Plant in the aralia family grown for its foliage. Leaves are shiny and divided, with leaflets arranged in whorls at the ends of long stems. Brassaia rarely flowers in the greenhouse; when it does, red flowers appear in round, dense clusters along a spiked branch.

Selected species and varieties. *B. actinophylla,* formerly designated *Schefflera actinophylla,* Australian umbrella tree, grows up to 6 feet tall. Young plants have three to five leaflets each 2 to 3 inches long; mature plants have up to 16 leaflets each up to 12 inches long.

Growing conditions. Australian umbrella tree grows best at 5,000 to 6,000 footcandles, but will tolerate light levels as low as 3,000 footcandles. Night temperature should be 65° to 70° F. Grow in average, well-drained, soilless medium that is allowed to dry out slightly between waterings. Fertilize twice yearly with 20-20-20; do not fertilize newly potted plants for six months. Australian umbrella tree tolerates low humidity. Wash or dust the foliage regularly. Plants may be cut back to keep them bushy and produce more stems. They are susceptible to spider mites, scales and mealybugs, and to leaf spot diseases.

Propagation. Propagate Australian umbrella tree by stem cuttings or air layering, or from seeds.

—

Brassavola (brass-a-VO-la)

Flowering plant in the orchid family. Foliage is fleshy; flowers are fragrant and appear singly or in small sprays. The blooms have narrow, spreading petals and a central, heart-shaped lip.

Selected species and varieties. *B. cordata* has long, linear leaves and 2-inch greenish white flowers with a white lip whose base is purple. It blooms in summer and fall. *B. digbyana* has long, thick foliage and 4- to 6-inch greenish yellow flowers with a creamy white, fringed lip. It blooms in spring and summer. *B. nodosa,* lady of the night, has long, linear leaves and 3-inch white or greenish yellow flowers with a white lip. It is fragrant only in the evening and blooms in fall and winter.

Growing conditions. Grow young brassavola plants at 1,200 to 1,500 footcandles because too much light when the plants are immature will burn the foliage. Grow plants that are more than two years old at 2,000 to 3,500 footcandles. Night temperature should be 60° to 65° F. Grow in a special orchid-potting medium, or a soilless medium with extra fir, redwood bark or osmunda fiber added. Brassavola may also be grown on a slab of tree fern bark. Fertilize monthly from midfall to midspring, and twice monthly from midspring to midfall. Use 30-10-10 fertilizer if the potting medium contains bark, and 20-20-20 if it contains osmunda fiber.

Allow the medium to dry out between waterings except when the plant is in bud or bloom; then the medium should not be allowed to dry out. As the bark in the potting medium breaks down over time, plants should be repotted at least every two years in spring or summer. Plants in fresh bark medium also need more frequent watering than those in older medium, as older medium retains more moisture. Humidity should be 60 to 70 percent, and constant air circulation is necessary. Plants should be placed in a shaded section of the greenhouse during the summer. Flowering stems need to be staked. Scales, slugs, snails and virus diseases may attack brassavola.

Propagation. Propagate brassavola by cuttings, by division or from seeds.

BRASSAIA ACTINOPHYLLA

BRASSAVOLA NODOSA

CALADIUM × HORTULANUM

CALCEOLARIA CRENATIFLORA

CAMELLIA JAPONICA

Bread palm see *Cycas*

Bunny-ears see *Opuntia*

Burn plant see *Aloe*

Burro's tail see *Sedum*

Butterhead lettuce see *Lactuca*

Cactus see *Cephalocereus; Echinocactus; Echinopsis; Epiphyllum; Gasteria; Lobivia; Mammillaria; Notocactus; Opuntia; Schlumbergera*

Caladium (ka-LAY-dee-um)
Elephant's ear, mother-in-law plant

Foliage plant in the arum family that grows from tubers. Leaves are lance-, heart- or arrow-shaped and appear at the ends of slender stems.

Selected species and varieties. *C. × hortulanum* grows 12 to 24 inches tall. The foliage is marked in green, white, silver, red, pink, rose, salmon or yellow.

Growing conditions. Grow elephant's ear at 3,000 to 5,000 footcandles. Night temperature should be 65° to 70° F. Grow in well-drained, soilless potting medium that has extra peat moss or other organic matter added. Keep the medium evenly moist and fertilize every two to three weeks with half-strength 20-20-20. Elephant's ear should be placed in a shaded section of the greenhouse during the summer. Tubers will rot if they are stored at temperatures below 50° F. The insects that most commonly attack elephant's ear are aphids and thrips.

Propagation. Divide tubers in early spring, making sure that there is at least one bud eye on each division. Plant the divisions 1 inch deep in peat moss and provide a temperature of 70° to 85° F. When roots form, transplant into potting medium. When the leaves start to wither in the fall, gradually withhold water until the foliage fades. Remove the tubers from the medium, allow them to dry out, and store them until spring in dry peat moss or vermiculite at 60° F. Elephant's ear may also be propagated from seeds.

Calceolaria (kal-see-o-LAR-ee-a)
Pocketbook plant

Flowering plant in the figwort family that has small "pockets," or pouches, at the front of the flowers.

Selected species and varieties. *C. crenatiflora* has 1-inch blooms of yellow, red, bronze or maroon. Some are spotted in orange or brown. Plants grow up to 2½ feet tall. The foliage is oval, toothed and 8 inches long at the base of the plant, becoming smaller at the tops of the stems.

Growing conditions. Grow pocketbook plant at 1,000 to 3,000 footcandles. Night temperature for seedlings should be 60° F. After three months of growth, lower the night temperature to 50° F until buds have set; then raise the temperature to 60° F. Seedlings and plants in bloom must be shaded from direct sun, which can burn the foliage and flowers. Grow in average, well-drained, soilless potting medium. Keep the soil barely moist and do not let water touch the leaves, which will rot. Fertilize once a month during the growth period with 20-20-20; stop fertilizing when buds set. Plants normally bloom in midspring; to force them into bloom earlier, place 100-watt bulbs 4 feet apart, 2 feet above the plants. Turn the lights on for four hours each night, starting three months before the desired bloom date. Plants may need to be staked. Damping-off may attack seedlings; do not plant them too deep when transplanting them or stem rot will occur. Aphids, thrips and whiteflies may attack pocketbook plant.

Propagation. Propagate pocketbook plant from seeds sown in late spring to early fall for blooming the following winter and spring. The seeds are fine and should not be covered during the germination period.

Calla lily see *Zantedeschia*

Camellia (ka-MEEL-ee-a)

Evergreen shrub in the tea family grown in the greenhouse for its single or double, waxy flowers of white, red, pink or combinations of these three colors. Plants grow to 4 feet in height and have glossy, leathery, dark green leaves.

Selected species and varieties. *C. japonica,* Japanese camellia, is a dense shrub with thick, oval, 3- to 4-inch leaves. Flowers 3 to 5 inches across bloom in winter and spring. *C. sasanqua,* Sasanqua camellia, is a loose shrub that has slender, 2-inch leaves. Flowers are 2 to 3 inches across and bloom in fall and winter.

Growing conditions. Grow camellias at 1,000 to 3,000 footcandles. Night temperature should be 40° to

60° F during flowering. After the flowers have bloomed, raise the temperature to 60° to 65° F during the period of new growth and setting of next season's buds, then lower it to below 60° F. Low temperatures during the blooming period will extend the bloom time. Grow in extra-rich, well-drained, acidic, soilless medium kept evenly moist at all times. Fertilize with a plant food for acid plants in early spring, late spring and midsummer. Humidity should be above 60 percent during the blooming period to induce buds to open and to prevent bud drop. Plants should be syringed and kept in a shaded part of the greenhouse from midspring to midfall. Prune after the plant has flowered. For larger flowers, disbud by removing all but one flower bud per stem. Camellias are susceptible to aphids, mealybugs, scales and spider mites.

Propagation. Camellias are most commonly propagated by stem cuttings taken in summer or fall or by grafting, but may also be propagated by layering or from seeds.

—

Cape leadwort see *Plumbago*
Cape primrose see *Streptocarpus*

—

Capsicum (KAP-si-kum)
Pepper

Member of the nightshade family that has small white flowers followed by green, red, yellow or purple fruit. Some varieties are grown as ornamental potted plants, others for their edible peppers.

Selected species and varieties. *C. annuum annuum* has two distinctive types of varieties. One is the edible pepper; it grows 20 to 30 inches tall. Fruits are either sweet or hot, and bell-shaped, tapered, cone-shaped, oval or round. 'Better Belle' is a sweet, green bell pepper 4½ inches long. 'Golden Bell' is a sweet, slightly tapered bell pepper that turns deep gold at maturity. 'Super Chili' is a compact plant that produces 2½-inch, cone-shaped, hot red peppers. The second type of plant in the species is called ornamental pepper. It grows 4 to 12 inches tall and has fruit that may be round, cone-shaped or tapered. Fruits change in color as they mature, from cream to purple, orange or red. With very few exceptions, the fruits of the ornamental pepper, although edible, are quite

hot. Ornamental peppers are usually grown for decorative value, especially during the winter holidays. 'Holiday Cheer' is an 8-inch plant with round fruit. 'Holiday Flame' produces slim fruits on 12-inch plants. 'Thai Hot' is an 8-inch plant that has very hot, cone-shaped fruit.

Growing conditions. Grow peppers at 5,000 or more footcandles. Supplemental lighting may be needed during the winter to produce a crop. Night temperature should be 60° to 65° F. Grow in well-drained, soilless medium and keep it barely moist at all times. Edible peppers may be planted in pots, in low benches or directly in large bags of potting medium. Fertilize very little or not at all. Ornamental peppers can be pinched to keep them bushy. Tap flowers to aid pollination and fruit set. Pick the peppers frequently to keep the plants producing and alive; discard the plants when they are no longer attractive or when they stop bearing fruit. Peppers are susceptible to aphids and to damping-off and virus diseases.

Propagation. Both edible and ornamental peppers are grown from seeds germinated at 65° to 70° F. Allow five months from the sowing date to produce fruit in fall, winter or spring; in summer, allow three and a half months from the sowing date.

—

Cardinal climber see *Ipomoea*
Carnation see *Dianthus*
Carolina jessamine
see *Gelsemium*
Carpet plant see *Episcia*
Carrion flower see *Stapelia*

—

Cattleya (KAT-lee-a)

Flowering plant in the orchid family. Foliage is thick, tough and leathery. Flowers have three narrow petals, two broader petals and a large tubular lip. Blooms appear in sprays and are fragrant.

Selected species and varieties. *Cattleya* species and hybrids have large, 5- to 7-inch flowers of white, yellow, pink, blue, green, red, lavender or purple. Plants grow 12 to 18 inches high. Depending on the species or variety, they bloom at different times of year.

CAPSICUM ANNUUM ANNUUM

CATTLEYA HYBRID

99

CEPHALOCEREUS SENILIS

CESTRUM NOCTURNUM

CHAMAEDOREA ELEGANS

Growing conditions. Grow young cattleya plants at 1,200 to 1,500 foot-candles. Plants more than two years old are grown at 2,000 to 3,500 foot-candles. Normal foliage is yellow-green. Too much light causes the foliage to yellow and burn. Insufficient light causes the foliage to turn solid green. Night temperature should be 60° to 65° F. Grow in a special orchid-potting medium, or in soilless medium with extra fir, redwood bark or osmunda fiber added. Cattleya may also be grown on a slab of tree fern bark. Fertilize monthly from midfall to midspring, and twice monthly from midspring to midfall. Use 30-10-10 fertilizer if the potting medium contains bark, and 20-20-20 if it contains osmunda fiber. Allow the medium to dry out between waterings except when the plant is in bud or bloom, when the medium should be kept evenly moist. As the bark in the potting medium breaks down over time, plants should be repotted at least every two years in spring or summer. Plants in fresh bark medium will also need more frequent watering than those in older medium. Humidity should be 60 to 70 percent, and constant air circulation is necessary. Plants should be placed in a shaded portion of the greenhouse during the summer. Flowering stems need to be staked. Flowering time with cattleyas can be manipulated with day length. Artificial lighting to provide longer days will delay flowering. Use of black shade cloth to shorten day length will promote flowering. Cattleya is susceptible to scales, slugs, snails and virus diseases.

Propagation. Propagate cattleya from seeds, or by division in spring or summer. The roots are made up of water- and food-storing tissue called pseudobulbs. Ensure that there are four to six pseudobulbs in each division. The root of the cattleya grows horizontally, so place the edge of the division at one side of the pot to allow it to grow to the other side of the pot.

—

Century plant see *Agave*

—

Cephalocereus
(sef-a-lo-SEER-ee-us)

Plant in the cactus family. The stem is erect, cylindrical and ribbed. Flowers open at night and are small, tubular to bell-shaped, and white, pink or red.

Selected species and varieties. *C. senilis,* old man cactus, grows to 12 inches tall. The stems are covered with long, hairy bristles and sharp spines. Flowers are rose-colored and bloom in the spring.

Growing conditions. Grow old man cactus at 5,000 to 8,000 foot-candles. Night temperature should be 60° to 65° F from spring through fall and should be lowered to 45° F in winter. Grow in soilless potting medium that has extra perlite or sharp sand added to ensure excellent drainage. From spring through fall, allow the top ¼ inch of the medium to dry out before watering; in winter, water only enough to keep the plants from shriveling. Do not feed newly potted plants for one year; fertilize mature plants once a year with 20-20-20. Humidity should be under 50 percent. Problems that affect old man cactus include mealybugs, spider mites, scales, rot and wilt diseases.

Propagation. Propagate old man cactus from cuttings taken at any time of year or from seeds.

—

Cestrum (SES-trum)

Evergreen shrub in the nightshade family that has leaves that may be linear or oval, and clusters of flowers that bloom either at the ends of the branches or from the leaf axils. Flowers are star-shaped, tubular and fragrant.

Selected species and varieties. *C. nocturnum,* night jessamine, has 1-inch greenish white to cream flowers that are fragrant at night. White berries follow the flowers.

Growing conditions. Grow night jessamine at 5,000 to 6,000 foot-candles. Night temperature should be 60° to 65° F. Grow in well-drained, soilless medium and keep it evenly moist. Fertilize every three to four months with 20-20-20. Prune the plant after the flowers fade. Mealybugs and scale are the insects that most commonly attack night jessamine.

Propagation. Propagate night jessamine from seeds or by cuttings taken from middle to late winter.

—

Chamaedorea
(kam-a-DOR-ee-a)

Plant in the palm family grown for its foliage. The stems are neat, green and bamboolike. Branches are arching and are covered with up to 20 dark green leaflets.

Selected species and varieties. *C. elegans,* parlor palm, grows up to 6 feet tall. Each leaflet is up to 8 inches long.

Growing conditions. Grow parlor palm at 2,000 to 3,000 footcandles. Night temperature should be 65° to 70° F. Grow in well-drained, soilless medium and keep it evenly moist but not wet. Allow the medium to dry out slightly between waterings in the winter. Fertilize monthly with 20-20-20 from early spring through early fall. Parlor palm is not susceptible to diseases, but it may be attacked by thrips, mealybugs and scales.

Propagation. Propagate parlor palm by division or from seeds. Parlor palm seeds must be fresh or they will not germinate.

—

Chamaerops (KAM-a-rops)
Fan palm

Plant in the palm family grown for its foliage. The plant is multistemmed; each stem is covered with black fibers. Leaves are stiff, upright and fan-shaped.

Selected species and varieties. *C. humilis,* European fan palm, grows 5 feet high. The leaves grow 1½ feet long and wide or more and are deeply cut. New leaves are covered with gray hairs; mature leaves are gray-green.

Growing conditions. Grow European fan palm at 3,000 to 4,000 footcandles. Night temperature should be 65° to 70° F; in the winter, it benefits from a night temperature of 50° to 55° F. Grow in well-drained, soilless medium and keep it evenly moist but not wet. Allow the medium to dry out slightly between waterings in the winter. Fertilize monthly with 20-20-20 from early spring through early fall. European fan palm is not susceptible to diseases; it is susceptible to thrips, mealybugs and scales.

Propagation. Propagate European fan palm by division, by offshoots or from seeds. Seeds must be fresh or they will not germinate.

—

Chandelier plant see *Kalanchoe*

Cholla see *Opuntia*

Christmas cactus
see *Schlumbergera*

Christmas heather see *Erica*

Chrysalidocarpus
(kri-sal-i-doh-KAR-pus)

Plant in the palm family grown for its foliage. Plants have many slender stems and arching branches covered with up to 60 fine leaflets that give the plant a feathery appearance.

Selected species and varieties. *C. lutescens,* yellow palm, areca palm, grows 5 feet tall or more. Branches arch, are 3 feet long and are covered with narrow, yellow-green leaflets.

Growing conditions. Grow yellow palm at 3,000 to 4,000 footcandles. Night temperature should be 65° to 70° F. Grow in well-drained, soilless medium and keep it evenly moist but not wet. Allow the medium to dry out slightly between waterings in the winter. The plant has a bulbous base that must be kept above the soil level. It grows best if it is slightly potbound. Fertilize monthly with 20-20-20 from early spring through early fall. Yellow palm likes a higher humidity than most palms; keep the greenhouse at 70 percent humidity or higher. Yellow palm is not susceptible to diseases, but it can be attacked by thrips, spider mites, mealybugs and scales.

Propagation. Propagate yellow palm from seeds. Seeds must be fresh or they will not germinate.

—

Chrysanthemum
(kri-SAN-the-mum)

Flowering plant in the composite family that is grown in the greenhouse either as a potted plant or to produce cut flowers. Many, but not all, of the flowers are daisylike.

Selected species and varieties. *C. frutescens,* Marguerite daisy, grows to 3 feet tall and has lacy, oblong to oval, 2- to 6-inch leaves. Flowers are 2 to 3 inches across and daisylike, with yellow centers and white, lemon yellow or pink petals. *C. × morifolium,* florist's chrysanthemum, grows up to 5 feet tall. Leaves are lance-shaped or oval, lobed, 3 inches long and have gray undersides. Flowers come in many types, including single, anemone, pompon, incurved, reflexed, spider, decorative and Fuji (large exhibition) forms. Size may vary from less than 1 inch to 8 inches across. Blooms are available in all colors except true blue.

Growing conditions. Grow Marguerite daisy at 3,000 to 10,000 foot-

CHAMAEROPS HUMILIS

CHRYSALIDOCARPUS LUTESCENS

101

CHRYSANTHEMUM × MORIFOLIUM

CISSUS RHOMBIFOLIA

candles. Night temperature should be 40° to 55° F. Grow in well-drained, soilless medium and keep it evenly moist. Fertilize every two to three weeks with 20-20-20.

Florist's chrysanthemums should be grown at 3,000 to 10,000 foot-candles. When light levels are below that in fall through spring, supplemental incandescent lighting should be used if plants are in their growth period. Lights should be set on a timer to go on and off in the middle of the night for two to five hours per night, depending on the time of year. Set 60-watt bulbs 4 feet apart, 2 feet above the plants.

Night temperature should be 60° F. Reducing the temperature to 55° F seven to 10 days before flowers open will deepen their color and improve their quality.

Florist's chrysanthemums intended as cut flowers may be grown either in pots or directly in the greenhouse bench. Grow them in well-drained, soilless medium that has a pH of 6.0 to 6.5. Tall plants grown in pots should have coarse sand added to weight the pots and prevent them from falling over.

When growing florist's chrysanthemums as potted plants, place five cuttings around the rim of a 6-inch pot, with one in the center. Set the cuttings at a 45° angle to produce a fuller plant. Pinch the cuttings by removing ½ inch of new growth when 1 inch of new growth has formed. Growth retardants may be applied two weeks after pinching to keep potted plants compact. Fertilize every two to three weeks with 20-20-20 when the plants are in growth.

Tall potted plants and plants grown for cutting flowers need to be tied, staked or supported with wire mesh. Disbudding the side buds as soon as they form will produce larger flowers.

Good air circulation is essential. The greenhouse must be cooled during the summer if the plants are in a growing period, as controlling temperature by placing plants in a shaded section of the greenhouse will cause legginess. Shading the plants during the summer if they are blooming will be of benefit to the flowers, because it prevents burning and fading.

Chrysanthemums naturally flower when the days are shorter than 14½ hours. It is possible to force them into bloom all year by manipulating the day length. When plants have reached their desired size and days are 14½ hours long or longer, extend black cloth or black polyethylene over the plants so that they are in complete darkness, to induce flower bud formation. Plants need at least 9½ hours of darkness to set buds and at least 10½ hours of darkness for the buds to open. It does no harm to shade the plants for 12 hours if this better fits your schedule. In the summer, do not extend the black cloth until the sun sets to prevent heat buildup inside the cloth, which will delay flowering. The shading can be stopped when the buds are 1 inch across or showing color, whichever comes first. Depending on the variety, it will take from seven to 15 weeks for a florist's chrysanthemum to flower after the days are naturally short enough or the plants are shaded. Black shade cloth or polyethylene should be replaced every two to three years.

To prevent plants from flowering during the period from midfall to midspring, light the plants during the night as described above.

Cut chrysanthemums for cut flowers when the buds are half to three-quarters open.

Chrysanthemums can be attacked by aphids, leaf miners, mealybugs, nematodes, spider mites, thrips and whiteflies. They are also susceptible to rust, leaf spot, root rot, stem rot, powdery mildew and wilt diseases.

Propagation. Propagate Marguerite daisy by stem cuttings. Propagate florist's chrysanthemum by stem cuttings or by division. The first time you grow florist's chrysanthemums, take precautions against verticillium wilt; start with purchased, culture-indexed cuttings—cuttings that have been professionally produced under laboratory conditions and are certified to be free of disease.

—

Cissus (SIS-us)
Grape ivy

Foliage plant in the grape family that has flexible stems and fleshy leaves; it is usually grown in a hanging basket.

Selected species and varieties. *C. antarctica,* kangaroo vine, has oval to oblong, leathery, glossy, dark green, 3- to 4-inch leaves that are often toothed. *C. discolor,* trailing begonia, has slender red stems. The foliage is 4 to 7 inches long, toothed, oval to heart-shaped and resembles that of the rex begonia. The upper sides of the foliage are velvety green with blotches of silvery white, pink or violet between the veins; the undersides are reddish purple. *C. rhombifolia,* Venezuela treebine, has hairy stems and coarsely toothed, three-lobed leaves, each section of the leaf being 1 to 4 inches long.

The upper sides of the foliage are metallic green with rust-colored veins showing through; the undersides are hairy. Leaves are bronze when new and change to deep green as they mature.

Growing conditions. Grape ivy grows best at 3,000 to 4,000 footcandles, but will tolerate lower light. Grow kangaroo vine and Venezuela treebine at a night temperature of 50° to 55° F, and trailing begonia at 65° to 70° F. Grow in well-drained, soilless medium and allow it to become slightly dry between waterings. Fertilize every two months with 20-20-20 during spring and summer only. Trailing begonia needs a humidity level of at least 60 percent; the others tolerate lower humidity. The ends of the branches may be pinched to keep the plant compact. Grape ivy may also be trained to grow up a trellis. It is susceptible to damage from spider mites.

Propagation. Propagate grape ivy by stem cuttings taken at any time.

Citrus (SIT-rus)
Lime, lemon, grapefruit, orange

Trees and shrubs in the rue family grown commercially to produce citrus fruits and as ornamentals in the greenhouse. Foliage is thick, leathery and shiny on stems that are usually spiny. Flowers are white, fragrant, lobed, up to 2 inches across, and bloom most abundantly in spring and fall. Blooms usually appear in clusters. Fruit follows the flowers and lasts on the plants for several months. Plants in the greenhouse grow 4 to 6 feet tall.

Selected species and varieties. *C. aurantiifolia,* lime, has oblong to oval 3-inch leaves and green to greenish yellow, 3-inch, oval fruit. *C. limon,* lemon, has oblong to oval 4-inch leaves and yellow, 3-inch, oval fruit. *C. × paradisi,* grapefruit, has oval 3-inch leaves and yellow, pinkish yellow or orange-yellow, round, 5-inch fruit. *C. sinensis,* orange, has oblong to oval 4-inch leaves and orange, round, 4-inch fruit.

Growing conditions. Grow citrus at 8,000 footcandles. Night temperature should be 50° to 55° F. Grow in slightly acid, well-drained, soilless medium and allow it to dry out slightly between waterings. Fruit will drop if the plant is either underwatered or overwatered. Fertilize in very early spring, early summer and late summer with 20-20-20. Humidity should

be 60 to 70 percent. Pinch growing tips to keep the plants compact. To ensure fruit formation, shake the flowers or transfer pollen with a brush. Citrus is susceptible to scales, spider mites and whiteflies, and to rust and scab diseases.

Propagation. Propagate citrus by grafting or by stem cuttings taken in late summer or fall. Plants will flower and fruit within one year. Citrus may also be grown from seeds, but these plants will rarely flower and fruit.

Cob cactus see *Lobivia*

Coleus (KO-lee-us)
Flame nettle

Plant in the mint family that is grown for its foliage, although it produces long, thin spikes of blue or violet flowers. Stems are square; foliage is variegated with splashy mixtures of green, red, chartreuse, white, gold, bronze, ivory, orange, salmon, rose, copper, yellow, apricot, pink or purple. Leaf edges may be lacy, smooth, fringed, wavy or toothed.

Selected species and varieties. *C. × hybridus* is a large group of hybrids including the 'Carefree', 'Dragon', 'Fiji', 'Poncho', 'Rainbow', 'Saber' and 'Wizard' cultivars. Depending on the variety, leaves are round to lance-shaped and 1 to 4 inches long.

Growing conditions. Grow flame nettle at 4,000 to 8,000 footcandles. Lower light will cause the foliage to lose its bright coloration. Growth is best when night temperature is 65° to 70° F, but coleus will tolerate 60° F. Grow in well-drained, soilless medium and keep it evenly moist. Fertilize once a month with half-strength 20-20-20. Pinch growing tips to keep the plant compact. Removing flowers will extend the life of the plant. Coleus is susceptible to mealybugs.

Propagation. Propagate flame nettle by stem cuttings taken at any time or from seeds.

Columnea (ko-LUM-nee-a)
Goldfish plant

Flowering plant in the gesneriad family that has trailing branches and is best used in hanging baskets. The flowers are 2 to 4 inches long, tubular, two-lipped, and are said to look like goldfishes when they are fully open. Flowers may appear all year

CITRUS SINENSIS

COLEUS × HYBRIDUS

COLUMNEA × BANKSII

CRASSULA ARGENTEA

CROCUS VERNUS

but bloom most abundantly in spring and summer.

Selected species and varieties. *C.* × *banksii* has oval to oblong, 1¾-inch leaves and red flowers. *C. gloriosa* has hairy stems and oval, 1¼-inch leaves that are covered with a dense purple or red fur. Flowers are red with a yellow throat and underside. *C. linearis* has narrow, 3½-inch, glossy, dark green leaves. The flowers are rose-pink and are covered with white hairs.

Growing conditions. Grow goldfish plant at 3,000 to 4,500 footcandles. Night temperature should be 65° to 70° F; plants benefit from a 50° to 60° F temperature during the winter. Grow in extra-rich, well-drained, soilless medium and keep it evenly moist. Allow the medium to dry out slightly between waterings in the winter if the plant is not in growth or in flower. Fertilize once a month with 20-20-20; do not fertilize in the winter if the plant is not actively growing or in flower. Keep humidity above 60 percent. Plants may be pinched or pruned after they flower to keep them compact. There are no diseases that bother goldfish plant. It is susceptible to mealybugs.

Propagation. Propagate goldfish plant from seeds, or by stem cuttings or root division during the summer.

—

Confederate jasmine
see *Trachelospermum*

Copperleaf see *Alternanthera*

Corn plant see *Dracaena*

Cow-tongue cactus see *Gasteria*

—

Crassula (KRASS-u-la)
Jade plant

Succulent plant usually grown as a foliage plant although it produces spikes of white or pink flowers at the ends of the branches if the conditions are right. Leaves are thick, fleshy, and oval or spoon-shaped.

Selected species and varieties. *C. argentea* has thick stems and grows up to 30 inches tall. Leaves are 1 to 2 inches long and jade green, often with a red margin.

Growing conditions. Grow jade plant at 4,000 to 8,000 footcandles. It will tolerate lower light, but will not flower. Night temperature should be 50° to 55° F. Grow in well-drained, soilless medium with extra perlite or sharp sand added. In spring, summer

and fall, water when the surface of the medium has dried out to keep the medium barely moist and reduce the chance of rotting. In winter, water enough only to keep the foliage from shriveling. Do not feed newly potted plants for six months; fertilize established plants once in summer with 20-20-20. Humidity should be under 50 percent. Jade plant can be attacked by mealybugs, spider mites and scales.

Propagation. Propagate jade plant by stem cuttings, by leaf cuttings or by air layering.

—

Creeping Charlie see *Pilea*
Creeping fig see *Ficus*
Cretan brake fern see *Pteris*

—

Crocus (KRO-kus)

Spring- or fall-flowering bulb in the iris family that can be forced into bloom in the greenhouse during the winter. Leaves are linear and grasslike. The flowers are white, yellow, lilac or purple, cup-shaped, and have six petals.

Selected species and varieties. *C. vernus,* Dutch crocus, contains many large-flowered hybrids and grows to 6 inches tall. Some flowers are striped; some have contrasting colors on the insides and outsides of the petals.

Growing conditions. Crocus corms are available either prechilled or not prechilled. Either start with prechilled corms, or chill them yourself before forcing them into bloom. To do so, pot the corms in early fall to midfall and store them between 40° and 48° F for 15 to 16 weeks. Plant the corms just below the surface of the medium, and place them in the dark or cover them with black plastic. Uncover and move them into the greenhouse at the end of the required storage period.

Prechilled corms should be stored at 63° F until they are ready to be planted and forced.

Plant 10 to 20 corms per 6-inch pot, adjusting the number for smaller or larger pots. Grow crocus at 4,000 to 6,000 footcandles. Night temperature should be 50° to 55° F. Grow in a soilless medium with excellent drainage and a pH of 5.5 to 6.5, and keep the medium evenly moist. Do not fertilize. Crocus will bloom within two weeks of being moved into the greenhouse. Crocus is generally pest- and disease-free.

Propagation. Crocus can be propagated from new cormels that develop at the base of the original corm after the foliage has faded, but better success will be achieved by planting new corms each year. The corms that were forced in the greenhouse can be planted in the garden.

Crossandra (kro-SAN-dra)
Firecracker flower

Flowering plant in the acanthus family that produces rounded, shrubby growth. The foliage may be oval or lance-shaped. Flowers are tubular at the base and open into five rounded lobes. Blooms appear in clusters at the ends of the branches.

Selected species and varieties. *C. infundibuliformis* grows up to 12 inches tall and has leaves that are glossy, wavy-edged and 2 to 5 inches long. The flowers are bright orange or salmon, 1¼ inches across and occur in 6-inch clusters. The plants bloom primarily in spring and summer and will bloom all year provided there is sufficient light.

Growing conditions. Grow firecracker flower at 3,000 to 5,000 footcandles. Plants should be placed in a shaded portion of the greenhouse during the summer. Night temperature should be 65° to 70° F. Grow in well-drained, soilless medium. Keep the medium evenly moist and fertilize every two weeks with half-strength 20-20-20 when the plant is in active growth or when it is flowering. Allow the medium to dry out slightly between waterings and do not fertilize during periods when the plant is not in growth or in flower. Humidity should be over 60 percent to encourage blooming and to prevent the leaves from curling. Plants can be pinched to keep them compact. Plants are susceptbile to spider mites.

Propagation. Propagate firecracker flower by taking cuttings at any time of year, or from seeds sown in spring.

Crown-of-thorns see *Euphorbia*

Cryptanthus (krip-TAN-thus)
East star

Plant in the bromeliad family grown primarily for its foliage. Leaves are stiff and sharply toothed and grow in a flat rosette that resembles a star. The flowers are white or greenish white, but are insignificant.

Selected species and varieties. *C. acaulis,* starfish plant, has 6-inch-long leaves that are striped in bright green and yellow on the upper surfaces, and white on the undersides. 'Roseus' has leaves tinted in rose-pink. *C. bivittatus* has 4-inch-long, wavy, greenish brown leaves that are cream-striped and tinted with pink.

Growing conditions. Grow starfish plant at 4,000 to 6,000 footcandles, and shade it from direct sun during the summer. Lower light will result in a loss of coloration of the foliage. Night temperature should be 65° to 70° F. Grow in well-drained, loose, soilless medium with coarse perlite, bark chips or osmunda fiber added. Keep the medium evenly moist but not wet, and make sure that the cup at the base of the plant is filled with water. Fertilize once a month in spring and summer with half-strength 20-20-20 by adding the fertilizer to the water in the cup. The humidity level should be more than 60 percent. Starfish plant is usually not bothered by insects or diseases, but occasionally it attracts scales or develops crown rot.

Propagation. Propagate starfish plant by removing and potting the offsets that form at the base of the plant.

Cucumber see *Cucumis*

Cucumis (KEW-kew-mis)

Member of the gourd family that has yellow flowers and edible fruit. Plants grow in either a bush or a vining habit.

Selected species and varieties. *C. sativus,* cucumber, has rough, medium green, three-pointed leaves, 1-inch flowers and cylindrical fruit. There are cucumber varieties especially developed for growing in the greenhouse. These are known as "European" varieties and have longer fruit than the cucumber varieties that are grown in the garden. European cucumbers do not need to be pollinated, which makes growing them in the greenhouse easier than using garden varieties. Garden varieties will grow very well in the greenhouse, but it is best to purchase varieties that are either self-pollinating or have both male and female flowers. The cucumbers that have only female flowers must be grown with a male pollinator plant, which will take up needed space in a small greenhouse. Good varieties for the greenhouse include the vining

CROSSANDRA INFUNDIBULIFORMIS

CRYPTANTHUS BIVITTATUS

CUCUMIS SATIVUS

105

CYATHEA COOPERI

CYCAS REVOLUTA

CYCLAMEN PERSICUM

types 'Cresta', 'Improved Telegraph', 'Super Slice', 'Sweet Slice' and 'Sweet Success', and the bush types 'Bush Crop' and 'Pot Luck'.

Growing conditions. Grow cucumbers at 5,000 or more footcandles. Supplemental lighting may be needed during the winter to produce a crop. Night temperature should be 60° to 70° F. Grow in well-drained, soilless medium and keep it barely moist at all times. Cucumbers may be planted in pots, in low benches or directly in large bags of potting medium. Fertilize every two weeks with 20-20-20 as soon as fruit starts to form. Humidity must be over 60 percent. Vining cucumbers will need to be trained on a string or a trellis. Tap flowers to aid pollination and fruit set unless you are growing the self-pollinating or European varieties. Keep the cucumbers picked to keep the plants producing and alive; discard the plants when they stop bearing fruit. Cucumbers are susceptible to aphids and spider mites and to downy mildew, damping-off, scab and virus diseases.

Propagation. Propagate cucumbers from seeds germinated at 80° F. It will take two to two and a half months to produce fruit during the summer, and three to four months to produce fruit during fall, winter and spring.

Cyathea (sy-ATH-ee-a)
Tree fern

Foliage plant in the fern family that has a distinct, treelike trunk and finely divided leaves.

Selected species and varieties. C. cooperi, also designated Alsophila cooperi, Australian tree fern, can grow up to 20 feet tall and has feathery fronds 2 feet long or more.

Growing conditions. Grow tree fern at 2,000 to 3,000 footcandles. Night temperature should be 60° to 65° F. Grow in very rich, well-drained, soilless medium to which lime, bone meal or other source of calcium has been added. Do not feed new plants for six months; fertilize established plants with half-strength 20-20-20 in early spring and again in early summer. Water to keep the medium constantly moist during the growing period; in the winter, water only to keep the fronds from wilting. Provide humidity of at least 70 percent to prevent brown leaf tips. Scales, mealybugs, aphids and

whiteflies are the insects that most commonly attack tree fern. Tree fern is also susceptible to botrytis blight.

Propagation. Propagate tree fern from spores.

Cycas (SY-kus)
Bread palm, funeral palm

Plant in the cycad family grown for its foliage. Foliage is palmlike, stiff, divided and arching, slowly growing in whorls from the base of the plant or from the top of the trunk.

Selected species and varieties. C. revoluta, sago palm, grows to 6 feet tall in the greenhouse. Fronds are 2 to 3 feet long and covered with glossy, leathery, narrow leaflets. When young, fronds emerge from a basal stub that develops into a trunk after 10 or more years.

Growing conditions. Grow sago palm at 3,000 to 4,000 footcandles. Night temperature should be 50° to 60° F. Grow in soilless medium with coarse sand or perlite added to ensure excellent drainage. Water heavily in spring, summer and fall, and then let the top ½ inch of the medium dry out before rewatering. In winter, water only to keep the fronds from wilting. Fertilize with 20-20-20 once a month during spring and summer. Spider mites, mealybugs and scales may infest sago palm.

Propagation. Propagate sago palm by removing and potting the suckers that develop at the base of the plant, or from seeds.

Cyclamen (SIK-la-men)
Persian violet

Flowering plant in the primrose family that has heart-shaped basal leaves that are blotched or marbled in light green, gray or silver on the upper surfaces. The flowers nod and the petals flare upward like wings.

Selected species and varieties. C. persicum, florist's cyclamen, has leaves up to 5½ inches across and 2-inch red, rose, pink, lilac, white or purple flowers with a purple blotch at the base. The species has fragrant flowers, but the newer hybrids have no fragrance. Florist's cyclamen is grown to flower during winter and spring. There are two types of cyclamen. The older varieties bloom in 12 to 15 months from seed; newer hybrids bloom in seven to eight months from seed.

Growing conditions. Grow young cyclamen plants at 3,500 to 4,000 footcandles. After several months, light intensity can be increased to 5,000 footcandles. Plants should be placed in a shaded section of the greenhouse during the summer. Night temperature should be 60° F until buds set; then the temperature should be lowered to 55° F. During the summer, mist the plants frequently to prevent foliage burn, which will result from high temperature if the greenhouse is not cooled. Grow in well-drained, soilless medium and keep it evenly moist. Do not allow water to fall on the crown when watering the plant or crown rot may develop. Fertilize young plants once a month with quarter-strength 20-20-20; increase feeding to half-strength 20-20-20 when buds form. Cyclamen may be affected by mites, nematodes, thrips and botrytis blight.

Propagation. Propagate cyclamen from seeds or by corms. Seeds should be soaked in water for 24 hours before sowing. After the seeds germinate, they form plants. When transplanting, set each corm so that the top half of it is visible above the medium. After a plant has flowered, the foliage will start to turn yellow. Gradually withhold water until the foliage has completely faded. Store each corm in its pot in a dark area at 45° F for three months, then start watering to encourage new growth. If the corms are large, they may be removed from the pots and divided.

—

Cymbidium (sim-BID-ee-um)

Flowering plant in the orchid family. Leaves are long, narrow and leathery. Flowers have five petals of equal size and central, lobed lips that are often of contrasting colors. Blooms appear in spikes of 10 to 30 flowers.

Selected species and varieties. Cymbidium hybrids grow up to 2 feet tall and have flowers of white, pink, yellow, green, maroon, bronze and mahogany. Blooms usually appear in fall and last through spring.

Growing conditions. Grow young cymbidium plants at 1,500 to 2,000 footcandles. Plants more than two years old are grown at 3,000 to 5,000 footcandles. Night temperature should be 50° to 55° F; for plants to bloom, temperature should be lowered to 45° to 50° F for six to eight weeks in fall or winter. Grow in a special orchid-potting medium, or in a

soilless medium with extra fir or redwood bark added. The pH must be between 5.5 and 6.5. Fertilize with 30-10-10 monthly from midfall to midspring, and twice monthly from midspring to midfall. The medium should be kept evenly moist at all times. As the bark in the potting medium breaks down over time, plants should be repotted at least every two years in spring or summer. Plants in fresh bark medium will need more frequent watering than those in older medium, which retains more moisture. Humidity should be 60 to 70 percent and constant air circulation is necessary. Plants should be moved into a shaded section of the greenhouse during the summer. Plants may be moved outdoors during the summer and returned inside just before the first frost. Scales, slugs, snails and virus diseases may affect cymbidium.

Propagation. Propagate cymbidium from seeds or by division in spring or summer. The roots are made up of structures called pseudobulbs, which are food- and water-storing tissue. Ensure that there are three to four pseudobulbs on each division.

—

Cyperus (sy-PEER-us)
Umbrella sedge

Plant in the sedge family grown for its foliage. Plants are semiaquatic, and have long stems on top of which are sprays of foliage.

Selected species and varieties. *C. alternifolius,* umbrella plant, grows to 4 feet tall. The foliage at the top of the stems consists of 4- to 12-inch, narrow, grassy leaves that radiate like the ribs of an umbrella.

Growing conditions. Grow umbrella plant at 3,000 to 4,000 footcandles. Night temperature should be 65° to 70° F. Grow in a soilless medium and keep it constantly wet by maintaining a saucer of water under the pot. Umbrella plant may also be grown directly in a container of water. Fertilize with half-strength 20-20-20 every two weeks during spring and summer. Mealybugs may infest umbrella plant.

Propagation. Propagate umbrella plant by division at any time of year or from seeds in spring or fall.

—

Cyrtomium (sir-TOH-mee-um)

Plant in the fern family that has leathery, divided foliage.

CYMBIDIUM HYBRID

CYPERUS ALTERNIFOLIUS

107

CYRTOMIUM FALCATUM

DAPHNE ODORA 'AUREOMARGINATA'

DAVALLIA FEJEENSIS

Selected species and varieties. *C. falcatum,* holly fern, grows 1 to 2 feet tall. The fronds are stiff and erect; the individual leaflets are dark green, shiny, 3 to 5 inches long, hollylike and often wavy.

Growing conditions. Grow holly fern at 2,000 to 3,000 footcandles. Night temperature should be 50° to 55° F. Grow in a very rich, well-drained, soilless medium to which lime, bone meal or other source of calcium has been added. Water to keep the medium constantly moist during the growing period; in the winter, water only to keep the fronds from wilting. Do not feed new plants for six months; fertilize established plants with half-strength 20-20-20 in early spring and again in early summer. Holly fern tolerates 50 percent humidity, which is lower than most ferns require. Scales, mealybugs, aphids and whiteflies may attack holly fern. It is also susceptible to botrytis blight.

Propagation. Propagate holly fern by division during spring or summer, or from spores.

—

Daffodil see *Narcissus*
Daily-dew see *Drosera*

—

Daphne (DAF-nee)

Flowering plant in the mezereum family that is shrubby in growth habit. Attractive, fragrant, bell-shaped flowers with four petals bloom in clusters at the ends of the branches.

Selected species and varieties. *D. × hybrida* has 3-inch, oblong, shiny leaves and dark pink flowers that appear in spring. *D. odora,* winter daphne, has 3-inch, smooth, shiny, narrow, oblong leaves and white, pink, red or purple flowers that bloom in fall and winter. Winter daphne is often grown as a source of cut flowers. 'Aureomarginata' has leaves with gold-colored edges.

Growing conditions. Grow daphne at 3,000 to 5,000 footcandles. Night temperature should be 40° to 45° F. Grow in well-drained, soilless potting medium and keep it barely moist. Fertilize once a year in the spring with 20-20-20. Plants may be kept compact by pruning after they flower. Daphne may be bothered by aphids, mealybugs and scales.

Propagation. Propagate daphne from seeds, by softwood cuttings in

spring, by hardwood cuttings in fall, by grafting or by layering.

—

Davallia (da-VAL-ee-a)

Plant in the fern family grown for both its foliage and its unusual rhizomes. Foliage is triangular, finely divided and feathery. The rhizomes grow above the surface of the medium and resemble animal paws; they are long, narrow, and covered with tan or brown hairs.

Selected species and varieties. *D. fejeensis,* rabbit's-foot fern, grows up to 2 feet across. The rhizomes are ½ inch thick and covered with long brown hairs. *D. trichomanoides,* squirrel's-foot fern, grows up to 18 inches across. The rhizomes are ¼ inch thick and covered with tan hairs.

Growing conditions. Grow davallia at 2,000 to 3,000 footcandles. Night temperature should be 50° to 65° F. Grow in very rich, well-drained, soilless medium to which fir or redwood bark and lime, bone meal or other source of calcium have been added. Water to keep the medium constantly moist during the growing period; in the winter, water only to keep the fronds from wilting. Do not feed new plants for six months; fertilize established plants with half-strength 20-20-20 in early spring and again in early summer. Davallia tolerates 50 percent humidity, which is lower than most ferns require. Because the rhizomes grow over the edge of the container, davallia is best grown in a wire hanging basket lined with sphagnum peat moss. The rhizomes can be pinned to the basket to create a rounded plant. Davallia is susceptible to scales, mealybugs, aphids, whiteflies and botrytis blight.

Propagation. Propagate davallia by division or from spores. Pieces of rhizome may also be cut, secured to the growing medium with wire clips and rooted.

—

Delphinium (del-FIN-ee-um)
Larkspur

Member of the buttercup family that is grown in the greenhouse for cutting flowers. Leaves are deeply divided; flowers bloom in tall, erect, dense spikes from late winter through early summer.

Selected species and varieties.
D. elatum grows 5 to 6 feet tall and has three- to seven-part leaves. Flowers are 1 inch across and white, pink, blue, lavender, purple or red. The center of each flower is a contrasting color, usually white. Pacific hybrids are the most satisfactory for forcing in the greenhouse.

Growing conditions. Grow larkspur at 4,000 to 8,000 footcandles. Night temperature should be 40° to 45° F from the time the seeds have germinated until midwinter, and 50° to 55° F from midwinter until the plants have finished flowering. Grow in well-drained, soilless medium and keep it evenly moist at all times. Fertilize every other week with 20-20-20. Plants need to be staked. Remove faded flowers to prolong the blooming period. It is best to discard larkspur plants after they have finished flowering because they cannot be satisfactorily reforced. Larkspur may be attacked by aphids, mites, thrips and mealybugs. It is also susceptible to powdery mildew.

Propagation. Larkspur is grown from seeds sown from midsummer to early fall; flowers will bloom nine to 12 months later.

—

Dendrobium (den-DRO-bee-um)

Flowering plant in the orchid family. This is a variable genus; some species have flat, thin leaves, and others have thick, leathery leaves. Flower size and shape are also variable.

Selected species and varieties.
D. aggregatum is a dwarf plant that has a 2-inch stem and one 3-inch, lance-shaped leaf. Flowers are flat, 1½ inches across, and gold or orange-yellow with a lip that has a deeper-colored base. Blooms appear in drooping clusters of three to 12 flowers in spring. *D. nobile* has 2- to 3-foot canelike stems and 4- to 5-inch strap-shaped leaves. Flowers have two narrow petals, three wider petals and a large, cup-shaped lip. Blooms are fragrant, 3 inches across, rose-lavender or white tipped in rose-purple, and have a white lip tipped in rose with a dark purple throat. Flowers bloom in winter and spring in clusters of two or three. *D. phalaenopsis* has 2-foot canelike stems and 7-inch strap-shaped leaves. Flowers have reflexed petals and appear from late spring to late fall in drooping clusters of four to 18 blooms. Flowers are rose-purple or white tinged in pink with a lip that has a dark purple

throat. There are many dendrobium hybrids that are purple, rose, magenta or white tinged in a contrasting color, with lips that may be spotted, blotched or of a contrasting color.

Growing conditions. Grow dendrobium at 2,500 to 4,000 footcandles. Night temperature should be 60° F. Grow in a special orchid-potting medium, or in a soilless medium with extra fir bark, redwood bark or osmunda fiber added. Dendrobium can also be grown on a slab of tree fern bark. Fertilize monthly from midfall to midspring, and twice monthly from midspring to midfall. Stop fertilizing if flower buds do not develop at the proper blooming time. Use 20-20-20 if the potting medium contains osmunda fiber, and 30-10-10 if it contains bark; a high concentration of nitrogen is needed because the bark uses nitrogen as it decomposes.

D. aggregatum should be kept constantly moist except when the plant starts to produce flower buds; then watering should be reduced. Other dendrobiums should be allowed to become almost dry between waterings when the plant is in growth. In late fall and winter, water only enough to keep the plant from shriveling. Keeping the medium dry in late fall and winter also induces flower bud set. Plants in fresh bark medium will need more frequent watering than those in older medium, as older medium retains more water. As the bark in the potting medium breaks down over time, plants should be repotted at least every two years in spring or summer. Repot carefully, as most dendrobiums do not like to be disturbed. Humidity should be 50 to 70 percent for *D. aggregatum* and 50 to 60 percent for other dendrobiums. Constant air circulation is necessary. Plants should be placed in a shaded section of the greenhouse during the summer. It is normal for dendrobiums other than *D. aggregatum* to lose some of their leaves during fall and winter. Scales, slugs and snails may attack dendrobium. Dendrobium is also susceptible to virus diseases.

Propagation. All dendrobiums can be propagated from seeds or by division. The roots contain water- and food-storing tissue called pseudobulbs; when dividing, make sure that there are four to six pseudobulbs per division. Dendrobiums that have canelike stems may also be propagated by cutting pieces of the stem and laying them atop moist sphagnum moss or osmunda fiber. Small plantlets will grow along the stems; they can be cut off and potted when they develop roots.

DELPHINIUM ELATUM PACIFIC HYBRID

DENDROBIUM NOBILE

109

DIANTHUS CARYOPHYLLUS

DIONAEA MUSCIPULA

DRACAENA FRAGRANS 'MASSANGEANA'

Dianthus (dy-AN-thus)
Pink

Annual or perennial plant in the pink family, one species of which is grown in the greenhouse for cutting flowers. The stems have swollen nodes; foliage is grasslike. Flowers may be single or double and may bloom one to a stem or in clusters.

Selected species and varieties. *D. caryophyllus,* carnation, has erect stems 2 to 4 feet tall and 3- to 6-inch blue-green leaves. Flowers are double, fragrant, 1 to 4 inches across, and appear in clusters of two to five blooms. Flower color may be white, pink, red, purple, yellow, apricot or white spotted in red.

Growing conditions. Grow carnations at 6,000 to 8,000 footcandles. Night temperature should be 50° to 55° F. The greenhouse should be cooled or the plants should be shaded during the summer. Grow in a well-drained, soilless medium that has a pH of 6.0 to 7.0. Plants may be grown in pots or directly in the greenhouse bench. Allow the medium to dry out slightly between waterings. During watering, to prevent disease, take care not to wet the foliage. Fertilize weekly with quarter-strength 20-20-20. Humidity should be under 50 percent. Newly planted carnations should be pinched 30 days after planting; a second pinch 30 days later on half of the stems will result in more evenly spaced flower production. Carbon dioxide should be introduced into the greenhouse to produce stronger stems, larger flowers and faster flower production. If CO_2 is used, night temperature may be raised by five degrees. Flowers may split if daytime temperature is more than 15 degrees higher than night temperature. Plants may be disbudded to produce larger flowers. Carnations may be attacked by aphids, thrips, spider mites, slugs, snails. They are also susceptible to leaf spot, wilt, botrytis, virus, root rot and stem rot diseases.

Propagation. Carnations are propagated from seeds or by stem cuttings rooted in winter or spring.

Dionaea (dy-o-NEE-a)

Member of the sundew family grown in the greenhouse as a curiosity. The plant has the ability to trap and digest flies and other insects. Leaves form in a basal rosette. Single flowers bloom in clusters in spring at the ends of long stems.

Selected species and varieties. *D. muscipula,* Venus flytrap, has leaves that are 5 inches long and flat. The upper portion of the leaf has a two-lobed, spiny, hinged reddish blade that closes over an insect when it senses its presence. Flowers are white and bloom on top of 3- to 15-inch stems.

Growing conditions. Grow Venus flytrap at 5,000 to 8,000 footcandles. Night temperature should be 55° F. Grow in sphagnum peat moss that is kept constantly wet. Plants should not be fertilized. Humidity should be at least 80 percent. Venus flytrap may be grown inside a sealed glass container to keep humidity high and to confine insects, although the plant does not need insects to survive. Flowers should be removed as soon as they form because they weaken the plant. There are no insects or diseases that bother Venus flytrap.

Propagation. Propagate Venus flytrap from seeds or by root division.

Dracaena (dra-SEE-na)

Foliage plant in the agave family. Plants are shrubby or treelike and have either broad or narrow leaves. As the plant grows and the lower leaves fall, a trunk that may be slender or thick becomes evident.

Selected species and varieties. *D. cincta* grows 24 inches high and has narrow, sword-shaped leaves that have reddish brown margins. The straight *D. derememsis* species is rarely grown, but several of its cultivars are common. 'Janet Craig' grows 2 to 5 feet tall and has strap-shaped, shiny, dark green, corrugated, 12- to 18-inch leaves. 'Warneckii', striped dracaena, grows 2 to 5 feet tall and has sword-shaped, stiff, corrugated leaves that have a milky green center and two white stripes at the margins. *D. fragrans* grows to 6 feet tall and has dark green, soft, arching, shiny foliage. 'Massangeana', corn plant, has leaves with a broad, light green to yellow stripe down the center. *D. sanderana,* Belgian evergreen, grows to 3 feet tall and has soft, slightly twisted, 7- to 9-inch leaves that have white stripes on the margins. *D. surculosa,* previously designated *D. godseffiana,* grows 18 to 24 inches tall and has shiny, leathery, oval leaves spotted in white.

Growing conditions. Grow dracaena at 3,000 to 4,000 footcandles. Night temperature should be

65° to 70° F. Grow in well-drained, soilless medium and keep it evenly moist at all times except in winter, when it should be allowed to dry out slightly between waterings. Fertilize monthly during spring and summer with 20-20-20. Humidity should be below 50 percent. Plants can be cut back if they grow too tall; new growth will originate at the top of the stem. Dracaena may develop leaf spot disease and may attract spider mites, mealybugs and scales.

Propagation. Propagate dracaena from seeds, by stem cuttings or by air layering.

Drosera (DRAH-ser-a)
Sundew, daily-dew

Member of the sundew family grown in the greenhouse as a curiosity. The plant has the ability to trap and digest insects. Leaves form in a basal rosette. Flowers are single and bloom one to a stem or in clusters at the ends of long stems in spring.

Selected species and varieties. *D. rotundifolia* has ½-inch, round, hairy leaves that appear at the ends of 2-inch stems. Flowers are white or pink and appear in clusters of up to 25 blooms on top of 2- to 12-inch stems.

Growing conditions. Grow sundew at 5,000 to 8,000 footcandles. Night temperature should be 50° to 55° F. Grow in sphagnum peat moss that is kept constantly wet. Plants should not be fertilized. Humidity should be at least 80 percent. Sundew may be grown inside a sealed glass container to keep humidity high and to confine insects, although the plant does not need insects to survive. Flowers should be removed as soon as they form because they weaken the plant. There are no insects or diseases that bother sundew.

Propagation. Propagate sundew from seeds, by root cuttings or by root division.

Dutch iris see *Iris*
Easter lily see *Lilium*
Easter-lily cactus see *Echinopsis*
East star see *Cryptanthus*

Echinocactus (ek-i-no-KAK-tus)

Plant in the cactus family. Plants are globe-shaped or cylindrical, ribbed and covered with sharp spines. Plants produce yellow flowers in spring.

Selected species and varieties. *E. grusonii*, barrel cactus, is a globe-shaped, light green plant that grows up to 12 inches across and has yellow or golden spines. Yellow flowers appear at the top of the plant.

Growing conditions. Grow barrel cactus at 5,000 to 8,000 footcandles. Night temperature should be 60° to 65° F from spring through fall, and should be lowered to 45° to 50° F in winter. Grow in soilless potting medium that has extra perlite or sharp sand added to ensure excellent drainage. From spring through fall, allow the top ¼ inch of medium to dry out before watering; in winter, water only enough to keep the plants from shriveling. Do not feed newly potted plants for one year; fertilize mature plants once a year in spring with 20-20-20. Humidity should be less than 50 percent. Barrel cactus is susceptible to rot and wilt diseases and can attract mealybugs, spider mites and scales.

Propagation. Propagate barrel cactus from seeds sown in late spring or early summer.

Echinopsis (ek-i-NOP-sis)
Sea-urchin cactus

Plant in the cactus family. Plants are globe-shaped or oblong, ribbed and covered with sharp spines. In spring they produce funnel-shaped flowers that open at night and close during the day.

Selected species and varieties. *E. multiplex*, Easter-lily cactus, is a globe-shaped, medium to dark green plant that grows up to 8 inches across and has yellow, black-tipped, 1-inch spines. Flowers are fragrant, rose-red, 6 to 10 inches across and bloom at the ends of 8-inch stems. Hybrids have showy flowers of white or pink.

Growing conditions. Grow Easter-lily cactus at 5,000 to 8,000 footcandles. Night temperature should be 60° to 65° F from spring through fall, and should be lowered to 45° to 50° F in winter. Grow in soilless potting medium that has extra perlite or sharp sand added to ensure excellent drainage. From spring through fall, allow the top ¼ inch of medium to dry out before watering; in winter, water only enough to keep the plants from shriveling. Do not feed newly potted plants for one year; fertilize mature plants once a year in spring with 20-20-20. Humidity should be less than 50 percent. Insects that attack Easter-lily cactus

DROSERA ROTUNDIFOLIA

ECHINOCACTUS GRUSONII

ECHINOPSIS MULTIPLEX HYBRID

111

EPIPHYLLUM CHRYSOCARDIUM HYBRID

EPISCIA CUPREATA

ERICA CANALICULATA 'ROSEA'

include mealybugs, spider mites and scales. The plants are susceptible to rot and wilt diseases.

Propagation. Propagate Easter-lily cactus from seeds sown in late spring or early summer, or by offshoots.

—

Egyptian star see *Pentas*
Elephant's ear see *Caladium*
English ivy see *Hedera*

—

Epiphyllum (ep-i-FY-lum)
Orchid cactus

Flowering plant in the cactus family. It is included in a group known as jungle cacti because it requires higher humidity, more water and richer soil than desert cacti. Branches are flat, drooping and lobed. Flowers are large, fragrant and tubular, with flaring petals opening into a cup or funnel shape. Some flowers open only during the day; others open only at night. All have showy stamens.

Selected species and varieties. *E. chrysocardium* has waxy branches up to 2 feet long. Flowers are white and 3 inches across and usually bloom in spring. There are thousands of hybrids that have flowers of purple, red, pink, white or yellow. Many of the hybrids bloom in winter.

Growing conditions. Grow orchid cactus at 2,000 to 4,000 footcandles. Night temperature should be 65° to 75° F from early spring to midfall, and 50° to 55° the rest of the year. Flowers will not form if the temperature is too high from midfall through winter. Grow in well-drained, soilless medium to which extra peat moss has been added. As soon as the temperature is lowered in midfall, allow the medium to dry out between waterings. When flower buds form in spring, increase watering and keep the medium evenly moist; if the medium is too dry after flower buds form, the buds will drop. Moving the plant may also cause bud drop. Fertilize every four weeks in spring and summer with 10-20-20. Branches can be pinched after the plant has flowered to keep it compact. Orchid cactus attracts spider mites and is susceptible to rot and wilt diseases.

Propagation. Orchid cactus may be propagated by stem cuttings taken in summer.

Episcia (e-PIS-ee-a)
Carpet plant

Flowering plant in the gesneriad family that is suitable for hanging baskets. Leaves are oval to elliptical and hairy. Flowers are 1 to 1½ inches long, tubular to bell-shaped, five-lobed, and bloom in spring and summer. The plant produces plantlets at the ends of runners.

Selected species and varieties. *E. cupreata,* flame violet, has 2- to 5-inch, wrinkled leaves that are clear green, reddish green, copper or marked with silver. Flowers are dark red with red-spotted yellow undersides. *E. lilacina* has 4-inch, quilted, green, reddish green or bronze leaves, often with rose-purple undersides. Flowers are lavender and have yellow throats. *E. punctata* has 3-inch, leathery, green leaves with reddish purple midribs. It is less hairy than other species. Flowers are creamy white and spotted in purple. *E. reptans,* flame violet, has 5-inch, quilted, dark green leaves that have pale green or silver midribs. Flowers are fringed and dark red with pink inside the tube.

Growing conditions. Grow carpet plant at 3,000 to 4,000 footcandles. Night temperature should be 65° to 70° F. Grow in well-drained, soilless medium to which extra peat moss has been added. Keep the medium evenly moist at all times; do not allow water to touch the leaves, or they will become spotted. Fertilize weekly during spring and summer with quarter-strength 20-20-20. Humidity should be at least 60 percent. Pinch the plant after it flowers to encourage fullness. Carpet plant is susceptible to spider mites, whiteflies, mealybugs and botrytis blight.

Propagation. Propagate carpet plant by stem cuttings or by rooting the plantlets that grow at the ends of the runners.

—

Erica (ER-i-ka)
Heath

Shrubby, flowering member of the heath family, some species of which are grown as greenhouse plants. Leaves are small, needlelike and held closely to the branches. Flowers are bell-shaped and bloom in nodding clusters at the ends of the branches.

Selected species and varieties. *E. canaliculata,* Christmas heather, has hairy branches and ¼-inch leaves that appear in threes. Flowers are ⅛ inch across, white or pink with black stamens, and bloom during winter. 'Rosea' has rose-pink flowers; 'Rubra' has red flowers.

Growing conditions. Grow Christmas heather at 4,000 to 8,000 footcandles. Night temperature should be 40° to 50° F. Grow in acidic, well-drained, soilless medium to which extra peat moss has been added. Allow the medium to dry out slightly between waterings. Fertilize once in early spring with 20-20-20. Scales may attack Christmas heather.

Propagation. Propagate Christmas heather by stem cuttings taken in spring.

—

Euphorbia (yew-FOR-bee-a)

Flowering, succulent plant that has tiny flowers surrounded by colorful bracts. One species, *E. pulcherrima,* is the poinsettia, traditionally used as a Christmas plant. All species contain a milky sap that may cause a skin rash.

Selected species and varieties. *E. milii splendens,* crown-of-thorns, is a shrubby plant growing 1 to 3 feet tall. The stems are brown, spiny and sparsely clothed with oblong to oval, 2- to 2½-inch leaves. Flowers are surrounded by ½-inch red bracts that appear in summer. *E. pseudocactus* forms a clump of thick, leafless, spiny branches. The branches are bright green and have fan-shaped markings. Flowers are surrounded by small yellow bracts. *E. pulcherrima,* poinsettia, grows 6 inches to several feet tall. Leaves are 4 to 7 inches long, toothed or lobed, and dull green. The flowers are surrounded in winter by showy bracts of red, pink, white or mottled combinations of all three colors. Three common cultivars are 'Annette Hegg', 'Eckespoint' and 'Mikkelsen'.

Growing conditions. Grow all euphorbias at 5,000 to 6,000 footcandles. Night temperature should be 60° to 65° F. Once poinsettia bracts are showing color, night temperature should be reduced to 58° to 62° F. Grow in well-drained, soilless medium that has a pH of 6.0 to 6.8. Large poinsettia plants should have extra sand added to the medium to weight the pots and prevent them from toppling over. Water crown-of-thorns and *E. pseudocactus* when the soil surface dries out; poinsettias should be kept evenly moist at all times. Fertilize crown-of-thorns and *E. pseudocactus* with 20-20-20 every

two weeks from spring through fall. Fertilize poinsettia with 20-20-20 every week from late spring until the bracts have fully developed their color. Crown-of-thorns may be pruned back in early spring to keep the plants compact.

To force a poinsettia to bloom for Christmas, shade it with black cloth or black polyethylene during the fall for 15 hours a night for 40 nights. The date to start the shading depends on the variety. 'Annette Hegg' blooms in eight and a half to nine weeks after the start of shading; 'Eckespoint' needs 11 weeks; 'Mikkelsen' needs nine and a half to 10 weeks;.

After a poinsettia has dropped its bracts in spring, it should be cut back to 4 to 6 inches. The original plant may be grown and forced again, or cuttings may be taken from the original plant and the original plant may then be discarded. Plants may be grown as single stem plants, or pinched to encourage branching. If plants are pinched, pinch out the growing tip when new shoots have three to four leaves. Pinching may continue until September 1. Growth regulators may also be applied to keep plants compact.

All of the euphorbias are susceptible to whiteflies, spider mites, aphids and mealybugs, and to botrytis blight, root rot and stem rot.

Propagation. Propagate poinsettias by stem cuttings. Crown-of-thorns and *E. pseudocactus* may be propagated by stem cuttings or from seeds.

—

European fan palm
see *Chamaerops*

Evening trumpet flower
see *Gelsemium*

—

Exacum (EK-sa-kum)

Flowering, shrubby plant in the gentian family that has small, four- or five-lobed flowers.

Selected species and varieties. *E. affine,* German violet, Persian violet, grows 6 to 12 inches tall. Leaves are light green, waxy and ½ to 1 inch long. Flowers are ½ inch across, starlike, fragrant, and blue, lavender or white. Blooms appear in clusters and each has a prominent deep yellow center.

Growing conditions. Grow German violet at 2,000 to 4,000 footcandles. The plant should be placed where it is shaded from direct sun

EUPHORBIA MILII SPLENDENS

EUPHORBIA PULCHERRIMA

EXACUM AFFINE

× FATSHEDERA LIZEI 'VARIEGATA'

FICUS BENJAMINA 'VARIEGATA'

during the summer. Night temperature should be 60° to 65° F. Grow in well-drained, soilless medium, and keep it evenly moist. Fertilize every two weeks with half-strength 20-20-20. Humidity should be above 50 percent. Remove faded flowers to extend the blooming period. After the plant has finished blooming, it will die. German violet is not susceptible to insects or diseases.

Propagation. Propagate German violet from seeds sown in winter or spring. Plants will bloom in four months. German violet may also be propagated from stem cuttings.

Fairy washboard see *Haworthia*
Fan palm see *Chamaerops*

× **Fatshedera** (fats-HED-e-ra)
Aralia ivy, tree ivy

Plant in the aralia family that is a cross between *Hedera* (ivy) and *Fatsia* (Japanese aralia). The plant is semi-climbing, with weak stems and large, glossy, leathery, dark green leaves that have three to five lobes. The leaves resemble those of ivy, but are larger, up to 10 inches across. The plant flowers, but is primarily grown for its foliage.

Selected species and varieties. × *F. lizei* grows 3 to 4 feet tall in the greenhouse. Leaves are 8 to 10 inches across. Flowers are small, light green to cream-colored and bloom in the fall in large, showy, branched clusters 6 to 10 inches long. Young branches are covered with rust-colored hairs. Plants are bushy when young, and become more vining in habit as they mature. 'Variegata' has leaves splashed with creamy white.

Growing conditions. Grow aralia ivy at 3,000 to 4,000 footcandles. Plants tolerate a wide range of night temperatures from 40° to 65° F. Grow in well-drained, soilless medium and keep it evenly moist. Fertilize with 20-20-20 once a month during spring and summer. Mature plants need to be tied to a trellis or staked. Stems that have become leggy or have dropped their foliage should be pruned back to the base of the plant. Pinch growing tips to encourage bushiness. Mealybugs, mites and scales may attack ivies.

Propagation. Propagate aralia ivy by stem cuttings or by air layering.

Ficus (FY-kus)
Fig

Large genus in the mulberry family that contains trees, shrubs and vines of varying sizes and descriptions, some of which are grown in the greenhouse for their foliage. All have milky sap.

Selected species and varieties. *F. benjamina,* weeping fig, grows 2 to 12 feet tall. Branches are slender and drooping, and covered with 2- to 5-inch, oval, thin, leathery, shiny leaves that are twisted at the tips. 'Variegata' has leaves with cream-colored margins. *F. carica,* common fig, grows to 8 feet tall. Leaves are 6 to 8 inches long, thick, three- to five-lobed, rough on the upper surfaces and hairy on the undersides. The edible fig is pear-shaped. *F. deltoidea,* mistletoe fig, grows 8 inches to 3 feet tall. Leaves are 1 to 3 inches long, rounded, leathery, dark green on the upper surfaces and rust-colored on the undersides. Branches are light gray. The inedible fruit is small, round, and yellow or red, resembling mistletoe. *F. elastica,* sometimes designated *F. robusta,* rubber plant, grows 2 to 12 feet tall. Leaves grow to 12 inches long and are thick, glossy and oblong to oval, with pointed tips. A rose-colored sheath encloses new leaves before they open. *F. lyrata,* fiddle-leaf fig, grows to 12 feet tall. Leaves are 12 to 18 inches long, thick, waxy, deep green and shaped like violins. Foliage has prominent white veins; the bark is shaggy. *F. pumila,* creeping fig, is a vining plant with 4-foot branches. Leaves are oval to heart-shaped, dark green and 1 inch long.

Growing conditions. Grow weeping, mistletoe and creeping figs at 3,000 to 4,500 footcandles. Grow common and fiddle-leaf figs and rubber plant at 5,000 to 6,000 footcandles. Night temperature should be 65° to 70° F. Grow in well-drained, soilless medium. Creeping fig needs extra peat moss added to the medium, and the medium should be kept evenly moist at all times; medium for the others should be allowed to dry out slightly between waterings. Do not fertilize newly potted plants for six months, then fertilize every six months with 20-20-20. Pinch growing tips to keep plants compact and bushy and to encourage branching. Keep the foliage of the large-leaved figs clean by frequent washing or dusting. Creeping fig may be grown in a hanging basket or trained to grow up a trellis or a wall. Figs benefit from being pot-bound.

They attract mealybugs, spider mites, scales and thrips, and are susceptible to leaf spot disease.

Propagation. Propagate all figs by stem cuttings; all but creeping fig may also be propagated by air layering.

—

Fiddle-leaf fig see *Ficus*

Fig see *Ficus*

Firecracker flower
see *Crossandra*

—

Fittonia (fi-TOH-nee-a)

Foliage plant in the acanthus family that has creeping stems and is suitable for a hanging basket. The leaves are marked with prominent veins that may be white or colored.

Selected species and varieties. *F. verschaffeltii*, red-nerve plant, has stems that grow to 12 inches long. Foliage is thick, oval, 3 to 4 inches long and dark olive green with deep red veins. *F. verschaffeltii argyroneura*, silver-nerve plant, has flat, thin, oval leaves that are vivid green with white veins.

Growing conditions. Grow fittonia at 2,000 to 3,000 footcandles. Leaf burn results when the light level is too high. Night temperature should be 65° to 70° F. Grow in well-drained, soilless medium. Keep the medium evenly moist in spring through fall, and allow it to dry out slightly between waterings in winter. Fertilize weekly during spring and summer with quarter-strength 20-20-20. Humidity should be above 60 percent. Pinch back growing tips to keep the plant compact. Spider mites, whiteflies and mealybugs may attack fittonia. It is susceptible to botrytis blight, root rot and stem rot.

Propagation. Propagate fittonia by stem cuttings taken in spring or early summer, or by layering.

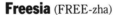

Flame nettle see *Coleus*

Flame-of-the-woods see *Ixora*

Flame violet see *Episcia*

Flamingo flower see *Anthurium*

Flowering tobacco
see *Nicotiana*

Forget-me-not see *Myosotis*

Fortunella (for-too-NEL-a)
Kumquat

Shrub or small tree in the rue family that can be grown in the greenhouse as a source of edible fruit. Leaves are thick and dark green on the upper surfaces, lighter green on the undersides. Flowers are five-lobed and white, and bloom in small clusters. The fruit is fleshy and has a thick, sweet-tasting rind.

Selected species and varieties. *F. margarita* has lance-shaped, 3- to 4-inch leaves. The flowers are fragrant, bloom in summer, and are followed in fall and winter by 1-inch, oval to round, orange to yellow fruits.

Growing conditions. Grow kumquat at 4,000 to 8,000 footcandles. Night temperature should be 50° to 55° F. Grow in well-drained, soilless medium and fertilize every two weeks during spring and summer with half-strength 20-20-20. Keep the medium evenly moist from spring through fall and slightly drier in the winter. Kumquat is susceptible to damage from thrips.

Propagation. Propagate kumquat by stem cuttings taken in summer or from seeds.

—

Freesia (FREE-zha)

Flowering bulb in the iris family that naturally blooms in late summer but can be forced into bloom in the greenhouse at any time of year. Blooms are very fragrant are funnel-shaped, grow on the upper side of wiry, arching spikes, and are generally produced for cutting flowers.

Selected species and varieties. *F. × hybrida* is a group of hybrids that have 2-inch single or double flowers of white, yellow, orange, red, bronze, lavender, blue, purple or pink.

Growing conditions. Grow freesia at 4,000 to 8,000 footcandles. Night temperature should be 45° to 50° F. Grow in well-drained, soilless medium. Keep the medium barely moist when the plant is growing; when it flowers, increase watering so the soil is constantly moist. Fertilize every two weeks with half-strength 20-20-20 when the plant is in bud or bloom. Plants can be grown either in pots or directly in greenhouse benches and will need to be staked. Freesia is generally pest- and disease-free.

FITTONIA VERSCHAFFELTII ARGYRONEURA

FORTUNELLA MARGARITA

FREESIA × HYBRIDA

FUCHSIA × HYBRIDA

GARDENIA JASMINOIDES

GASTERIA VERRUCOSA

Propagation. Plant corms 1 inch deep and so they are just touching; they will bloom in three to four months. After the plant has flowered, gradually withhold water until the foliage fades; then remove the corms from the medium and store them in the dark at 45° F. Replant the corms the following season. Freesia may also be propagated from seeds that are soaked in hot water for 24 hours before sowing.

—

Fuchsia (FEW-sha)
Lady's-eardrops

Flowering plant in the evening primrose family that has delicate drooping flowers shaped like hoop skirts. The flowers are generally two-toned and have long, showy stamens. Fuchsia is splendid in a hanging basket.

Selected species and varieties. *F. × hybrida* has 1- to 3-foot stems, 4-inch oval leaves and flowers up to 3 inches long. Blooms are in combinations of white, pink, magenta, rose, red or purple. Flowers may appear all year, but bloom is most abundant from midspring to midfall.

Growing conditions. Grow lady's-eardrops at 2,000 to 4,000 footcandles. The plant should be grown where it is shaded from direct sun in the summer. Night temperature should be 45° to 50° F. Grow in well-drained, soilless medium. From spring through fall, keep the medium evenly moist; in winter, let the medium dry between waterings. Fertilize weekly with quarter-strength 20-20-20 during spring and summer. Humidity should be above 50 percent. Pinch growing tips to keep the plant compact, and cut stems back after flowering. Spider mites, aphids, mealybugs, whiteflies and scales may attack lady's-eardrops.

Propagation. Propagate lady's-eardrops by stem cuttings. Lady's-eardrops is occasionally grown from seeds.

—

Funeral palm see *Cycas*

—

Gardenia (gar-DEEN-ya)

Flowering plant in the madder family. It has fragrant blooms that are often used as cut flowers.

Selected species and varieties. *G. jasminoides* grows 1 to 3 feet tall. Leaves are shiny, dark green and 4 to

6 inches long. Flowers are double, 3 to 5 inches across and have thick, waxy petals. Blooms appear during winter and spring.

Growing conditions. Grow gardenia at 4,000 to 8,000 footcandles. Night temperature should be 60° to 65° F; night temperature should be 60° to 62° F for bud set. Light shade may be needed during the summer to control temperature. Grow in acidic, well-drained, soilless medium. Fertilize monthly with 20-20-20. Humidity should be 60 to 70 percent. Pinch plants to encourage branching; stop pinching five months before desired bloom time. To have plants in bloom for the winter holidays, either apply black cloth for 15 hours per night for three weeks beginning in mid-July, or remove any flower buds that form before mid-September. Handle cut flowers carefully, as any bruising will cause them to turn brown. New growth that turns yellow is a sign of iron chlorosis and should be treated with iron sulfate. Insects that may attack gardenia include aphids, mealybugs, spider mites, thrips and nematodes. Gardenia is susceptible to leaf spot diseases.

Propagation. Propagate gardenia by rooting stem cuttings under mist from midfall through midspring.

—

Gasteria (gas-TEER-ee-a)
Cow-tongue cactus

Succulent plant in the lily family grown chiefly for its foliage, although it may produce loose spikes of red or rose-colored flowers in spring and summer. Leaves are thick and fleshy, and are covered with light green or white spots or small growths.

Selected species and varieties. *G. caespitosa*, pencil-leaf gasteria, grows 4 to 6 inches high. Leaves are triangular, 5½ inches long, curve backward and grow in a flat plane. *G. verrucosa*, warty aloe, wart gasteria, rice gasteria, has lance-shaped leaves 4 to 9 inches long, 1½ inches wide and dull green with raised white spots. Flowers are up to 1 inch long. There are many hybrids with thick, tongue-shaped leaves that grow in spirals. Foliage is dark green and turns purple as it matures.

Growing conditions. Grow cow-tongue cactus at 3,000 to 5,000 footcandles. Night temperature should be 50° to 55° F. Grow in soilless medium that has extra perlite or coarse sand added to ensure excellent drainage. Water when the surface has dried out to keep the medium barely moist and prevent rotting. In winter, water just enough to keep the foliage from shriveling. Do not feed newly potted plants for one year; feed established plants monthly in spring and summer with 20-20-20. Humidity should be less than 50 percent. Mealybugs, spider mites and scales may attack cow-tongue cactus.

Propagation. Propagate cowtongue cactus by stem cuttings, from seeds or by removing and rooting offsets that form at the base of the plant.

—

Gelsemium (jel-SEE-mee-um)
Yellow jessamine, Carolina jasmine

Vining plant in the logania family that has funnel-shaped, five-lobed flowers that appear singly or in small clusters in the leaf axils.

Selected species and varieties. *G. sempervirens,* evening trumpet flower, has slender branches and lance-shaped, narrow, shiny, 1½- to 4-inch leaves. The flowers are fragrant, bright yellow and 1 to 1½ inches long.

Growing conditions. Grow evening trumpet flower at 4,000 to 6,000 footcandles. Night temperature should be 50° to 55° F. Grow in well-drained, soilless medium, and keep it evenly moist. Fertilize monthly in winter, spring and summer with 20-20-20. Prune plants after they have flowered. Grow evening trumpet flower in a hanging basket or on a trellis. Mealybugs and scales may attack.

Propagation. Propagate evening trumpet flower from seeds sown in spring, by cuttings taken in spring or by air layering in spring.

—

Geranium see *Pelargonium*

—

Gerbera (jer-BEER-a)

Flowering member of the composite family that is grown in the greenhouse either as a potted plant or to produce cut flowers. Leaves grow in a basal rosette. Flowers are daisylike and bloom singly on top of thick, leafless stems.

Selected species and varieties. *G. jamesonii,* Transvaal daisy, grows 1½ to 2 feet tall. The leaves are hairy, oblong, deeply lobed or divided, and up to 10 inches long.

Flowers are single or semidouble, 4 inches across, and white, pink, red, scarlet, orange, salmon or yellow. Gerbera is usually grown to flower in winter and spring, but may flower at any time of year.

Growing conditions. Grow gerbera at 5,000 to 8,000 footcandles. Night temperature should be 50° to 55° F. Grow in well-drained, soilless medium that has extra peat moss added and a pH of 6.0 to 6.5. When the plant is growing or flowering, keep the medium evenly moist but not wet; at other times, allow it to dry out slightly between waterings. Fertilize every two weeks with half-strength 20-20-20 during spring and summer. Plants may be grown in pots or directly in the greenhouse bench. Ensure that the plant's crown is above the medium or rot will occur. Divide plants once a year. Plants are susceptible to leaf miners, mealybugs, spider mites, thrips, whiteflies, powdery mildew and root rot.

Propagation. Propagate gerbera from seeds or by division. Plants grown from seeds will flower in 11 to 12 months. Plants from divisions will flower in four to five months.

—

German ivy see *Senecio*
German violet see *Exacum*
Goldfish plant see *Columnea*
Grapefruit see *Citrus*
Grape hyacinth see *Muscari*
Grape ivy see *Cissus*
Hairy toad plant see *Stapelia*

—

Haworthia (ha-WOR-thee-a)

Succulent plant in the lily family grown primarily for its foliage, although it may produce loose spikes of white flowers in spring and summer. Leaves are thick and fleshy, and are covered with small growths. Foliage grows erect in basal rosettes.

Selected species and varieties. *H. fasciata,* zebra haworthia, grows 2 to 4 inches high. Leaves are triangular, 1½ inches long, tapered and inward-curving. They are dark green and have bands of white wartlike growths across the upper surfaces. *H. limifolia,* fairy washboard, grows 2 to 4 inches high. Leaves are

GELSEMIUM SEMPERVIRENS

GERBERA JAMESONII

HAWORTHIA FASCIATA

HEDERA HELIX

HIBISCUS ROSA-SINENSIS

HIPPEASTRUM 'MINERVA'

concave, sharply pointed and outward-curving. They are dark brownish green and have horizontal ribs. *H. retusa* is 2 inches high and 6 inches across. Leaves are triangular, toothed, outward-curving and have pale green lines running lengthwise.

Growing conditions. Grow haworthia at 3,000 to 5,000 footcandles. Night temperature should be 50° to 55° F. Grow in soilless medium that has extra perlite or coarse sand added to ensure excellent drainage. In spring, summer and fall, water when the surface has dried out to keep the medium barely moist and reduce the chance of rotting. In winter, water enough only to keep the foliage from shriveling. Do not feed newly potted plants for one year; feed established plants with 20-20-20 once a year in spring. Humidity should be lower than 50 percent. Insects that attack haworthia include mealybugs, spider mites and scales.

Propagation. Propagate haworthia from seeds, by stem cuttings, or by removing and rooting the offsets that form at the base of the plant.

—

Heath see *Erica*

—

Hedera (HED-er-a)
Ivy

Vining plant in the aralia family grown for its lobed foliage.

Selected species and varieties. *H. helix,* English ivy, has five-lobed, 2- to 4-inch, dark green foliage with white veins. There are many varieties that differ in size, shape and coloration.

Growing conditions. Grow English ivy at 4,000 to 6,000 footcandles. Night temperature should be 55° to 60° F. Grow in well-drained, soilless medium and keep it barely moist. Do not fertilize newly potted plants for three months; then fertilize every two weeks during spring and summer with 20-20-20. Grow in a hanging basket, train up a pole or train into a form over chicken wire. Pinch growing tips to encourage branching. English ivy is susceptible to aphids, scales, spider mites, crown rot and leaf spot diseases.

Propagation. Propagate English ivy by layering or by stem cuttings.

Helxine see *Soleirolia*

—

Hibiscus (hy-BIS-kus)
Rose mallow

Shrubby, flowering plant in the mallow family that has large, funnelshaped, five-petaled flowers with prominent projections from the center of the bloom. Flowers are white, yellow, red, pink, purple or blue.

Selected species and varieties. *H. rosa-sinensis,* Chinese hibiscus, grows 3 to 6 feet tall. Leaves are 6 inches long, oval, toothed and shiny dark green. Flowers are single or double and have 2- to 5-inch papery petals. Each flower lasts one day, but is quickly replaced by another. Plants may bloom all year, but flowering is most abundant in summer and fall.

Growing conditions. Grow Chinese hibiscus at 5,000 to 8,000 footcandles. Night temperature should be 60° to 65° F. Grow in well-drained, soilless medium, and keep it evenly moist. Fertilize monthly with 20-20-20. Humidity should be 50 to 60 percent. If plants stop blooming in winter, lower the temperature to 55° F, stop fertilizing and reduce watering. Prune in early spring to encourage branching and bushiness. To keep plants compact, apply growth regulator when new shoots are 1 to 1½ inches long. Scales may attack Chinese hibiscus.

Propagation. Propagate Chinese hibiscus from cuttings or seeds.

—

Hippeastrum (hip-ee-AS-trum)
Amaryllis

Bulb in the amaryllis family that is forced in the greenhouse for winter and early-spring bloom. Leaves are strap-shaped; flowers are trumpetshaped and when fully open bend downward slightly.

Selected species and varieties. Amaryllis hybrids have 6- to 10-inch white, pink, rose, red, scarlet or orange flowers that bloom in clusters of three or four on top of 18- to 24-inch, hollow stems. Some flowers are variegated or striped. Varieties include pink 'Amethyst', blush pink 'Apple Blossom', red and white striped 'Cinderella', red with white center 'Minerva', crimson 'Red Lion' and orange 'Orange Star'.

Growing conditions. Amaryllis bulbs should be planted so that only 1 inch lies between a bulb and the rim of its pot. The top third to half of the bulb should be exposed above well-drained, soilless medium. Water after potting and do not water again until growth starts; thereafter the medium should be kept evenly moist. Night temperature should be 60° to 70° F until flower buds form; then the temperature should be lowered to 55° to 60° F. Grow at 4,000 to 8,000 footcandles throughout the entire growth cycle. Fertilize once a month with 20-20-20 from the time growth starts until the foliage ripens and turns brown. After the plant has flowered, maintain watering until the foliage turns brown in late summer, then store the bulb dry for two to three months in a dark, 50° F area. The cycle then repeats itself. Mealybugs, scales, spider mites and thrips may attack amaryllis.

Propagation. Amaryllis may be propagated from seeds or by removing and potting the small bulblets that form around the main bulb. It will take two to three years to produce flowering plants.

—

Holly fern see *Cyrtomium*
Hyacinth see *Hyacinthus*

—

Hyacinthus (hy-a-SIN-thus)
Hyacinth

Spring-flowering bulb in the lily family that can be forced into bloom in the greenhouse during the winter and early spring. Leaves are strap-shaped. Flowers are small, waxy and bell-shaped, and bloom in dense, cylindrical clusters.

Selected species and varieties. *H. orientalis* grows to 18 inches tall and has very fragrant flowers. Varieties include white 'Carnegie', pink 'Pink Pearl' and 'Anne Marie', yellow 'City of Haarlem', red 'Amsterdam', and blue 'Blue Jacket' and 'Delft Blue'.

Growing conditions. There are two types of hyacinth bulbs. Prepared bulbs, the first type, are developed for early- to midwinter forcing. The second, called regular bulbs, is developed for mid- to late-winter and early-spring forcing. Store prepared bulbs at 48° to 55° F until planting; store regular bulbs at 60° to 65° F until planting.

Both types of bulbs require cold treatment before forcing. Plant bulbs in midfall in well-drained, neutral,

soilless medium and water well. Plant one bulb in a 4-inch pot, three bulbs in a 6-inch pot, and increase pot size proportionately. Bulbs may be placed outdoors under heavy mulch if the proper temperatures exist; otherwise, they must be cooled in a dark refrigerator. Prepared bulbs are held at 48° to 50° F for four weeks; then at 41° F for four weeks or until shoots are 1½ inches high; then at 32° to 35° F for two to five weeks, until shoots are 3 to 4 inches long. Pots are then moved into the greenhouse. To complete forcing, night temperature should be 65° to 73° F.

Regular bulbs follow a similar schedule for the first eight weeks, until the time when the temperature is reduced to 32° to 35° F. They must remain at that temperature for the next five to 14 weeks, when pots are moved into the greenhouse. To complete forcing, night temperature should be 60° to 65° F.

Once hyacinths are moved indoors, grow them at 4,000 to 6,000 footcandles. Keep the medium evenly moist at all times. When flower buds show color, reducing the night temperature to 50° F will result in longer-lasting flowers, but is not necessary. Large flowers will need to be staked. Do not fertilize. Blooms will appear in 10 to 20 days.

Few insects or diseases attack hyacinths. Blooms may "spit," which means stems break off at or just above the soil level, if the bulbs are planted too early, if too-high temperatures are maintained during cold treatment or as a result of poor drainage during cold treatment.

Propagation. It is difficult if not impossible to propagate your own hyacinth bulbs. After bulbs are forced, plant them in the garden, and for the greenhouse, start with new bulbs the following season.

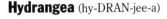

Hydrangea (hy-DRAN-jee-a)

Shrubby, flowering member of the saxifrage family with rounded or pyramidal clusters of white, pink or blue flowers. Plants naturally bloom in late summer, but are often forced in the greenhouse for spring flowering.

Selected species and varieties. *H. macrophylla macrophylla,* French hydrangea, is grown indoors and grows 18 to 24 inches tall. Leaves are shiny, oval, dark green, serrated and 2 to 6 inches long. Flowers are pink or blue and form in round clusters 8 to 10 inches across.

HYACINTHUS ORIENTALIS

HYDRANGEA MACROPHYLLA MACROPHYLLA

119

IPOMOEA × MULTIFIDA

IRIS XIPHIUM

Growing conditions. Grow hydrangea at 5,000 to 8,000 footcandles. To prevent sunburn, the plants should be moved to a shaded part of the greenhouse when flowers start to open. Grow in well-drained, soilless medium and keep it evenly moist when the plant is growing and when it is flowering. At other times, keep the medium barely moist. Humidity should be 50 to 60 percent.

Night temperature should be 55° to 65° F from midspring to midfall. In midfall, lower the night temperature to 33° to 40° F or move the plants outdoors into a cold frame or other frost-protected area for six weeks, because a cold period is necessary to initiate flower buds. To prevent disease, remove the foliage before cold storage. During the cold storage period, the plants must be kept in the dark.

After cold storage, return the plants to the greenhouse. If a night temperature of 60° F is maintained, plants will leaf out and bloom in three months. If the temperature is set at 70° F, the plants will bloom in two to two and a half months. When plants are flowering, night temperature should be 55° F to extend the blooming period. After the plant has flowered, cut it back by one-half and repeat the cycle.

The flower color of the hydrangea depends on the pH of the medium and on the amount of phosphorus in the fertilizer. For blue flowers, the medium should have a pH of 4.5 to 5.5 and the plants should be fertilized with 15-0-15 every two weeks while they are growing and flowering. If blue flowers are too purple, add aluminum sulfate to the fertilizer solution. For pink flowers, the medium should have a pH of 6.0 to 7.0 and the plants should be fertilized with 15-30-15 every two weeks while they are growing and flowering.

Aphids, mites and thrips may attack hydrangeas. The plants are also susceptible to botrytis blight, leaf spot diseases and powdery mildew.

Propagation. Propagate hydrangea by stem cuttings or by leaf-bud cuttings taken after the plant has flowered.

—

Ipomoea (ip-o-MEE-a)
Morning glory

Vining annuals and perennials in the morning glory family that grow to 8 feet tall in the greenhouse. Stems are thin and covered with oval to heart-shaped leaves. Flowers are tubular and five-lobed.

Selected species and varieties. *I. alba,* moonflower, is a perennial that has bright green, shiny, broadly oval, 5- to 8-inch leaves that are often three-lobed. Flowers are white, fragrant, up to 6 inches long and open at night. *I.* × *multifida,* cardinal climber, is an annual with finely cut, oval, 4½-inch leaves. Flowers are 2 inches long and red with white centers.

Growing conditions. Grow morning glory at 5,000 to 8,000 footcandles. Night temperature should be 60° to 65° F. Grow in well-drained, soilless medium, and keep it barely moist at all times. Fertilize monthly with half-strength 20-20-20; stop fertilizing if flowers do not form during the summer. Morning glory must be trained on a trellis or other support. To extend the blooming period, remove flowers as they fade. Prune moonflower back after blooming has ceased. Cardinal climber will die after it has bloomed and should be discarded. Aphids, scales, mealybugs, thrips and whiteflies may attack morning glory.

Propagation. Propagate morning glory from seeds. Nick the hard seed coat before sowing to hasten germination.

—

Iris (I-ris)

Spring-flowering member of the iris family. Some varieties can be forced into bloom in the greenhouse for potted plants and for cutting flowers during the winter. Some irises grow from bulbs, others from rhizomes. Leaves are narrow and grassy or lance-shaped. Flowers consist of three outer segments, called falls, which curve downward, and three inner segments known as standards, which grow erect.

Selected species and varieties. Dutch irises, the irises most commonly used for forcing, are hybrids of *I. xiphium* crossed with other irises. Flowers are 2½ to 4 inches high and bloom on top of 2-foot stems. Blooms are most commonly blue or purple, but there are white and yellow varieties. Many have golden yellow blotches on the falls.

Growing conditions. Dutch iris bulbs may be purchased either prechilled or not prechilled. If bulbs have not been prechilled, pot them 3 inches apart, and position the bulbs so that the tops are even with the surface of the medium. Chill them at 48° to 50° F, either in a refrigerator or outdoors, for four to eight weeks. At the end of the chilling period, the tops will have grown 2 to 6 inches high and the plants should be moved into the greenhouse. Bulbs that have been prechilled may be potted as above and placed directly in the greenhouse.

Grow iris at 5,000 to 8,000 footcandles. Night temperature should be 55° to 60° F. Grow in well-drained, soilless medium and keep it constantly moist. Do not fertilize. The greenhouse must be well ventilated. Iris will bloom two and a half to three months after being placed in the greenhouse. Cut flowers when the buds begin to show color. If flowers do not "blast," or fully develop, the failure may have been caused by growing temperatures above 60° F, by planting bulbs too closely together or by allowing the medium to dry out. Insects that attack iris include aphids, mites and nematodes. The plants are susceptible to rot and virus diseases.

Propagation. Iris is difficult if not impossible to propagate yourself. After a bulb has flowered, discard it or plant it outdoors in the garden and start with new bulbs for the greenhouse the following season. Once an iris bulb has been forced it cannot be reforced successfully.

—

Ivy see *Hedera*

Ivy geranium see *Pelargonium*

—

Ixora (ik-SOR-a)

Shrubby, flowering member of the madder family having tubular flowers that end in four or five spreading lobes.

Selected species and varieties. *I. coccinea,* flame-of-the-woods, grows 2 to 3 feet tall in the greenhouse. Leaves are oblong, leathery, shiny and 3 to 4 inches long. New foliage is bronze; mature foliage is dark green. Flowers are 2 inches long and 1 inch wide, red and four-lobed, blooming in 4- to 6-inch round clusters. Flowers appear most abundantly in summer but may bloom on and off all year.

Growing conditions. Grow flame-of-the-woods at 5,000 to 8,000 footcandles. Plants should be shaded from direct sun during the summer. Night temperature should be 60° to 65° F. Grow in well-drained, soilless medium and keep it moist when the plant is growing and when it is flowering. At other times, allow the medium

to become slightly dry between waterings. Fertilize every two weeks during spring and summer with 20-20-20. Humidity should be 60 to 70 percent. Prune the plant after it flowers to keep it compact. Aphids, mealybugs and scales may attack flame-of-the-woods.

Propagation. Propagate flame-of-the-woods from stem cuttings in spring or from seeds.

—

Jade plant see *Crassula*
Jasmine see *Jasminum*

—

Jasminum (JAS-mi-num)
Jasmine

Member of the olive family that has divided leaves and clusters of tubular flowers.

Selected species and varieties. *J. polyanthum* is a vine that grows to 10 feet high. Each leaf has seven leathery, lance-shaped, dark green leaflets. Flower buds are pink and open into white, fragrant, ¾-inch, tubular, star-shaped flowers. Blooms appear in winter and spring.

Growing conditions. Grow jasmine at 5,000 to 8,000 footcandles. Night temperature should be 55° to 60° F during spring, summer and fall, and 40° to 45° F during winter. Grow in well-drained, soilless medium and keep it evenly moist during spring and summer. In fall and winter, allow the medium to dry out slightly between waterings. Fertilize every two weeks during spring and summer with 20-20-20. Jasmine should be trained on a trellis or other support. Prune the plant back to 6 inches after it has bloomed. Insects that may attack jasmine include mealybugs, scales and whiteflies.

Propagation. Propagate jasmine by stem cuttings in summer or by layering.

—

Jerusalem cherry see *Solanum*
Joseph's coat see *Alternanthera*

—

Kalanchoe (kal-an-KO-ee)

Succulent plant grown either for its colorful flowers or for its unusual foliage, depending on the species.

IXORA COCCINEA

JASMINUM POLYANTHUM

KALANCHOE BLOSSFELDIANA

LACTUCA SATIVA 'DARK GREEN BOSTON'

Selected species and varieties. *K. blossfeldiana* grows 6 to 12 inches high. Foliage is oval, 1 to 3 inches long, waxy, thick and dark green with lobed, red edges. Flowers are ¼ to ½ inch across; red, orange or yellow; have four petals; and bloom in round clusters. Flowers naturally appear in winter and spring, but can be forced into bloom at any time of year by changing the day length. *K. diagremontiana* grows 10 to 15 inches tall. Leaves are oblong, 1½ to 3 inches long, blue-green or brown-green, and blotched in reddish purple. The leaf edges are deeply toothed, and small plantlets grow between the teeth. It rarely blooms, but when it does, flowers are tubular and purplish gray, and bloom in drooping clusters.

K. tomentosa, panda plant, grows 6 to 10 inches high. Leaves are 2 to 3 inches long, oblong, soft and covered with silvery hairs. The leaf margins are spotted in brown. Panda plant seldom blooms; when it does, its flowers are tubular, yellow on the outside, purple on the inside and appear in loose clusters. *K. tubiflora,* chandelier plant, grows 12 to 18 inches tall. Foliage is green tinged with pink and spotted in purplish brown, narrow, cylindrical and up to 6 inches long. The leaf tips are toothed; plantlets form between the teeth. Flowers are orange or red, tubular, narrow, 1 inch long, and appear in clusters that contain both erect and drooping blooms.

Growing conditions. Grow *K. blossfeldiana* and *K. tomentosum* at 3,000 to 6,000 footcandles; grow *K. diagremontiana* and *K. tubiflora* at 5,000 to 8,000 footcandles. Night temperature should be 55° to 60° F for *K. blossfeldiana* and *K. tomentosum* and 50° to 55° F for *K. diagremontiana* and *K. tubiflora.* Lowering night temperature to 50° F when flower buds show color will intensify the flower color of *K. blossfeldiana.* Grow all kalanchoes in well-drained, soilless medium and allow the medium to dry out slightly between waterings. Do not allow water to touch the foliage to avoid spotting and reduce disease. Fertilize *K. blossfeldiana* every two weeks with 20-20-20 until flower buds form; then discontinue fertilizing. Fertilize other kalanchoes every two weeks during spring and summer with 20-20-20. *K. blossfeldiana* may be forced into bloom by shading it with black cloth for 14 hours every night for six weeks. Kalanchoe may be damaged by aphids, thrips, mealybugs, mites, crown rot, stem rot and powdery mildew.

Propagation. All kalanchoes may be propagated by stem cuttings or by leaf cuttings. *K. diagremontiana* and *K. tubiflora* may be propagated by removing and potting the plantlets that form on the foliage. *K. blossfeldiana* may also be propagated from seeds; it will produce flowering plants in 11 months.

—

Kangaroo vine see *Cissus*
Kumquat see *Fortunella*

—

Lactuca (lak-TOO-ka)
Lettuce

Plant in the composite family grown in the greenhouse for its leaves, which are used as salad greens. Foliage grows in basal rosettes.

Selected species and varieties. *L. sativa,* garden lettuce, is available in four types. Two of these, butterhead and leaf, are best for growing in the greenhouse. Butterhead lettuce has crisp, fleshy leaves that form a small head. 'Bibb' has loosely folded, dark green leaves sometimes tinged in brown. 'Buttercrunch' has dark green, crumpled leaves that form a compact head. 'Dark Green Boston' has tight heads of dark green leaves. Leaf lettuce is nonheading, with crinkled, curled or frilled leaves. 'Grand Rapids' has light green, very frilled, crisp leaves. 'Red Sails' has ruffled and fringed reddish bronze leaves. 'Salad Bowl' has wavy, deeply lobed, lime green leaves.

Growing conditions. Grow lettuce at 4,000 to 6,000 footcandles. Night temperature should be 45° to 55° F. Grow in well-drained, soilless medium and keep the medium evenly moist. Plants may be grown in pots, directly in the greenhouse bench, or in bags of potting medium laid on the bench or on the floor. Fertilize monthly with 20-20-20. Lettuce can be harvested by removing the outer leaves as soon as they are large enough, leaving the center of the plant to continue growing, or by pulling up the entire plant. It will take eight to 10 weeks to produce butterhead lettuce in fall and spring, and 11 to 12 weeks in winter. Leaf lettuce matures about 14 days earlier. Lettuce is usually not grown in the greenhouse in summer because high heat causes the plants to bolt (form flowers). Bolting results in bitter leaves and causes premature death of the plant. Lettuce may be damaged by aphids; it is also prone to damping-off and botrytis blight.

Propagation. Lettuce is propagated from seeds. For a continuous supply, sow seeds every two to four weeks.

—

Lady of the night see *Brassavola*
Lady's-eardrops see *Fuchsia*

—

Laelia (LEE-lee-a)

Flowering plant in the orchid family. Flowers have three narrow petals, two broader petals and a three-lobed lip.

Selected species and varieties. *L. anceps* has one or two strap-shaped, 8- to 12-inch leaves. Stems are wiry, slightly arching and 2 to 4 feet long. Flowers are 2 to 4 inches wide, often fragrant, and bloom in clusters of two to five during fall and winter. The species has rose-pink flowers with a long, deep purple, yellow-blotched lip; cultivars are white, pink, rose or purple, often with lips of contrasting colors. *L. autumnalis* has two or three leathery 8-inch leaves. Flowers are fragrant, 4 inches across, and appear in clusters of four to nine on 2½-foot stems during fall and winter. The species has rose-purple flowers with a white lip; cultivars have white, deep rose or purple flowers.

Growing conditions. Grow laelia at 3,000 to 5,000 footcandles. Night temperature should be 55° to 65° F; lowering the temperature to 45° to 50° F in early fall will aid the setting of flower buds. Grow in a special orchid-potting medium, or in a soilless medium with extra fir bark, redwood bark or osmunda fiber added. Laelia can also be grown on a slab of tree fern bark. When the plants are growing and when they are flowering, allow the plants to become slightly dry between waterings; after they have flowered, withhold water until new growth appears. Plants in fresh bark medium will need more frequent watering than those in older medium because older medium retains more water. As the bark in the potting medium breaks down over time, plants should be repotted at least every two years in spring or summer. When plants are growing and when they are flowering, fertilize twice monthly. Use 30-10-10 if the potting medium contains bark, and 20-20-20 if it contains osmunda fiber. Humidity

should be 50 to 60 percent. Constant air circulation is necessary. Place the plants in a shaded section of the greenhouse during the summer. Scales, slugs, snails and virus diseases may damage laelia.

Propagation. Laelia can be propagated from seeds or by division. The roots contain water and food-storing tissue called pseudobulbs; when dividing, be sure to take four pseudobulbs per division.

—

Lantana (lan-TAY-na)
Shrub verbena

Shrubby, flowering plant in the verbena family. Small, tubular flowers bloom in 2-inch clusters; flower colors change as the blooms age.

Selected species and varieties. *L. camara,* yellow sage, grows to 4 feet tall but can be pruned to a lower height. Leaves are dark green, shiny and rough-textured. Flowers are fragrant, yellow aging to orange and red, and bloom from early spring through summer. It is possible to have all three colors in a flower cluster at the same time.

Growing conditions. Grow yellow sage at 4,000 to 6,000 footcandles. Night temperature should be 60° to 65° F during spring, summer and fall, and 55° F during winter. Yellow sage will tolerate higher temperatures if the humidity is raised above 60 percent. Grow in well-drained, soilless medium and keep it constantly moist during spring, summer and fall. Allow the medium to dry out slightly between waterings in winter. Fertilize twice a month during spring and summer with 20-20-20. In early winter, before growth starts, prune plants back to 6 inches; pinch the tips back during the first six weeks of growth, to encourage compactness. Yellow sage may be trained as a standard. Mealybugs, mites, thrips and whiteflies may attack yellow sage.

Propagation. Propagate yellow sage from stem cuttings taken in fall or from seeds sown in spring.

—

Larkspur see *Delphinium*
Leadwort see *Plumbago*
Lemon see *Citrus*
Lettuce see *Lactuca*

LAELIA ANCEPS

LANTANA CAMARA

LILIUM LONGIFLORUM

LITHOPS PSEUDOTRUNCATELLA

Lilium (LIL-ee-um)
Lily

Summer-flowering bulb in the lily family that can be forced in the greenhouse for spring bloom. Lilies can be grown either as potted plants or for cutting flowers. Plants have erect stems covered with narrow leaves, and showy, funnel-shaped flowers that may be erect, outward-facing or nodding.

Selected species and varieties. *L. longiflorum* has 3-foot stems and narrow, pointed, dark green, 5- to 7-inch leaves. The flowers are outward-facing, fragrant, white and up to 7 inches long. *L. longiflorum eximium* is the well-known Easter lily; it is similar in appearance but slightly taller and with longer flowers. *L. speciosum,* Japanese lily, grows 4 to 5 feet tall. The foliage is lance-shaped, leathery and up to 7 inches long. The flowers are 4 to 6 inches across, fragrant and drooping; the petals curve back so much that the flowers appear to be flat. Blooms are white suffused with pink or red, and have raised spots. The Asiatic hybrids are a group of lilies that includes the Mid-Century hybrids. Plants grow 2 to 5 feet high and have 4- to 6-inch flowers of white, yellow, orange, pink, lavender or red. Blooms are often spotted. 'Enchantment' and 'Connecticut Yankee' are widely grown varieties with orange flowers.

Growing conditions. Lilies benefit from prechilling before they are forced. Plant the bulbs, one to a 6-inch pot, with the top of the bulb 2 inches below the surface of the medium. Water well and maintain the pots at a temperature of 35° to 45° F for six weeks. Then move them into the greenhouse and force them at a night temperature of 63° to 65° F. Plants will bloom in another 16 to 17 weeks. If faster blooming time is desired, force at 68° to 70° F. If slower blooming time is desired, force at 55° F.

Grow lilies at 5,000 to 8,000 footcandles. Grow in rich, soilless medium that has a pH of 6.0 to 7.0 and excellent drainage, and keep it evenly moist. Fertilize weekly with quarter-strength 20-20-20 beginning when the shoots appear and continuing until the flowers have faded. Growth regulator may be applied when the plants are 3 to 6 inches high to keep them compact. After the plants have flowered and the leaves have withered, discard the bulbs or move them into the garden. Lilies cannot be successfully reforced. Lilies are susceptible to aphids,

mealybugs, scales, thrips, botrytis blight, leaf spot diseases and viruses.

Propagation. Propagate lilies by removing and potting the bulblets that form at the base of the bulb or by peeling off and potting the scales. Lilies may also be propagated from seeds. It will take two to four years to produce plants of flowering size.

—

Lily see *Lilium*
Lily-of-the-Nile see *Agapanthus*
Lime see *Citrus*

—

Lithops (LITH-ops)
Living-stones

Stemless succulent plant in the carpetweed family grown as a curiosity in the greenhouse. It is made up of a pair of thick, fleshy leaves that resemble stones. Yellow or white daisylike flowers bloom in late summer and fall from the crevice between the leaves. The leaves shrivel and die after the plant has flowered, and a new pair of leaves forms in spring.

Selected species and varieties. *L. bella* is 1 inch high and has brownish yellow leaves with green or dark brown markings. Flowers are 1 inch across, fragrant and white. *L. marmorata* grows 1½ inches tall and has beige leaves marked in brown. Flowers are 1¼ inches across, fragrant and white. *L. pseudotruncatella* grows to 1¼ inches in height and has gray leaves tinged with purple and golden yellow flowers that are 1⅜ inches across. There are many varieties and hybrids of living-stones; they may be gray, yellowish green, beige, reddish brown or yellow-brown, spotted in contrasting colors or marked with transparent spots.

Growing conditions. Grow living-stones at 5,000 to 8,000 footcandles. They will tolerate lower light, but the leaf markings will not be as evident, and the plants will not flower. Night temperature should be 55° to 60° F from fall through spring. In summer, lithops tolerates temperatures as high as 80° F. Grow in a soilless medium to which coarse sand or perlite has been added to ensure excellent drainage. In spring through fall, water when the medium dries out. After the flowers fade in fall, do not water until the following spring. Do not fertilize. The humidity must be under 50 percent and the greenhouse must be well ventilated. There are no insects that attack living-stones. It is susceptible to rot caused by overwatering or high humidity.

Propagation. Propagate living-stones by division in spring or summer, or from seeds.

—

Living-stones see *Lithops*
Living-vase see *Aechmea*

—

Lobivia (lo-BIV-ee-a)
Cob cactus

Plant in the cactus family. Plants may be globe-shaped or cylindrical, and are ribbed and covered with sharp spines. Flowers are funnel- or bell-shaped, bloom in spring and summer, and close at night.

Selected species and varieties. *L. binghamiana* is globe-shaped, 3½ inches across, and green with white markings and yellow spines. Flowers are 2 inches across and purplish red.

Growing conditions. Grow cob cactus at 5,000 to 8,000 footcandles. Night temperature should be 60° to 65° F from spring through fall, and should be lowered to 40° to 45° F in winter. Grow in soilless potting medium that has extra perlite or sharp sand added to ensure excellent drainage. Let the top ¼ inch of medium dry out before watering from spring through fall; in winter, water enough only to keep the plants from shriveling. Do not feed newly potted plants for one year; fertilize mature plants once a year in spring with 20-20-20. Humidity should be less than 50 percent. Cob cactus attracts mealybugs, scales and spider mites. It is susceptible to rot and wilt diseases.

Propagation. Propagate cob cactus from seeds sown in spring or by removing and potting the offsets that form at the base of the plant.

—

Lobster claws see *Vriesea*

—

Lycopersicon (ly-ko-PER-si-kon)
Tomato

Member of the nightshade family that can be forced in the greenhouse for its edible fruit. Tomatoes are available in sizes ranging from the ¾-inch cherry tomatoes to the beefsteak types that grow 5 inches or more across. Fruit

may be round, oval, globular or pear-shaped, and is usually red, although there are yellow, orange and pink varieties.

Selected species and varieties. *L. lycopersicum* plants generally belong to either of two groups: determinate or indeterminate. Determinate tomatoes are bushy plants whose fruit ripens at the same time. This type of tomato can be eaten fresh or used for canning, juice and cooking. Indeterminate tomatoes are vining plants that flower and produce fruit continuously. These are best used fresh in salads.

When choosing tomato plants, consider the available space in the greenhouse. If it is limited, choose a dwarf variety that can be grown in a small container or in a hanging basket. These varieties are all determinate and include 'Goldie Hybrid', which is 14 inches tall and produces 1-inch golden yellow fruit; 'Minibel', which is 24 inches high and produces 2-inch fruit; and 'Tiny Tim', which is 15 inches tall and produces ¾-inch cherry tomatoes.

There are varieties developed for greenhouse forcing that require lower light conditions and are more compact in growth. These are all indeterminate, produce standard-sized tomatoes and include 'Park's Greenhouse Hybrid 130', 'Tuckcross 520' and 'Tuckcross 533'. Many garden tomatoes can be successfully forced indoors, especially 'Better Boy', 'Better Bush' and 'Early Girl'. When selecting tomatoes, choose those with disease resistance; this is indicated by the letters *V, F, N, T* or *A* after the variety name. The initials stand for the variety's resistance to verticillium wilt, fusarium wilt, nematodes, tobacco mosaic virus and alternaria.

Growing conditions. Grow tomatoes at 5,000 to 8,000 footcandles. Night temperature should be 62° to 65° F. Grow in well-drained, soilless medium and keep it evenly moist. Tomatoes may be grown in pots, directly in the greenhouse bench, or in bags of potting medium laid on the floor or on the greenhouse bench. When plants are young, fertilize monthly with quarter-strength 20-20-20; as soon as the plants start to set fruit, increase the fertilization to weekly. Tap the flowers to aid in pollination. Vining tomatoes will need to be staked, or trained as a single stem on a wire or string. To keep the plants producing, pick the fruit as soon as it ripens. Tomatoes are susceptible to aphids, nematodes, whiteflies, viruses and wilt diseases.

LOBIVIA BINGHAMIANA

LYCOPERSICON LYCOPERSICUM

MAMMILLARIA COMPRESSA

MANGIFERA INDICA

Propagation. Propagate tomatoes from seed. It will take three to five months to produce fruit after sowing seed, depending on the variety and the time of year.

___

Madagascar jasmine
see *Stephanotis*

Magic flower see *Achimenes*

Maidenhair fern see *Adiantum*

___

Mammillaria (mam-i-LAR-ee-a)
Pincushion

Plant in the cactus family. Plants may be hemispherical or oblong, are covered with small, rounded projections, and grow in clumps. Sharp spines grow from the center of each projection. The plants are often covered with woolly or hairy growth, and contain a milky juice. Flowers bloom in winter and spring, and close at night. They form in a circular ring at the top of the plant.

Selected species and varieties. *M. compressa* grows to 8 inches high and 3 inches thick. Spines are white; flowers are ⅝ inch across and purplish red. *M. schiedeana* grows 4 inches high and 1½ inches thick. Spines are white with yellow tips; flowers are ¾ inch across and white.

Growing conditions. Grow pincushion at 5,000 to 8,000 footcandles. Night temperature should be 60° to 65° F from spring through fall, and should be lowered to 40° to 45° F in winter. Grow in a soilless potting medium that has extra perlite or sharp sand added to ensure excellent drainage. From spring through fall, allow the top ¼ inch of medium to dry out before watering; in winter, water enough only to keep the plants from shriveling. Do not feed newly potted plants for one year; fertilize mature plants once a year in spring with 20-20-20. Humidity should be less than 50 percent. Pincushion attracts mealybugs, spider mites and scales. It is susceptible to rot and wilt diseases.

Propagation. Propagate pincushion from seeds sown in spring or by removing and potting the plantlets that form at the base of the plant.

___

Mangifera (man-JIF-er-a)
Mango

Tropical tree in the cashew family that can be grown in the greenhouse as a source of edible fruit.

Selected species and varieties. *M. indica* can grow to 15 or more feet indoors, but can be kept smaller by pruning and by growing it in a container that restricts its root growth. Leaves are stiff, lance-shaped, and 8 or more inches long. Flowers are pink or white, hairy, and bloom in winter or early spring. The fruit is oval, 3 to 5 inches long, green-, yellow- or red-skinned, and with orange pulp. Fruits are borne from spring to fall. Some people are allergic to the flowers and to the skin of the mango.

Growing conditions. Grow mango at 5,000 to 8,000 footcandles. Night temperature should be 60° to 65° F. Grow in rich, well-drained, soilless medium and allow it to dry out slightly between waterings. Fertilize with 20-20-20 once a month. Shake the flowers or hand-pollinate to ensure fruit set. If the plants are growing too large, prune them after they have fruited. Mango may be damaged by mealybugs, mites, scales and thrips.

Propagation. Propagate mango by stem cuttings, by budding or by grafting.

___

Mango see *Mangifera*

___

Maranta (ma-RAN-ta)

Foliage plant in the arrowroot family that has thin leaves with distinctive markings.

Selected species and varieties. *M. leuconeura,* prayer plant, grows 6 to 12 inches high. The leaves are oval to elliptical, up to 5 inches long and fold at night like a pair of praying hands. Foliage is green with red veins and dark brown spots on both sides of the midrib. The variety *M. leuconeura erythroneura* is similar, but the leaves are more oblong and the markings are larger and darker.

Growing conditions. Grow prayer plant at 2,000 to 3,000 footcandles. Too much light causes the leaves to become papery and lose their markings. Night temperature should be 65° to 70° F. Grow in well-drained, soilless medium and keep it constantly moist during spring and summer. In fall and winter, allow the medium to become dry on the surface between waterings. Do not fertilize newly potted plants for three months; after that, fertilize monthly during spring and summer with 20-20-20. Humidity should be 60 to 70 percent to prevent brown leaf tips. The plants should be placed in a shaded part of the greenhouse during the summer. Prayer plant is very sensitive to fluorides in water, which cause leaf tips and edges to turn brown. It is also susceptible to spider mites, root rot and stem rot.

Propagation. Propagate prayer plant either by division or by leaf-stem cuttings.

—

Marguerite daisy
see *Chrysanthemum*

—

Matthiola (math-ee-O-la)
Stock

Flowering plant in the mustard family that is grown in the greenhouse for cutting flowers. Flowers are cross-shaped, single or double, heavily fragrant and bloom in spikes on 12- to 18-inch stems.

Selected species and varieties. *M. incana* has stiff spikes of 1-inch white, blue, purple, reddish, pink or yellowish flowers. The columnar types, usually grown in the greenhouse, produce clusters of blooms on single spikes. There are also types that branch, producing several spikes. Stock is grown to flower between January and June; attempts to grow it at other times of the year usually result in plants that do not flower.

Growing conditions. Grow stock at 5,000 to 8,000 footcandles. Night temperature should be 60° F until the plants have formed 10 leaves. Then, night temperature should be reduced to 40° to 50° F for three weeks to induce flower buds. No flowers will form if daytime temperature is above 65° F during this period. After flower buds have formed, plants should be grown at a night temperature of 50° to 60° F. Grow in a soilless medium that has excellent drainage and a pH of 5.5 to 6.5. Stock may be grown in pots or directly in the greenhouse bench. The medium must be kept evenly moist at all times. Fertilize weekly with quarter-strength 20-5-30. Stock has a high potassium requirement; insufficient potassium causes the foliage to fall from the plant. Growth regulator may be applied when the plants have four leaves to keep them compact. The greenhouse must be well ventilated. Stock may be attacked by aphids and thrips. It is susceptible to botrytis blight and stem rot.

Propagation. Propagate stock from seeds. Soak seeds in 129° F water for 10 minutes before sowing to destroy seedborne bacteria. Thin the plants after they have six leaves; those that have notched or lobed leaves will produce double flowers. Plants will bloom 15 to 22 weeks after seeds are sown, depending on the time of year. Seeds sown to produce June-flowering plants will require less time to flower than seeds sown to produce January-flowering plants.

—

Miltonia (mil-TOH-nee-a)
Pansy orchid

Flowering plant in the orchid family. Leaves are thin. Flowers are flat, with five equal-sized petals and a spreading lip. Flowers are often marked in contrasting colors and resemble the garden pansy.

Selected species and varieties. *M. vexillaria* has six to eight light green, 10-inch leaves. Flowers are 3 to 4 inches across and bloom in sprays of three to nine on 24-inch stems. The species has flowers of white, or white flushed with rose, pink or lavender. Hybrids have flowers of white, pink, rose or red, often with yellow markings. Blooms appear in spring and summer.

Growing conditions. Grow pansy orchid at 1,000 to 1,500 footcandles from midspring to midfall, and at 2,500 footcandles from midfall to midspring. Leaves turn red or yellow if light intensity is too high. Night temperature should be 45° to 50° F. Grow in a special orchid-potting medium, or in soilless medium with extra fir bark, redwood bark or osmunda fiber added. Plants should be kept evenly moist at all times except when they are flowering; then they should be allowed to dry out slightly between waterings. Plants in fresh bark medium will need more frequent watering than those in older medium because older medium retains more water. As the bark in the potting medium breaks down over time, plants should be repotted at least every two years in spring or summer. Fertilize every four to six weeks during the winter. Use 30-10-10 if the potting medium contains bark, and 20-20-20 if it contains osmunda fiber. Humidity should be 60 to 70 percent. Constant air circulation is necessary. Place the plants in a shaded section of the greenhouse during the summer. Scales, slugs, snails and viruses may damage pansy orchid.

MARANTA LEUCONEURA ERYTHRONEURA

MATTHIOLA INCANA

MILTONIA HYBRID

MONSTERA DELICIOSA

MUSA ACUMINATA

Propagation. Pansy orchid can be propagated from seeds or by division. The roots contain water and food-storing tissue called pseudobulbs; when dividing, be sure to take four pseudobulbs per division.

Mistletoe fig see *Ficus*

Monstera (mon-STAIR-a)
Windowleaf

Foliage plant in the arum family that has a semivining habit. Leaves are shiny, leathery and dark green. Young leaves are heart-shaped and undivided; mature leaves are lobed and perforated with round to oblong holes.

Selected species and varieties. *M. deliciosa,* split-leaf philodendron, Swiss-cheese plant, grows to 6 feet or more high. Mature leaves are 18 inches or more across and deeply lobed. *M. obliqua* has 8-inch, narrow, heart-shaped leaves that are not as deeply lobed as those of the split-leaf philodendron.

Growing conditions. Grow windowleaf at 3,000 to 4,000 footcandles. If the light level is too low, leaves will lose their lobes and their holes. Night temperature should be 65° to 70° F. Grow in well-drained, soilless medium and keep it evenly moist from spring through fall. In winter, allow the medium to dry out slightly between waterings. Do not fertilize newly potted plants for four to six months; then fertilize monthly from midspring to midfall with 20-20-20. Humidity should be 50 percent. Keep the leaves clean by frequent dusting or washing. As the plant grows, it produces aerial roots. If a slab of bark is placed in the pot, the roots will cling to the bark. Water the bark as well as the medium when watering. The aerial roots may be removed without damaging the plant. Mealybugs and leaf spot disease may damage windowleaf.

Propagation. Propagate windowleaf from seeds, by stem cuttings or by air layering.

Moonflower see *Ipomoea*
Morning glory see *Ipomoea*
Mother fern see *Asplenium*
Mother-in-law plant
see *Caladium*

Moth orchid see *Phalaenopsis*

Musa (MEW-za)
Banana

Tropical treelike herb in the banana family grown in the greenhouse either as an ornament or as a source of edible fruit. Leaves are long and spirally arranged around the stem. Flowers appear in erect or drooping clusters, usually in late spring or early summer, and are followed by long, fleshy fruits with green or yellow skin and white or yellowish pulp.

Selected species and varieties. *M. acuminata,* edible banana, plantain, grows to 12 feet or more. The stems grow in clumps and are covered with leaves that grow to 9 feet long. The foliage is green on the upper surface, often flecked in brown or black, and green or purple on the lower surface. Flowers are red, purple or yellow and are spirally tiered on drooping clusters. The bananas, which are up to 5 inches long, form upside-down on the top half of the clusters after the flowers fade. *M. ornata,* flowering banana, grows to 9 feet tall. Leaves are 3 to 6 feet long and medium green with reddish purple undersides. Flowers are pale pink tipped with yellow, and bloom in erect clusters. The fruit is yellow-green, 3 inches long and inedible.

Growing conditions. Grow banana at 3,000 to 5,000 footcandles. Night temperature should be 60° to 65° F. Grow in well-drained, soilless medium to which extra peat moss or other organic matter has been added. Keep the medium constantly moist and fertilize twice a month with 20-20-20. Humidity must be 60 to 70 percent. Flowers are self-pollinating. After a banana plant has fruited, it dies, and a new plant grows from the base. It takes 18 months to three years for fruit to be produced. Banana plant is susceptible to mealybugs, nematodes, scales, leaf spot disease and wilt diseases.

Propagation. Propagate bananas by root cuttings or by offsets. Edible bananas may also be propagated from seeds.

Muscari (mus-KAR-ee)
Grape hyacinth

Spring-flowering bulb in the lily family that can be forced into bloom in winter in the greenhouse. Foliage is slender, grasslike and blue-green. Flowers are fragrant and bell-shaped, and bloom in spikes.

Selected species and varieties. *M. armeniacum* grows to 9 inches tall. Flowers are oblong, ⅜ inch long and blue to deep violet with white edges. *M. botryoides* grows to 12 inches tall. Flowers are round, ⅛ inch long and blue with white edges. 'Album' has white flowers.

Growing conditions. Grape hyacinth bulbs must be chilled before being forced. Pot the bulbs in the fall, water them well and store them in a dark area at 40° F for eight to 12 weeks. They may be placed outdoors in a cold frame or other protected area if the proper temperature exists. At the end of the chilling period, move the pots into the greenhouse.

Grow grape hyacinth at 4,000 to 6,000 footcandles. Night temperature should be 45° to 55° F. Grow in well-drained, soilless medium and keep it evenly moist. Continue to water after the plants have flowered, until the foliage fades. When flower buds start to show color, fertilize once with 20-20-20. After the foliage has faded, store the bulbs in dry peat moss in a dark area at 50° F until the following fall. Grape hyacinth is not susceptible to insects or diseases.

Propagation. Propagate grape hyacinth by removing and potting the bulblets that form around the base of the bulb.

Myosotis (my-o-SO-tis)
Forget-me-not

Flowering plant in the borage family that is grown in the greenhouse as a potted plant or for cutting flowers. Plants have hairy foliage and stems and clusters of small flowers.

Selected species and varieties. *M. sylvatica* has airy clusters of ¼-inch flowers that are usually blue, but often pink or white, all with a yellow eye. Plants grow 6 to 10 inches high.

Growing conditions. Grow forget-me-not at 1,000 to 3,000 footcandles. Night temperature should be 45° to 50° F. Grow in well-drained, soilless medium and keep it evenly moist. Fertilize monthly with 20-20-20. To prolong bloom, keep flowers cut. After the plant has ceased to flower, it will die. Aphids may attack.

Propagation. Propagate forget-me-not from seeds. Plants will bloom six months after seeds are sown.

Narcissus (nar-SIS-us)
Daffodil

Spring-flowering bulb, member of the amaryllis family, that can be forced in the greenhouse for winter and spring bloom. Foliage is narrow and flat. The center of the flower is tubular or cup-shaped and is surrounded by six petals. Bulbs may be forced either for potted plants or for cutting flowers.

Selected species and varieties. Based on flower shape and on species derivation, daffodils are divided into 11 categories, two of which are commonly forced in the greenhouse. One is Division I, Trumpet daffodils, which have tubular centers that are longer than the petals. Flowers may be all-yellow or all-white, or have white trumpets and yellow petals. Varieties include 'King Alfred' and 'Unsurpassable'. The other is Division VIII, Tazetta daffodils, which have 18-inch leaves and clusters of small, fragrant, yellow or white flowers. 'Paper White' and 'Soleil d'Or' are widely planted varieties.

Growing conditions. Daffodils can be forced to bloom if they are planted in a pot, and then given a cold treatment so that they will develop roots and embryonic flowers. Plant five or six bulbs in a 6-inch pot so that they are almost touching, with the tip of each bulb 1 inch below the surface of the medium. Water the potted bulbs well. Then place the pot in an area where temperatures are between 35° and 45° F for a minimum of 12 weeks, or until roots protrude from the drainage holes. Keep the growing medium moist.

Some bulbs are sold prechilled, which means they have been given a partial cold treatment by the nursery. If you use prechilled bulbs, give them another five weeks' cold treatment after you pot them. When the cold treatment is done, the bulbs may be moved into the greenhouse for forcing, or they may be kept at 33° to 35° F until you are ready to force them.

If you want to store bulbs for forcing later, place them in an area where temperatures are between 55° and 60° F before potting them, and then give them a cold treatment as above.

Grow daffodils at 4,000 to 8,000 footcandles. If you are growing daffodils for potted plants, night temperature should be 60° to 62° F. If you are growing them for cutting flowers, night temperature should be 50° to 55° F, as the lower temperature results in longer stems. Grow in well-drained, soilless medium with a pH of

MUSCARI ARMENIACUM

MYOSOTIS SYLVATICA

NARCISSUS 'KING ALFRED'

NARCISSUS 'PAPER WHITE'

NEPHROLEPIS EXALTATA

NERIUM OLEANDER

6.0, and keep the medium evenly moist. Tazetta daffodils may be grown in pebbles and water. Fertilizing is not necessary. Tall plants may need to be staked. Bulbs will bloom 10 days to three weeks after being moved into the greenhouse. Tazetta daffodils should be discarded after being forced; trumpet daffodils can be planted in the garden to rebloom naturally, but cannot be successfully reforced. Daffodils may be damaged by mites and nematodes; they are also susceptible to rot.

Propagation. Daffodils can be propagated by removing and potting the bulblets that form around the base of the bulb, but bulblets take several years to grow to full size. Greater success will be achieved from purchasing new bulbs each year.

Nasturtium see *Tropaeolum*

Natal ivy see *Senecio*

Nephrolepis (ne-FROL-e-pis)
Sword fern

Plant in the fern family that has sword-shaped fronds with long, narrow, closely spaced leaflets.

Selected species and varieties. *N. exaltata* has stiff, erect fronds that can grow to 5 feet long. The plant produces runners that root as they creep along the soil. The species is rarely grown, but many of its varieties are widely cultivated. 'Bostoniensis', Boston fern, has bright green, drooping, 3-foot fronds with 3- to 4-inch lobed leaflets. 'Dallas' grows 12 inches high and has dark green, slightly drooping fronds and lobed leaflets. 'Fluffy Ruffles' grows 12 inches high and has stiff, erect, dark green fronds with ruffled leaflets.

Growing conditions. Grow sword fern at 2,000 to 4,000 footcandles. Night temperature should be 55° to 60° F. Grow in a very rich, well-drained, soilless medium to which lime, bone meal or other source of calcium has been added. Water to keep the medium constantly moist from spring through fall; in the winter, water only enough to keep the fronds from wilting. Do not feed newly potted plants for six months; fertilize established plants with 20-20-20 in early spring and again in early summer. Humidity should be 50 to 60 percent. Sword fern may be damaged by scales, mealybugs, aphids

and whiteflies. It is susceptible to botrytis blight.

Propagation. Propagate sword fern by division in spring, or by pinning the runners to the surface of the medium, where they will root and form new plants. The varieties of sword fern described here are sterile and do not produce spores.

Nerium (NEER-ee-um)
Oleander

Shrubby, flowering plant in the dogbane family that has narrow, lance-shaped foliage in whorls of three. Tubular flowers bloom in clusters at the ends of the branches.

Selected species and varieties. *N. oleander*, rosebay, grows to 6 feet tall in the greenhouse, but can be kept lower by pruning and pinching. The willowy leaves are dark, dull green, leathery and 10 inches long. Five-petaled flowers may be white, yellow, rosy red, pink or reddish purple, and bloom in summer. Blooms are often fragrant. 'Album' has white flowers; 'Roseum' has rose-pink flowers; 'Variegata' has rose-red flowers and foliage striped and edged in yellow or creamy white. All parts of oleander are poisonous.

Growing conditions. Grow oleander at 5,000 to 8,000 footcandles. Night temperature should be 50° to 55° F from spring through fall, and 45° to 50° F in winter. Grow in well-drained, soilless medium and allow it to dry out slightly between waterings. Fertilize every two weeks with 20-20-20 while the plants are growing or flowering. Prune the plants back by one-half after the flowers have faded, and keep the plants compact and branching by pinching when growth starts in spring. The greenhouse must be well ventilated. Aphids, mealybugs and scales may attack oleander.

Propagation. Propagate oleander by cuttings taken after the plant has flowered.

Nicotiana (ni-ko-shi-AY-na)

Annual or perennial member of the nightshade family that is forced in the greenhouse as a flowering potted plant. Plants are upright-growing and have fuzzy, sticky leaves and spikes of trumpet-shaped flowers.

Selected species and varieties. *N. alata,* flowering tobacco, is an annual relative of the commercially grown tobacco plant. It has loose spikes of yellow, purple, green, red, pink or white flowers. 'Domino' and 'Nicki' are the most readily available varieties; both grow 8 to 12 inches high. *N. × sanderae* has 2- to 3½-inch-long flowers borne in loosely branched clusters; petals are 2 inches across and generally red, but may vary from white to deep violet.

Growing conditions. Grow flowering tobacco at 5,000 to 8,000 footcandles. Night temperature should be 50° to 60° F. Grow in well-drained, soilless medium and keep it constantly moist. Fertilize every two weeks after flower buds have appeared with half-strength 20-20-20. To extend the blooming period, remove flowers as they fade. After the plant has ceased to flower, it will die. Insects that most commonly attack flowering tobacco are aphids and whiteflies.

Propagation. Propagate flowering tobacco from seeds. Seeds sown in midsummer will produce blooming plants in six months.

—

Night jessamine see *Cestrum*

—

Notocactus (no-toh-KAK-tus)
Ball cactus

Plant in the cactus family. Plants are globe-shaped when young, cylindrical when mature. Daisylike flowers bloom at the top of the ribbed plants during the spring.

Selected species and varieties. *N. apricus* grows to 2 inches thick. It is dark green and densely covered with reddish yellow spines that curve upward and intertwine. Flowers are 3 inches across and yellow. *N. haselbergii* is 3 to 5 inches across. The plant is covered with soft, fine, yellow-tipped, silvery spines. Flowers are ⅝ inch across and red or orange. *N. ottonis* is 2 to 5 inches thick and glossy green, with short yellow to brown spines. Flowers are yellow and 2½ inches across. *N. varasii* grows 6 to 7 inches high and wide, with soft yellow-gold spines and bright yellow flowers.

Growing conditions. Grow ball cactus at 5,000 to 8,000 footcandles. Night temperature should be 60° to 65° F from spring through fall, and should be lowered to 40° to 45° F in winter. Grow in soilless potting me-

dium that has perlite or sharp sand added to ensure excellent drainage. From spring through fall, let the top ¼ inch of medium dry out before watering; in winter, water enough to keep the plants from shriveling. Do not feed newly potted plants for one year; fertilize mature plants once a year in spring with 20-20-20. Keep humidity under 50 percent. Ball cactus may be damaged by mealybugs, spider mites and scales; it is also susceptible to rot and wilt diseases.

Propagation. Propagate ball cactus from seeds sown at any time or by removing and potting the plantlets that form at the base of the plant.

—

Ocimum (o-SY-mum)
Basil

Member of the mint family that is grown in the greenhouse for use as an herb. The stems are square; the foliage is often toothed. Flowers are two-lipped and bloom in long, narrow spikes.

Selected species and varieties. *O. basilicum,* common basil, grows 6 to 18 inches high. The leaves are aromatic, oval, 3 to 5 inches long, and may be green or purple. Some varieties have leaves that are curled at the edges. Flowers are white or lavender and appear in summer.

Growing conditions. Grow basil at 4,000 to 6,000 footcandles. Night temperature should be 45° to 55° F. Grow in a well-drained, soilless medium and keep it constantly moist. Fertilize once a month with 20-20-20. Leaves may be harvested continually as they are needed. To prolong the life of the plant, pick off flower spikes as soon as they start to develop. The plant will start to decline after about nine months. Basil is not susceptible to insects or diseases.

Propagation. Propagate basil from seeds sown in early spring.

—

Old man cactus
see *Cephalocereus*

Oleander see *Nerium*

—

Opuntia (o-PUN-cha)
Prickly pear, cholla

Plant in the cactus family. Plants have either cylindrical or flat segments that are dotted with short, spiny tufts.

NICOTIANA × SANDERAE

NOTOCACTUS VARASII

OCIMUM BASILICUM

OPUNTIA MICRODASYS 'ALBISPINA'

OXALIS RUBRA

PASSIFLORA × ALATOCAERULEA

Selected species and varieties. *O. microdasys,* bunny-ears, grows slowly to 3 feet and is divided into flat, oval segments 3 to 6 inches long. New growths that resemble a rabbit's ears appear at the top of the older segments. The segments are bright green and are dotted with tufts of white, yellow or brownish red spines. Showy yellow flowers bloom in spring. 'Albispina' has white spines.

Growing conditions. Grow bunny-ears at 5,000 to 8,000 foot-candles. From spring through fall, night temperature should be 60° to 65° F; in winter, the temperature should be lowered to 40° to 45° F. Grow in a soilless potting medium that has extra perlite or sharp sand added to ensure excellent drainage. From spring through fall, allow the top ¼ inch of the medium to dry out before watering; in winter, water enough only to keep the plants from shriveling. Do not feed newly potted plants for one year; fertilize mature plants once a year in spring with 20-20-20. Humidity should be less than 50 percent. Bunny-ears attracts mealybugs, spider mites and scales; it is also susceptible to rot and wilt diseases.

Propagation. Propagate bunny-ears from seeds sown at any time or by removing and potting the growth that forms at the top of the plant.

▬

Orange see *Citrus*
Orchid cactus see *Epiphyllum*
Ornamental pepper see *Capsicum*

▬

Oxalis (OK-sa-lis)
Wood sorrel

Flowering plant in the sorrel family that has bulbous, tuberous or rhizomatous roots. Leaves are 2 to 4 inches across and cloverlike, and often fold up at night. Flowers have five petals.

Selected species and varieties. *O. rubra* is a tuberous species that grows 6 to 12 inches tall and has leaves consisting of three leaflets. Flowers are rose-pink, sometimes veined with violet or white, and ¾ inch long; they are borne in umbels above the foliage and bloom in winter.

Growing conditions. Plant wood sorrel tuberous roots in autumn 2 inches deep and up to 4 inches apart.

Grow plants at 5,000 to 8,000 foot-candles. Night temperatures should be 50° to 60° F. Grow in well-drained, soilless medium and keep it evenly moist. Fertilize once a month with 20-20-20. After the plants have flowered, gradually withhold water and stop fertilizing. When the foliage withers, remove the tubers from the pot and store them in a dark area at 45° F until it is time to repot them. Wood sorrel is susceptible to aphids and mites.

Propagation. Propagate wood sorrel from seed or by division, when a tuber reaches the size of a golf ball.

▬

Panda plant see *Kalanchoe*
Pansy orchid see *Miltonia*
Paper flower see *Bougainvillea*
Parlor ivy see *Senecio*
Parlor palm see *Chamaedorea*
Parsley see *Petroselinum*

▬

Passiflora (pas-i-FLOR-a)
Passionflower

Vigorous vine in the passionflower family that has leaves with five or more deep lobes. Flowers have 10 outer petals; the center is composed of a crownlike ring that surrounds a profusion of filaments, stamens and pistils. The odd shape of the flower was a religious symbol to early missionaries.

Selected species and varieties. *P. × alatocaerulea* grows 6 to 10 feet high. Leaves have three lobes; flowers are 4 inches across, fragrant, white outside and pink to purple inside, and have variegated coronas. *P.caerulea,* blue passionflower, has gray-green leaves 4 to 5 inches across, and five to nine deep lobes. The outer petals of the flowers are white to off-white; the filaments are purple, blue and white. Plants bloom in spring and summer, and often into fall; each flower lasts only one day.

Growing conditions. Grow passionflower at 5,000 to 8,000 foot-candles. Night temperature should be 55° to 65° F. Grow in well-drained, soilless medium kept constantly moist during the growing and flowering period. At other times, let the medium dry out slightly between waterings. Fertilize every two weeks with 20-20-20 when the plant is growing and flowering. Keep humidity at 60 to 70 percent. After the plant has flowered, cut it back to 6 inches. Plants must be trained to a trellis or other support. Mealybugs and nematodes may attack passionflower.

Propagation. Propagate passionflower from seeds or by stem cuttings taken after the plant has flowered.

—

Passionflower see *Passiflora*

—

Pelargonium (pel-ar-GO-nee-um)
Geranium

Member of the geranium family that is grown for its showy flowers or for its scented leaves, depending on the species. All will flower in the greenhouse from spring through fall, and will flower in winter if given sufficient light.

Selected species and varieties. *P. × domesticum,* Martha Washington geranium, grows 18 to 24 inches tall. Leaves are 2 to 4 inches across and toothed, lobed or deeply divided. Flowers are white, red, pink or purple, and blotched in contrasting colors. *P. graveolens,* rose geranium, is grown primarily for its rose-scented, deeply lobed, soft, hairy leaves. Plants are bushy and grow 24 to 36 inches high; flowers are lavender-pink marked with purple. *P. × hortorum,* zonal geranium, garden geranium, grows 18 to 24 inches tall. Leaves are round to heart-shaped, 3 to 5 inches across, scalloped, and often zoned in brown or black. Flowers bloom in round clusters on long stalks and are white, pink, rose, red, coral, salmon or violet. *P. peltatum,* ivy geranium, has stems up to 3 feet long and is best grown in a hanging basket. Leaves are 2 to 3 inches across and lobed. Flowers of white, pink, red or lavender bloom in loose, 2- to 3-inch clusters. *P. tomentosum,* peppermint geranium, is grown primarily for its peppermint-scented, three-lobed, soft, hairy, bright green leaves. It grows up to 36 inches tall. Flowers are pink or white.

Growing conditions. Grow scented geraniums at 4,000 to 6,000 footcandles; grow the others at 5,000 to 8,000 footcandles. Night temperature should be 45° to 50° F for Martha Washington geraniums and 55° to 60° F for the others. Grow in well-drained, soilless medium and allow it to dry out slightly between waterings. If the plant is not flowering in winter, water enough only to keep the foliage from shriveling. Fertilize every two weeks from early spring to midfall with 20-20-20. Growth regulator may be applied when plants are 6 weeks old to keep them compact. If there is not enough light to force plants into bloom in winter, install four 4-foot, cool-white fluorescent lights 12 to 15 inches above the plants for each 6 square feet of greenhouse space. Leave the lights on for 16 hours each day. To keep the plant vigorous and neat, remove flowers as they fade. After the plant has ceased to flower, it may be cut back. After several years, geranium plants become woody and do not produce new stems, foliage or flowers well; when this happens, discard the plants. Geraniums may be attacked by aphids, mealybugs, mites and whiteflies. They are also susceptible to damping-off, botrytis blight, virus disease, root rot and stem rot.

Propagation. Propagate geraniums from stem cuttings taken at any time or from seeds. Only some varieties of ivy and zonal geraniums can be propagated from seeds.

—

Pencil-leaf gasteria
see *Gasteria*

—

Pentas (PEN-tas)

Flowering plant in the madder family that has oval to lance-shaped leaves and clusters of flowers at the ends of the branches.

Selected species and varieties. *P. lanceolata,* star cluster, Egyptian star, can grow to 4 feet tall but is most attractive if kept at 12 to 18 inches high. Leaves are bright green, hairy, 3 to 4 inches long and often deeply veined. Flowers are star-shaped, tubular, ½ inch across, and bloom in 4-inch clusters most abundantly in winter and spring. Flower colors include white, rose, red and lavender.

Growing conditions. Grow star cluster at 5,000 to 8,000 footcandles. Night temperature should be 50° to 60° F. Grow in well-drained, soilless medium and keep it evenly moist while the plant is growing and flowering. For two months after the plants have flowered, allow the medium to dry out between waterings. Fertilize every two weeks with half-strength 20-20-20 during the growing and flowering period. Pinch the plants to keep them compact and bushy. Scales are the major insect problem.

PELARGONIUM × HORTORUM

PENTAS LANCEOLATA

133

PERSEA AMERICANA

PETROSELINUM CRISPUM

Propagation. Propagate star cluster by stem cuttings taken either in spring or in summer.

—

Pepper see *Capsicum*

Peppermint geranium
see *Pelargonium*

—

Persea (PER-see-a)
Avocado

Tropical tree in the laurel family that is grown in the greenhouse as a source of edible fruit. Leaves are deeply veined. Small, greenish flowers bloom in clusters. Fruit is pear-shaped to oval.

Selected species and varieties. *P. americana* grows to 6 feet indoors and can be kept lower with pruning. Leaves are oval to oblong, leathery and 4 to 8 inches long. The fruit is ¼ inch in diameter and has yellow-green, green or brown skin, and buttery, yellow-green flesh. The fruit contains a large pit, which is the seed.

Growing conditions. Grow avocado at 5,000 to 8,000 footcandles. Night temperature should be 55° to 60° F. Grow in a soilless medium that has excellent drainage, and keep the medium evenly moist. Fertilize every two weeks during spring and summer with 20-20-20. Humidity should be maintained at 50 to 60 percent; when the humidity is too low, leaf tips turn brown. Prune plants when they are young to encourage branching, and pinch out growing tips as plants grow to prevent them from becoming leggy. Shake the plants when they are flowering to aid pollination, or pollinate by hand. Avocado is susceptible to scales and to scab.

Propagation. Propagate avocado by cuttings, by grafting, or from seeds grown in spring and summer. The pit may be planted in moist growing medium, with one-quarter of its tip exposed, or germinated in water. Make sure that only the base of the pit rests in the water. After roots have formed, transfer the plant to a growing medium.

—

Persian buttercup
see *Ranunculus*

Persian violet see *Cyclamen; Exacum*

Petroselinum
(pe-tro-se-LY-num)
Parsley

Biennial in the carrot family grown in the greenhouse for use as an herb or a garnish.

Selected species and varieties. *P. crispum* grows 12 inches tall. Leaves are dark green and may be flat, curled or crisped. Parsley blooms in its second year, with flat clusters of yellow-green flowers. Because the foliage becomes bitter when the plant is mature enough to flower, plants are seldom grown to maturity.

Growing conditions. Grow parsley at 1,000 to 3,000 footcandles. Night temperature should be 45° to 55° F. Grow in well-drained, soilless medium and keep it evenly moist. Fertilize monthly with 20-20-20. Cut leaves of parsley with scissors as needed. Parsley is generally insect-free, but is susceptible to root rot and leaf spot diseases.

Propagation. Propagate parsley from seeds soaked in warm water for 24 hours before sowing. Plants will be mature enough to begin harvesting in four months.

—

Phalaenopsis (fal-e-NOP-sis)
Moth orchid

Flowering plant in the orchid family. Leaves are shiny, erect or arching, and grow in groups of five or six. Flowers are flat, with five round petals and a small, three-lobed lip. Flowers bloom in arching sprays and resemble moths in flight.

Selected species and varieties. *P. amabilis* has 10- to 12-inch leaves. Flowers are 2 to 2½ inches across, white with a red-spotted yellow crest on the lip, and bloom in sprays during winter and spring. Hybrids have flowers of white, pink, rose, red, yellow or purple, often with stripes or spots in contrasting colors. Blooms appear at any time of year.

Growing conditions. Grow moth orchid at 500 to 1,500 footcandles. Night temperature should be 60° to 65° F in winter, spring and summer, and 50° to 60° F in fall. Grow in a special orchid-potting medium, or in soilless medium with extra fir bark, redwood bark or osmunda fiber added. Keep the medium evenly moist at all times, but avoid spilling water on the foliage. Plants in fresh bark medium will need more frequent watering than those in older medium because older medium retains more water. As the bark in the potting medium breaks down over time, plants should be repotted at least every two years in spring or summer. Fertilize every two weeks during the growing period. Use 30-10-10 if the potting medium contains bark, and 20-20-20 if it contains osmunda fiber. Humidity should be 60 to 70 percent. Constant air circulation is necessary. Place the plants in a shaded section of the greenhouse during the summer. Flowering stems will need to be staked. Scales, slugs, snails and virus diseases can damage moth orchid.

Propagation. Moth orchid can be propagated from seeds or by removing and potting the plantlets that form on the flowering spike.

Philodendron (fil-o-DEN-dron)

Foliage plant in the arum family. Plants have a variety of sizes, shapes and growing habits. They may be either vining or self-heading. Self-heading plants have stems growing from a central point at the base of the plant. Foliage is shiny and leathery. Foliage is usually unlobed when young, and often changes to lobed as it matures. Foliage of vining types is larger if the plant is trained upright than if the plant is grown in a hanging basket. Any philodendron may send out aerial roots.

Selected species and varieties. *P. erubescens,* red-leaf philodendron, is a vining plant growing to 6 feet tall. Leaves are arrow-shaped, to 10 inches long, dark green edged in red on the upper surfaces and copper on the undersides. *P. scandens,* heart-leaf philodendron, is a vining plant that has 6-inch, heart-shaped leaves. The variety *P. scandens oxycardium,* formerly designated *P. cordatum,* common philodendron, has heart-shaped, 3- to 4-inch leaves. *P. selloum* is a self-heading type growing to 6 feet high and wide. Young leaves are oval; mature leaves are 2 feet long, deeply cut and have wavy margins.

Growing conditions. Grow philodendron at 3,000 to 4,000 footcandles. Night temperature should be 55° to 65° F. Grow in a well-drained, soilless, acidic medium that is allowed to dry out slightly between waterings. Do not fertilize newly potted plants for four months; then fertilize twice a month in spring and sum-

mer with 20-20-20. Philodendron prefers to be grown slightly pot-bound. Upright-growing plants should be staked on a slab of bark; water the bark slab as well as the medium. Vining types can be pinched to keep them compact. Clean large leaves by frequently dusting or washing. Aerial roots can be removed without damage to the plants. Mealybugs, scales and leaf spot diseases may damage philodendron.

Propagation. Vining philodendrons are propagated by stem cuttings. Self-heading philodendrons are propagated by removing and potting the offsets that form at the base of the plant, by air layering or from seeds.

Piggyback plant see *Tolmiea*

Pilea (PY-lee-a)

Foliage plant in the nettle family that may be upright or vining. Leaves are oval, oblong or round, quilted, and often marked in a contrasting color.

Selected species and varieties. *P. cadierei,* aluminum plant, grows 10 to 12 inches high. Leaves are 3 inches long, oval, toothed and medium green with silver markings. *P. microphylla,* artillery plant, is a vining plant with dense, 12-inch branches. Leaves are oblong and ¼ to ½ inch long. *P. nummularifolia,* creeping Charlie, is a fast-growing, vining plant with ¼- to ¾-inch circular leaves.

Growing conditions. Grow pilea at 2,000 to 3,500 footcandles. Night temperature should be 60° to 65° F. Grow in a well-drained, soilless medium that is allowed to dry out between waterings. Fertilize every two weeks during spring and summer with 20-20-20. Maintain humidity at 50 to 60 percent. Pinch growing tips to keep the plants compact. Pilea is not long-lived and may need to be replaced every two years. Insects that can attack pilea include mealybugs and whiteflies; diseases include leaf spot, root rot and stem rot.

Pincushion see *Mammillaria*
Pineapple see *Ananas*
Pink see *Dianthus*
Pitcher plant see *Sarracenia*

PHALAENOPSIS HYBRID

PHILODENDRON SELLOUM

PILEA CADIEREI

PITTOSPORUM TOBIRA 'VARIEGATA'

PLATYCERIUM BIFURCATUM

PLECTRANTHUS AUSTRALIS

Pittosporum (pi-TOS-po-rum)

Shrubby, flowering plant in the pittosporum family that has whorled leaves and clusters of flowers that bloom in spring and summer.

Selected species and varieties. *P. tobira* has glossy, leathery, thick, oval, dark green, 2- to 4-inch leaves. Flowers are creamy white, fragrant, ½ inch long and bloom in 3-inch clusters. Plants grow 3 to 4 feet tall. 'Variegata' has thin, dark green leaves with irregularly marked white margins.

Growing conditions. Grow pittosporum at 4,000 to 6,000 footcandles. Night temperature should be 60° to 65° F during spring, summer and fall, and 45° to 50° F during winter. Grow in a well-drained, soilless medium that is kept evenly moist while the plant is growing or flowering. In fall, allow the medium to dry out slightly between waterings; in winter, water enough only to keep the foliage from shriveling. Fertilize every two weeks during spring and summer with 20-20-20. Prune in early spring before growth starts to shape the plants. Pittosporum attracts aphids, mealybugs, mites and scales.

Propagation. Propagate pittosporum by stem cuttings, by air layering or from seeds.

—

Plantain see *Musa*

—

Platycerium (plat-i-SEER-ee-um)
Staghorn fern

Foliage plant in the fern family. Staghorn fern has two types of fronds: sterile fronds, which are round, platelike and papery brown, and clasp the support on which the plant is grown; and fertile fronds, which are branched or forked and resemble antlers.

Selected species and varieties. *P. bifurcatum,* common staghorn fern, has round to kidney-shaped, overlapping, sterile fronds at the base of the plant. The fertile fronds are gray-green, hairy, drooping and 2 to 3 feet across. Small plantlets form at the base of the parent plant.

Growing conditions. Grow common staghorn fern at 2,000 to 4,000 footcandles. Plants should be placed in a shaded section of the greenhouse during the summer. Night tempera-ture should be 50° to 55° F. Only very young plants can be grown in pots; the medium must be very rich, well-drained, soilless, and have lime, bone meal or some other source of calcium added. Once a plant starts to mature, it must be grown on a piece of bark, on tree fern bark, or on a board to which a ball of sphagnum peat moss has been attached. When first attaching a staghorn fern to a support, tie it gently; in time the basal fronds will grow around the support and keep the plant attached. Although the basal fronds turn brown, they should never be removed, as they provide attachment and help the support retain moisture. From spring through fall, water to keep the medium or the support constantly moist; in winter, water only enough to keep the fronds from wilting. Do not fertilize staghorn ferns. Humidity should be 60 to 70 percent. Maintain good air circulation. Staghorn fern may be damaged by aphids, scales, mealybugs and whiteflies. It is also susceptible to botrytis blight.

Propagation. Propagate common staghorn fern from spores, or by removing and potting the offsets that form at the base of the plant.

—

Plectranthus (plek-TRAN-thus)
Swedish ivy

Plant in the mint family that is grown for its foliage, although it does produce spikes of bell-shaped flowers. Stems are fleshy and square.

Selected species and varieties. *P. australis* has rapid-growing, trailing branches that grow 2 to 3 feet long, and is excellent in a hanging basket. Leaves are waxy, thick, round, scalloped, bright green and 1 to 1½ inches across. Small, pale purple or white flowers bloom in 8-inch, upright spikes in spring.

Growing conditions. Grow Swedish ivy at 3,000 to 4,500 footcandles. Night temperature should be 55° to 65° F. Grow in well-drained, soilless medium and keep the medium evenly moist. Fertilize once a month with 20-20-20 while the plant is actively growing. Pinch back growing tips to keep the plant bushy. Swedish ivy is especially susceptible to spider mites.

Propagation. Propagate Swedish ivy by stem cuttings taken at any time of year.

Plumbago (plum-BAY-go)
Leadwort

Member of the leadwort family that has rounded spikes of bell-shaped flowers at the ends of the branches during late winter, spring and early summer.

Selected species and varieties. *P. auriculata,* formerly designated *P. capensis,* Cape leadwort, grows 2 to 4 feet tall and has arching stems. Leaves are oblong and 2 inches long. Flowers are slender, tubular, five-petaled, usually blue but sometimes white, and 1½ inches long.

Growing conditions. Grow Cape leadwort at 4,000 to 6,000 foot-candles. Night temperature should be 55° to 60° F during spring, summer and fall, and 50° F in winter. Grow in well-drained, soilless medium and keep it evenly moist from spring through fall. In winter, allow the soil to dry out between waterings. Fertilize monthly with 20-20-20 during spring and summer. During the winter, before new growth starts, prune the plants to shape them and control their height. Mealybugs and scales are the insects that most commonly attack Cape leadwort.

Propagation. Propagate Cape leadwort from seeds, by division and by stem cuttings. Plants propagated in spring will bloom by the following winter.

Pocketbook plant
see *Calceolaria*

Poinsettia see *Euphorbia*

Polypodium (pol-i-PO-dee-um)
Polypody

Plant in the fern family grown for both its foliage and its unusual rhizomes. Leaves are deeply cut. The rhizomes grow above the surface of the medium and resemble animal paws; they are long, thick and covered with hairs.

Selected species and varieties. *P. aureum,* rabbit's-foot fern, grows 2 to 3 feet high and across. The rhizomes are covered with rusty brown fur. The leaves are 1½ to 2 feet long and are deeply cut; the leaflets are metallic light green, thin and leathery, and have wavy margins.

Growing conditions. Grow rabbit's-foot fern at 2,000 to 4,000 footcandles. Night temperature

should be 55° to 60° F. Grow in a very rich, well-drained, soilless medium to which fir or redwood bark and lime, bone meal or some other source of calcium have been added. Rabbit's-foot fern can also be grown on a slab of bark or tree fern bark, or in a wire hanging basket lined with sphagnum peat moss. The rhizomes can be pinned to the basket to create a rounded plant. From spring through fall, water to keep the medium constantly moist; in the winter, water only to keep the leaves from wilting. Do not feed new plants for six months; fertilize established plants with half-strength 20-20-20 in early spring and again in early summer. Humidity should be 50 to 60 percent. Rabbit's-foot fern may be damaged by aphids, mealybugs, scales and whiteflies. It is also susceptible to botrytis blight.

Propagation. Propagate rabbit's-foot fern by division or from spores. Pieces of the rhizome may also be cut, secured to the growing medium with wire clips and rooted.

Polypody see *Polypodium*
Pomegranate see *Punica*
Prayer plant see *Maranta*
Prickly pear see *Opuntia*
Primrose see *Primula*

Primula (PRIM-u-la)
Primrose

Flowering plant in the primrose family that grows 9 to 12 inches tall. Leaves grow at the base of the plant; flowers are funnel-shaped and bloom in rounded clusters in winter and spring.

Selected species and varieties. *P. malacoides,* fairy primrose, has light green, papery, toothed leaves with hairy undersides. Flowers are less than 1 inch across; white, pink, rose, lavender or red; and bloom in clusters arranged in tiers on thin stems. *P. obconica,* German primrose, has 10-inch, round to heart-shaped, rough, hairy leaves that often cause a skin rash. Flowers are fragrant; 1 to 2 inches across; and white, pink, lavender or red with a green eye. *P. × polyantha,* polyanthus primrose, has oval or oblong leaves and fragrant, 1- to 2-inch flowers of white, yellow, pink, red, lavender, purple, orange or maroon, often with a white eye.

PLUMBAGO AURICULATA

POLYPODIUM AUREUM

PRIMULA × POLYANTHA

PTERIS CRETICA

PUNICA GRANATUM 'NANA'

Growing conditions. Grow primrose at 4,000 to 5,000 footcandles. The plants should be placed in a shaded section of the greenhouse during the summer. Night temperature should be 50° to 55° F for fairy and German primroses and 40° to 45° F for polyanthus primrose. Grow in well-drained, soilless medium and keep it evenly moist. Fertilize every two weeks in spring, summer and fall with 20-20-20. Humidity should be maintained at 50 to 60 percent. Primroses are often short-lived and are usually discarded after two years. Mites, whiteflies, mealybugs and aphids are the insects that most commonly attack primrose; crown rot and damping-off are the most common diseases.

Propagation. Propagate primrose by division or from seeds. Seeds must be sown in spring or fall because they will not germinate in summer heat. Plants will bloom in seven to 12 months.

Pteris (TEER-is)
Brake fern, table fern

Foliage plant that is a member of the fern family. It grows 12 to 18 inches tall and has delicate, divided fronds.

Selected species and varieties. *P. cretica,* Cretan brake fern, has wiry stems and 6- to 18-inch fronds. The leaflets are dark green, 3 to 6 inches long, and have crisped or wavy edges.

Growing conditions. Grow brake fern at 2,000 to 4,000 footcandles. Night temperature should be 50° to 55° F. Grow in a very rich, well-drained, soilless medium to which lime, bone meal or some other source of calcium has been added. From spring through fall, water to keep the medium constantly moist; in the winter, water only enough to keep the fronds from wilting. Do not feed newly potted plants for six months; fertilize established plants with 20-20-20 in early spring and again in early summer. Humidity should be 60 to 70 percent. Brake fern may be damaged by scales, mealybugs, aphids, whiteflies and botrytis blight.

Propagation. Propagate brake fern from spores or by division in spring.

Punica (PEW-ni-ka)
Pomegranate

Small tree or shrub in the pomegranate family that is grown in the greenhouse as a source of edible fruit.

Selected species and varieties. *P. granatum* grows to 10 feet indoors. Leaves are 1 to 3 inches long, oblong and shiny. Flowers are 1½ inches across, and have a purple tube and five to eight crinkled, orange-red lobes. They bloom most abundantly in spring and summer. The flowers are followed by 2½- to 5-inch, yellow, orange, red or purplish fruit. 'Nana', dwarf pomegranate, is usually grown indoors. It grows 2 to 4 feet high and has narrow, bright green, shiny, ¾- to 1½-inch leaves. Flowers are bright red or orange-red and 1 inch across. The fruit is red to orange-red and 2 inches long. Plants will start to produce fruit when they are three or four years old.

Growing conditions. Grow pomegranate at 5,000 to 8,000 footcandles. Night temperature should be 50° to 55° F except in winter, when it should be 45° to 50° F. Grow in rich, well-drained, soilless medium and keep it evenly moist from early spring to midfall. During late fall and winter, water enough only to keep the plant from withering. It is normal for leaves to fall from the plant during this period. Fertilize every two weeks during spring and summer with half-strength 20-20-20. Prune the plant in early spring to shape and control its size. Fruit will ripen better if it is picked and allowed to ripen off the plant. Insects that attack pomegranate include aphids, mealybugs, mites, scales, thrips and whiteflies.

Propagation. Propagate pomegranate from seeds, by layering or by stem cuttings.

Queen Victoria century plant
see *Agave*

Rabbit's-foot fern see *Davallia; Polypodium*

Ranunculus (ra-NUN-kew-lus)

Flowering member of the buttercup family that is grown in the greenhouse as a potted plant or for cutting flowers. Blooms appear from late fall through spring.

Selected species and varieties. *R. asiaticus,* florist's ranunculus, Persian buttercup, grows 1½ feet tall. Leaves have three narrow, toothed leaflets. Flowers are 1½ inches across, slightly hairy, single or double, and white, yellow, pink, orange or red. The double flowers have many layers of swirled, papery petals.

Growing conditions. Ranunculus may be grown from tuberous roots; if so, the roots should be soaked for 24 hours and then planted 2 inches deep. They may also be grown from seedling plants, with the crown set on the surface of the medium. Grow ranunculus at 4,000 to 6,000 footcandles. Night temperature should be 40° to 45° F. Grow in well-drained, soilless medium, and keep it evenly moist. Do not allow the leaves to get wet during watering. Fertilize every two weeks with half-strength 20-20-20 while the plant is growing and flowering. Maintain humidity at 50 to 60 percent. After the plant has flowered, gradually withhold water until the foliage has withered. Then, remove the roots from the pots and store them in a dry area at 40° F until replanting the following fall. Aphids, mealybugs, mites, crown rot and botrytis blight may attack ranunculus.

Propagation. Propagate ranunculus from seeds or by division of the tuberous roots.

—

Red-nerve plant see *Fittonia*
Rex begonia see *Begonia*

Rhododendron
(ro-doh-DEN-dron)
Rhododendron, azalea

Shrubby, flowering plant in the heath family. Plants and foliage vary greatly in size. Flowers are funnel-shaped, single or double, and come in many colors. Plants can be forced to bloom from early winter through spring.

Selected species and varieties. *R. simsii,* Sims's azalea, Indian azalea, grows 12 inches high indoors. Leaves are dark green, leathery, 1½ to 2 inches long and oblong to oval. Flowers are 2 inches across, white, rose or red, and often spotted in darker tones.

Growing conditions. Grow rhododendron at 6,000 to 8,000 footcandles. Night temperature should be 65° F from early spring, when plants start to grow, until fall, when the flower buds are formed. Then plants should be held at 35° to 50° F for four to eight weeks to complete the development of the flower buds. The cooling can be done outdoors if temperatures are appropriate, in a refrigera-

tor or in an unheated greenhouse. At the end of the cooling period, plants are forced into bloom at 60° to 65° F. They will bloom in about four weeks. Grow in a rich, well-drained, soilless medium that has a pH of 5.0 to 5.5. Fertilize every two weeks with half-strength 20-20-20 during spring and summer. Growth regulator applied when new growth is 1 inch long will help to keep the plants compact. Humidity should be 50 to 60 percent. Remove faded flowers and prune the plants back after they have flowered. If leaves turn yellow, treat the plants with iron sulfate. Insects that attack rhododendron include aphids, thrips, mites, mealybugs and nematodes; diseases include botrytis blight, leaf spot, root rot and stem rot.

Propagation. Propagate rhododendron by cuttings or from seeds.

—

Rosa (RO-za)
Rose

Flowering plant in the rose family that is grown in the greenhouse as a potted plant or for cutting flowers. Leaves have five, seven or nine leaflets; flowers are single or double and often fragrant. Blooms may be white, yellow, orange, red, pink, apricot or mauve, or blends of two or three colors. Roses will flower all year in the greenhouse if they receive sufficient light.

Selected species and varieties. Several different classes of hybrid roses, including hybrid teas, grandifloras, floribundas and miniatures, can be grown in the greenhouse. Hybrid teas produce high-centered flowers, one to a stem, and are the most commonly grown for cutting flowers. Grandifloras produce hybrid-tea-type flowers in clusters. Floribundas are shorter, bushier plants than hybrid teas and grandifloras, and are good subjects for potted plants. Miniatures are small plants with small flowers and may be grown either as potted plants or for cutting flowers.

Roses sold for the garden, except miniatures, generally do not force well in the greenhouse. Roses bred for greenhouse use are referred to as "started eyes"; greater success will be achieved with them than with other roses.

Growing conditions. Grow roses at 6,000 to 10,000 footcandles. A light shading is often applied to the greenhouse covering during the summer to prevent the petals from burn-

RANUNCULUS ASIATICUS

RHODODENDRON SIMSII

ROSA (HYBRID TEA)

ROSMARINUS OFFICINALIS

ing. Night temperature for newly potted plants should be 50° F for two weeks to encourage root growth; after that, night temperature should be 58° to 60° F. Grow roses in a rich, well-drained, soilless medium that has a pH of 6.5. Roses grown for cutting flowers can be grown in pots or directly in the bench or on the floor of the greenhouse. Keep the medium evenly moist at all times. Fertilize every two weeks with 20-20-20 during spring, summer and fall, and once a month during winter.

Good air circulation is essential. Adding carbon dioxide to the atmosphere will increase flower production. It will take five to eight weeks for a rose to rebloom, depending on the variety and the time of year. Although it is not necessary, roses will benefit from being given a dormant period each year. To do this, withhold water completely for two to three months, and prune the plants to 18 to 24 inches. Roses that are not given a dormant period will usually need to be replaced in four years. Roses can be damaged by aphids, mites, nematodes, thrips and powdery mildew.

Propagation. Miniature roses are propagated by stem cuttings. Hybrid teas, grandifloras and floribundas are propagated by budding. Any type of rose can be propagated from seeds, but the plants will not come true to variety.

Rose see *Rosa*

Rosebay see *Nerium*

Rose geranium see *Pelargonium*

Rose mallow see *Hibiscus*

Rosemary see *Rosmarinus*

Rosmarinus (ros-ma-RY-nus)
Rosemary

Flowering plant in the mint family that is grown in the greenhouse as a decorative plant or as an herb for seasoning. Leaves are aromatic and needlelike; flowers are tubular and two-lipped and bloom in spikes from midwinter to early spring.

Selected species and varieties. *R. officinalis* grows 1 to 3 feet high. Leaves are ½ to 1½ inches long, dark green, shiny on the upper surfaces and fuzzy white on the undersides. Flowers are fragrant and usu-

ally blue or violet, but sometimes white or pink.

Growing conditions. Grow rosemary at 5,000 to 8,000 footcandles. Night temperature should be 50° to 55° F. Grow in well-drained, soilless medium and allow it to dry out between waterings. Fertilize every two months from midspring to midfall with 20-20-20. Pinch growing tips to keep the plants compact. Leaves may be cut off at any time and used fresh or dried in cooking. Rosemary is generally insect-free, but it is susceptible to root rot.

Propagation. Propagate rosemary from seeds or by stem cuttings taken in spring or summer.

Rubber plant see *Ficus*

Sago palm see *Cycas*

Saintpaulia (saint-PAUL-ee-a)
African violet

Flowering plant in the gesneriad family that grows 4 to 6 inches high and has rosettes of hairy, heart-shaped, green, bronze or mottled leaves. The flowers, which resemble violets, are white, pink, rose, blue, purple or two-toned. Blooms may be single or double, and some varieties have ruffled or frilled petals.

Selected species and varieties. *S. ionantha* has 2½-inch leaves and 1-inch flowers. There are many hybrids, including the Ballet and the Optimara series, which resemble the species but are more free-flowering. Plants bloom most abundantly from summer to fall, but will bloom all year if there is sufficient light.

Growing conditions. Grow African violet at 1,000 to 2,000 footcandles. The plants should be placed in a shaded section of the greenhouse during the summer. Night temperature should be 65° to 70° F. Grow in well-drained, soilless medium to which extra peat moss has been added. Keep the medium evenly moist. Water only with warm water to prevent leaf distortion; never allow water to touch the foliage, or the leaves will become spotted. Fertilize weekly with quarter-strength 20-20-20 when the plants are actively growing and flowering. Humidity should be 60 to 70 percent. Good air circulation is essential. When planting, make sure that the crown of the plant is on or above the surface of the medium to prevent crown rot.

Leaves that touch the rim of the pot are often killed by their contact with the soluble salts that build up on the rim. Coating the rim with paraffin or aluminum foil will prevent this. African violet is susceptible to aphids, mealybugs, mites, thrips, botrytis blight, crown rot and root rot.

Propagation. Propagate African violet by division, by leaf cuttings or from seeds.

Sarracenia (sar-a-SEE-nee-a)
Pitcher plant

Plant in the pitcher plant family that is grown in the greenhouse as a curiosity. The roots are rhizomatous. Leaves are tubular or trumpet-shaped and grow from a basal rosette. The leaves end in a broad hood that holds water; hence the name pitcher plant. Flowers are nodding and appear on leafless stems.

Selected species and varieties. *S. purpurea*, common pitcher plant, has 12-inch leaves that are veined in red or purplish red. Flowers are purple or green and 2½ inches across.

Growing conditions. Grow pitcher plant at 4,000 to 8,000 footcandles. Night temperature should be 40° to 45° F. Grow in sphagnum peat moss and keep it constantly wet by placing the pot in a saucer of water. Plants should not be fertilized. Humidity should be at least 70 percent. Pitcher plant may be grown inside a sealed glass container to keep humidity high. There are no insects or diseases that attack pitcher plant.

Propagation. Pitcher plant is propagated by division or from seeds.

Saxifraga (saks-IF-ra-ga)

Member of the saxifrage family that has varying growth habits and foliage. Flowers bloom in airy, nodding clusters in late spring and summer.

Selected species and varieties. *S. stolonifera*, strawberry geranium, mother of thousands, has hairy, round, scalloped, 3- to 4-inch leaves that grow in a rosette at the base of the plant. The leaves are dark green and have silver veins and red undersides. The plants produce runners that grow up to 24 inches long; small plants form at the ends of the runners. Strawberry geranium is an ex-

cellent plant for a hanging basket. Flowers are 1 inch across and white, and appear on thin stems.

Growing conditions. Grow strawberry geranium at 4,000 to 6,000 footcandles. Plants should be placed in a shaded section of the greenhouse during the summer. Night temperature should be 45° to 60° F. Grow in well-drained, soilless medium and keep it evenly moist from spring through fall. In winter, allow the soil to dry out slightly between waterings. Fertilize with 20-20-20 every two months from spring through fall. Maintain humidity at 60 to 70 percent. Strawberry geranium is generally insect-free; it is susceptible to root rot disease.

Propagation. Propagate strawberry geranium from seeds, by division or from the plantlets that form at the ends of the runners.

Schefflera see *Brassaia*

Schlumbergera
(shlum-BER-je-ra)

Flowering plant in the cactus family. This plant is included in a group known as jungle cacti because it requires higher humidity, more water and richer soil than desert cacti. Branches are flat and made up of 1½- to 2-inch jointed segments. Flowers are drooping; white, pink, red, lavender, purple or orange; and, depending on the species, bloom in fall or winter. Flowers are 3 inches long and tubular, with flaring petals opening into a cup or funnel shape.

Selected species and varieties. *S. bridgesii*, Christmas cactus, has branches made up of 2-inch segments that have rounded margins. It naturally blooms during the winter. *S. truncata*, Thanksgiving cactus, has branches made up of 2-inch segments that have pointed or toothed margins. It naturally blooms in the fall.

Growing conditions. Grow Christmas cactus and Thanksgiving cactus at 2,000 to 4,000 footcandles. Plants should be placed in a shaded part of the greenhouse during the summer. Night temperature should be 65° to 70° F from early spring to fall, 50° to 55° F until flower buds form in fall, and 60° to 65° F from the time buds form until the plants have finished flowering. Grow in well-drained, soilless medium to which

SAINTPAULIA IONANTHA

SARRACENIA PURPUREA

SAXIFRAGA STOLONIFERA

SCHLUMBERGERA TRUNCATA

SEDUM MORGANIANUM

SENECIO ROWLEYANUS

peat moss has been added. Keep the medium evenly moist at all times until the temperature is lowered in fall. Then let the medium dry out between waterings until flower buds appear, when regular watering should be resumed. If the medium is too dry after flower buds form, the buds will drop. Moving the plant after buds have formed will also cause buds to drop. Fertilize monthly with 10-20-20 in spring and summer, and when the plant is flowering.

To force a Christmas cactus to bloom by Christmas, lower the temperature on September 15 and cover the plant with black shade cloth or black polyethylene for 16 hours per night until October 10. To ensure that Thanksgiving cactus blooms by Thanksgiving, lower the temperature on August 15 and cover the plant with black shade cloth or black polyethylene for 12 hours each night until September 10.

Spider mites, rot and wilt diseases may damage either plant.

Propagation. Thanksgiving cactus and Christmas cactus are propagated by stem cuttings taken in spring, by grafting or from seeds.

—

Sea-urchin cactus
see *Echinopsis*

—

Sedum (SEE-dum)
Stonecrop

Large genus of succulent plants with variable plant habits and foliage, one species of which is grown in the greenhouse in a hanging basket.

Selected species and varieties. *S. morganianum,* burro's tail, has 18- to 36-inch trailing branches that are densely covered with plump, cylindrical, pointed, blue-green, 1- to 1½-inch leaves. The leaves are covered with a whitish dust known as a "bloom."

Growing conditions. Grow burro's tail at 4,000 to 6,000 footcandles. Night temperature should be 50° to 55° F. Grow in soilless medium to which coarse sand or perlite has been added to ensure excellent drainage. In spring, summer and fall, allow the medium to dry out slightly between waterings. In winter, water only enough to keep the foliage from withering. Do not fertilize newly potted plants for four to six months; fertilize established plants with 20-20-20

once a month during spring and summer. Leaves will fall from the plant if it is disturbed. Burro's tail may be damaged by mealybugs, spider mites, scales, rot and wilt diseases.

Propagation. Burro's tail is propagated by rooting the leaves.

—

Senecio (se-NEE-see-o)

A genus of plants that belong to the composite family, that may be bushing or vining, and may be annual or perennial. All species produce daisy-like or buttonlike flowers, but in the greenhouse several species are grown in hanging baskets, primarily for their foliage.

Selected species and varieties. *S. macroglossus,* Natal ivy, wax vine, has trailing, 12- to 18-inch branches. Foliage is waxy, leathery, 1½ to 2½ inches across and three- to five-lobed, resembling ivy. Flowers are yellow, daisylike and 1 inch across. 'Variegatum' has green leaves with creamy white margins. *S. mikanioides,* parlor ivy, German ivy, has 12- to 18-inch branches. Foliage is thin, soft, 2 to 4 inches across and five- to seven-lobed, resembling ivy. Flowers are buttonlike, ¼ to ½ inch across, yellow and fragrant, and appear in clusters. *S. rowleyanus,* string-of-beads, has thin, 2- to 3-foot branches. Leaves are ¼ inch across, round and resemble beads. There is a thin, translucent band across each leaf. Flowers are buttonlike, ¼ to ½ inch across, purple or white, fragrant, and appear in clusters.

Growing conditions. Grow Natal ivy and string-of-beads at 4,000 to 6,000 footcandles; grow parlor ivy at 2,000 to 4,000 footcandles. Night temperature should be 50° to 60° F. Grow in soilless medium to which coarse sand or perlite has been added to ensure excellent drainage. In spring, summer and fall, allow the medium to dry out slightly between waterings. In winter, water only enough to keep the plant from withering. Do not fertilize newly potted plants for three to four months; fertilize established plants monthly from spring through fall with 20-20-20. Pinch the growing tips to keep the plants compact. Aphids and spider mites are the insects that most commonly attack senecio.

Propagation. Propagate Natal ivy, parlor ivy and string-of-beads by stem cuttings or from seeds. String-of-beads may also be propagated by leaf cuttings.

—

Shrub verbena see *Lantana*
Silver-nerve plant see *Fittonia*
Snapdragon see *Antirrhinum*
Snowflower see *Spathiphyllum*

—

Solanum (so-LAY-num)

Genus of plants in the nightshade family that are grown either as a source of food or as decorative plants.

Selected species and varieties. *S. pseudocapsicum,* Jerusalem cherry, is a shrubby plant that grows 12 to 18 inches tall. Leaves are dark green, glossy, oval and 2 to 4 inches long. Flowers are ½ inch across, star-shaped, white and bloom in summer. Fruits are ½ inch across, round and green, ripening first to yellow and then to red. Plants are grown to produce fruits for the winter holidays. The fruits are poisonous.

Growing conditions. Grow Jerusalem cherry at 3,000 to 5,000 footcandles. Night temperature should be 55° to 60° F in late winter and spring. Plants should be moved outdoors into a protected spot during the summer for maximum fruit set, and then returned indoors to a night temperature of 50° to 55° F until after the fruits have dropped. Grow in well-drained, soilless medium and keep it evenly moist at all times. Fertilize once a month during spring and summer with 10-20-20. Plants can be pinched until early summer to keep them compact. After the fruits have dropped, cut the plants back to 6 inches. Plants are generally discarded after the second year. Aphids, thrips and mealybugs are the main problems of Jerusalem cherry.

Propagation. Jerusalem cherry is propagated from seeds sown in midwinter or by stem cuttings.

—

Soleirolia (so-le-RO-lee-a)

Creeping plant in the nettle family that has threadlike branches and is best grown in a hanging basket.

Selected species and varieties. *S. soleirolii,* formerly designated *Helxine soleirolii,* baby's tears, grows into a dense, mosslike mat that is 3 inches high. Leaves are bright green, round, ¼ inch across and hairy. The flowers are greenish and inconspicuous.

Growing conditions. Grow baby's tears at 3,000 to 4,000 footcandles. Night temperature should be 50° to 55° F. Grow in rich, well-drained, soilless medium and keep the medium constantly moist. Fertilize once in spring with 20-20-20. Maintain humidity at 60 to 70 percent. Baby's tears is not susceptible to insects or diseases.

Propagation. Propagate baby's tears by stem cuttings.

—

Spathe flower see *Spathiphyllum*

—

Spathiphyllum (spath-i-FIL-um)
Spathe flower

Flowering plant in the arum family. Leaves are shiny and oblong. The flowers are fragrant, white and tiny, and form along a tail-like structure called a spadix. The spadix is surrounded by a white or green bract called a spathe. Flowers appear most abundantly in spring and summer.

Selected species and varieties. *S. floribundum,* snowflower, grows 12 inches high. Leaves are dark green and satiny. The spathe is 3 inches long and white. *S.* × *hybridum* grows 30 inches tall. Narrow leaves are 10 inches long; the spathe is large and white, and has a green midrib on the underside. *S. wallisii* grows 12 to 18 inches high. Leaves are thin and narrow; the spathe is white when it first appears and matures to green.

Growing conditions. Grow spathe flower at 2,000 to 3,500 footcandles. Night temperature should be 65° to 70° F. Grow in well-drained, soilless medium and keep it evenly moist at all times. Fertilize with 20-20-20 every two months from spring through fall. Maintain humidity at 50 to 60 percent. Keep the foliage clean by frequent dusting or washing. Spathe flower is generally insect-free. It is susceptible to leaf spot diseases.

Propagation. Propagate spathe flower by division at any time of year.

—

Spiderwort see *Tradescantia*
Split-leaf philodendron see *Monstera*
Staghorn fern see *Platycerium*

SOLANUM PSEUDOCAPSICUM

SOLEIROLIA SOLEIROLII

SPATHIPHYLLUM × HYBRIDUM

STAPELIA NOBILIS

STEPHANOTIS FLORIBUNDA

STRELITZIA REGINAE

Stapelia (sta-PEE-lee-a)
Carrion flower, starfish flower

Flowering, succulent plant in the milkweed family. It has one or more fingerlike stems that are thick, fleshy, upright and usually leafless. The flowers are large, showy, often mottled or striped, five-pointed and resemble starfish. The flowers have an offensive odor.

Selected species and varieties. *S. hirsuta,* hairy toad plant, grows 8 inches high. The flowers are hairy, 4 to 5 inches across, dark purplish brown with cream-colored or yellow stripes, and grow from the bottom of the plant. *S. nobilis* has mustard yellow flowers with crimson ridges and fine purplish hairs. *S. pasadensis* has 5-inch, wine red flowers.

Growing conditions. Grow carrion flower at 5,000 to 8,000 footcandles. It will tolerate less light, but will not flower. Night temperature should be 60° to 65° F. Grow in soilless medium to which coarse sand or perlite has been added to ensure excellent drainage. From spring through fall, let the medium dry out slightly between waterings. In winter, water only enough to keep the plant from shriveling. Fertilize monthly with 20-20-20 in spring and summer. Carrion flower may attract flying insects when it is in bloom, but the insects may not do any damage. It is susceptible to rot diseases.

Propagation. Carrion flower is propagated by cuttings taken in summer or by seeds sown in spring.

—

Star cluster see *Pentas*
Starfish flower see *Stapelia*
Starfish plant see *Cryptanthus*
Star jasmine
see *Trachelospermum*

—

Stephanotis (stef-a-NOT-is)

Vining, flowering plant in the milkweed family that has leathery leaves and funnel-shaped, five-lobed flowers that bloom in racemes.

Selected species and varieties. *S. floribunda,* Madagascar jasmine, grows 10 to 15 feet tall. Leaves are oval, pointed, 2 to 4 inches long, thick, shiny and dark green. Flowers are waxy, fragrant, white, 1 to 2 inches long, and bloom in 4- to 6-inch racemes during spring and summer.

Growing conditions. Grow Madagascar jasmine at 5,000 to 8,000 footcandles. Night temperature should be 60° to 65° F. Grow in well-drained, soilless medium and keep it evenly moist from midspring to midfall. From midfall to midspring, allow the medium to dry out slightly between waterings. Fertilize with 20-20-20 once a month from midspring to midfall. Maintain humidity at 60 to 70 percent. Madagascar jasmine needs to be supported on a trellis or on wires. Plants may be pinched back to keep them bushy. Floodlights may be turned on for four hours during the night in winter to encourage the plants to bloom. Mealybugs, nematodes and scales are the insects that most commonly attack Madagascar jasmine.

Propagation. Propagate Madagascar jasmine by stem cuttings at any time of year or from seeds.

—

Stock see *Matthiola*
Stonecrop see *Sedum*
Strawberry geranium
see *Saxifraga*

—

Strelitzia (stre-LIT-zee-a)
Bird-of-paradise

Flowering plant in the strelitzia family that has clumps of large, erect leaves and showy flowers that bloom in summer and fall. The flowers resemble birds' heads.

Selected species and varieties. *S. reginae* grows 3 to 6 feet tall. Leaves are 1 to 1½ feet long, stiff, oblong, leathery and blue-green, and have a yellow or red midrib. Flowers have yellow or orange petals and a deep blue tongue, and grow from a green, boatlike bract that is edged in purple or red.

Growing conditions. Grow bird-of-paradise at 4,000 to 6,000 footcandles. Night temperature should be 50° to 55° F. Grow in well-drained, soilless medium. From spring through fall, keep the medium barely moist; in winter, allow the medium to dry out slightly between waterings. Fertilize with 20-20-20 every two weeks in spring and summer. Maintain humidity at 60 to 70 percent. Bird-of-paradise is susceptible to damage from mealybugs, scales and root rot disease.

Propagation. Bird-of-paradise is propagated by division in the spring or from seeds. Seeds are not long-lived and must be sown immediately. They may take six months or more to germinate and plants will not reach blooming size for several years.

—

Streptocarpus
(strep-toh-KAR-pus)
Cape primrose

Flowering plant in the gesneriad family that has trumpet-shaped, five-lobed flowers. Blooms may appear at any time of year but they occur most abundantly in late spring through fall.

Selected species and varieties. *S.* × *hybridus* has basal rosettes of 10- to 12-inch, oblong, scalloped, wrinkled leaves. Flowers are 2 to 5 inches long and bloom on 6-inch leafless stems. Blooms are white, pink, rose, red, blue or purple, often with a contrasting color in the throat.

Growing conditions. Grow Cape primrose at 3,000 to 5,000 footcandles. Night temperature should be 60° to 70° F. Grow in well-drained, soilless medium and keep it evenly moist in spring, summer and fall. Plants will usually go dormant in winter; then, soil should be allowed to dry out between waterings. Fertilize with 20-20-20 every two weeks during spring and summer. Maintain humidity at 50 to 60 percent. Grow Cape primrose in shallow pots to avoid root rot. Aphids, mealybugs and thrips may attack Cape primrose.

Propagation. Propagate Cape primrose by division during winter, by leaf cuttings in spring and summer, and from seeds in winter and spring.

—

String-of-beads see *Senecio*

Sundew see *Drosera*

Swedish ivy see *Plectranthus*

Sword fern see *Nephrolepis*

Table fern see *Pteris*

Tailflower see *Anthurium*

Thanksgiving cactus
see *Schlumbergera*

—

Thunbergia (thun-BER-jee-a)

Erect or vining plant in the acanthus family that has flowers with five rounded lobes.

Selected species and varieties. *T. alata*, black-eyed Susan vine, grows 2 to 6 feet long. Leaves are oval to triangular, toothed and 1 to 3 inches long. Flowers are 1 to 2 inches across and have thin, creamy white, yellow or orange petals. Flowers have dark purple or black centers and appear in spring and summer.

Growing conditions. Grow black-eyed Susan vine at 5,000 to 8,000 footcandles. Night temperature should be 50° to 60° F. Grow in well-drained, soilless medium and allow it to dry out slightly between waterings when the plant is growing. When the plant starts flowering, increase watering to keep the medium evenly moist. Fertilize every two weeks during spring and summer with 20-20-20. Maintain humidity at 50 to 60 percent. Remove flowers as they fade to extend the blooming period. Black-eyed Susan vine may be grown on a trellis or in a hanging basket. Mealybugs and scales are the insects that most commonly attack black-eyed Susan vine.

Propagation. Propagate black-eyed Susan vine from seeds. Plants will flower from seed in six months.

—

Thyme see *Thymus*

—

Thymus (THY-mus)
Thyme

Shrubby plant in the mint family that has square stems, creeping branches, small aromatic leaves, and clusters of bell-shaped white, blue or lilac flowers.

Selected species and varieties. *T. vulgaris*, common thyme, grows 6 to 15 inches high and wide. Leaves are narrow, ½ inch long and grow on wiry stems. Flowers are ¼ inch long, white or lilac, and bloom in spring and summer. Leaves are used fresh or dried as an herb.

Growing conditions. Grow thyme at 4,000 to 6,000 footcandles. Night temperature should be 45° to 55° F. Grow in well-drained, soilless medium and keep it evenly moist in spring, summer and fall. In winter, let the medium become dry between waterings. Fertilize monthly with 20-20-20 during spring and summer. Cut plants back to 6 inches in late winter before growth starts. Harvest leaves for use in cooking at any time. Thyme is susceptible to mealybugs, botrytis blight and root rot.

STREPTOCARPUS × HYBRIDUS

THUNBERGIA ALATA

THYMUS VULGARIS

TOLMIEA MENZIESII

TRACHELOSPERMUM JASMINOIDES

Propagation. Thyme is propagated by division in spring, by cuttings in summer or from seeds sown in spring.

▬

Tolmiea (TOL-mee-a)

Member of the saxifrage family that forms a clump of heart-shaped, lobed, hairy leaves. Flowers are greenish white or reddish brown and inconspicuous.

Selected species and varieties. *T. menziesii,* pickaback plant, grows 6 to 12 inches high and wide. Leaves are bright green and 4 inches across. The plant rarely flowers, but when it does, blooms appear in summer. New plants form at the base of the leaves.

Growing conditions. Grow pickaback plant at 3,000 to 4,500 footcandles. Night temperature should be 40° to 55° F for best growth, but pickaback plant will tolerate night temperatures of up to 65° F. Humidity should be increased at higher temperatures. Grow in well-drained, soilless medium and keep it evenly moist from spring through fall. In winter, allow the medium to become dry between waterings. Fertilize monthly during spring and summer with 20-20-20. Pickaback plant may be damaged by mealybugs.

Propagation. Propagate pickaback plant by potting the small plantlets that form at the base of the leaves.

▬

Tomato see *Lycopersicon*

▬

Trachelospermum
(tra-ke-lo-SPER-mum)
Star jasmine, Confederate jasmine

Vining plant in the dogbane family that has milky sap and loose clusters of very fragrant, tubular, star-shaped flowers.

Selected species and varieties. *T. jasminoides* grows to 8 feet tall. Leaves are oblong, leathery, shiny, long-stalked and 2½ to 4 inches long. Flowers are white and ½ to 1 inch across. Blooms appear most abundantly in spring and summer.

Growing conditions. Grow star jasmine at 2,000 to 4,000 foot-

candles. Night temperature should be 50° to 55° F. Grow in well-drained, soilless medium and allow the medium to become slightly dry between waterings. Fertilize every two to three months with half-strength 20-20-20. Star jasmine should be trained to a trellis or other support. To keep the plant compact, pinch growing tips. Star jasmine may be attacked by scales and whiteflies.

Propagation. Propagate star jasmine by stem cuttings taken at any time.

▬

Tradescantia
(trad-e-SKAN-shi-a)
Spiderwort

Erect or trailing plant in the spiderwort family. The bases of the leaves surround the stem. It is grown in the greenhouse as a foliage plant, but occasionally produces blue, rose, purple or white single flowers.

Selected species and varieties. *T. fluminensis,* wandering Jew, has stems that grow 12 to 24 inches long. Leaves are oval, pointed, 1½ inches long, green on the upper surfaces and purple on the undersides. Flowers are white. *T. sillamontana,* white velvet plant, has 8-inch stems. Leaves are elliptical and 2½ inches long. Flowers are rose- to magenta-colored. The leaves and the branches are covered with soft, white hairs.

Growing conditions. Grow spiderwort at 3,000 to 6,000 footcandles. Night temperature should be 50° to 60° F. Grow in well-drained, soilless medium; during spring, summer and fall, keep the medium evenly moist. In winter, allow the medium to dry out slightly between waterings. Fertilize every two weeks during spring and summer with 20-20-20. Pinch growing tips to keep the plant compact. Spiderwort grows best in a hanging basket. It is susceptible to aphids, botrytis blight and root rot.

Propagation. Propagate spiderwort by division, by stem cuttings or from seeds.

▬

Trailing begonia see *Cissus*
Transvaal daisy see *Gerbera*
Tree fern see *Cyathea*
Tree ivy see *Fatshedera*

Tropaeolum (tro-PEE-o-lum)
Nasturtium

Member of the nasturtium family that may be bushy or vining, annual or perennial. Leaves are lobed and flowers are yellow, orange or red.

Selected species and varieties. *T. majus* is an annual that has round, dull green, long-stalked, 2- to 7-inch leaves. Flowers are 2½ to 3½ inches across, fragrant, single or double, and sometimes spotted or striped. Depending on the variety, plants may be bushy or vining. The double-flowered forms are sometimes used for cutting flowers. Nasturtium is best grown to flower from midfall to midspring because it does not grow well in summer heat. Flower buds and seeds are used as seasoning; leaves may be used in salads.

Growing conditions. Grow nasturtium at 4,000 to 8,000 footcandles. Night temperature should be 45° to 50° F. Grow in well-drained, soilless medium and keep it evenly moist at all times. Fertilize every two weeks with half-strength 20-20-20 after the flower buds have formed. Vining types may be grown in hanging baskets and should be pinched to keep them compact. After the plant has finished flowering, it should be discarded. Aphids, mites and thrips may attack nasturtium.

Propagation. Propagate nasturtium from seeds. Plants will flower within six months.

—

Tulip see *Tulipa*

—

Tulipa (TOO-li-pa)
Tulip

Spring-flowering bulb in the lily family that can be forced in the greenhouse for winter and early-spring bloom. Foliage is dull green, long and pointed, and grows from the base of the plant and along the flower stems. Flowers may be single or double and are available in all colors. Bulbs are forced for potted plants and for cutting flowers.

Selected species and varieties. Hybrid tulips are classified in 15 groups by their shape, time of bloom or species derivation; those most commonly used for forcing are cottage, Darwin, double early and double late tulips. Cottage tulips are single and have egg-shaped flowers. They grow 1½ to 2½ feet high.

Darwin tulips are single and have flowers with square bases. They grow 2 to 3 feet high. Double early and double late tulips have double flowers and grow 8 to 16 inches high. They differ only in their blooming time, the double early blooming prior to the double late.

Growing conditions. Tulips can be forced to bloom if they are planted in a pot and then given a cold treatment so they will develop roots and embryonic flowers. Plant five or six bulbs in a 6-inch pot, and arrange them so that the flattened side of each is against the inside wall of the pot (this is because the first leaves emerge from the flat side and will cascade over the rim of the pot). The tips of the bulbs should be just below the surface of the growing medium for potted plants, and 1 inch below the surface for flowers that are to be used for cuttings. Water the medium well. Then place the pot in an area where temperatures are between 35° and 45° F for 12 weeks or until roots protrude from the drainage holes. Keep the medium moist throughout.

Some bulbs are sold prechilled, which means they have been given a partial cold treatment by the nursery. The gardener will need to give such prechilled bulbs an additional chilling for about five weeks after potting them. When the cold treatment is completed, the bulbs may be moved into the greenhouse, or they may be kept at 33° to 35° F until the gardener is ready to force them.

Grow tulips at 4,000 to 8,000 footcandles. Bulbs forced to bloom from January to mid-February should be covered with newspaper or black cloth for several days as soon as they are brought into the greenhouse to encourage stretching of the stems. If you are forcing bulbs for cutting flowers, night temperature should be 55° F for two weeks; then night temperature should be raised to 58° to 60° F. If you are forcing bulbs for potted plants, night temperature should be 63° F. Day temperature should be no more than five degrees higher or stems will be weak. Grow in well-drained, soilless medium with a pH of 6.0, and keep the medium evenly moist. Tulips grown for cutting flowers may be grown in pots or directly in the greenhouse bench. Fertilize weekly, alternating 20-20-20 and calcium nitrate; calcium is needed to prevent a disease known as tulip topple, which causes the flower stalks to fall over. Tall plants need to be staked. Tulips will bloom within three weeks of being moved into the greenhouse. Tulips cannot be suc-

TRADESCANTIA SILLAMONTANA

TROPAEOLUM MAJUS

TULIPA (DARWIN TULIP)

147

VANDA TRICOLOR

VRIESEA CARINATA

cessfully reforced but can be moved to the garden to rebloom naturally. Tulips attract aphids and mites. They are susceptible to botrytis blight and virus diseases.

Propagation. Tulips can be propagated by removing and potting the bulblets that form around the base of the bulb, but bulblets take several years to grow to full size and may never develop into satisfactory plants. Greater success will be achieved by purchasing new bulbs each year.

—

Umbrella sedge see *Cyperus*
Urn plant see *Aechmea*

—

Vanda (VAN-da)

Flowering plant in the orchid family. Leaves may be either strap-shaped or cylindrical. Flowers have five usually round petals and three-lobed lips that have short spurs. They are usually flat, and some vandas have ruffled petals. Flower color may be white, brown, green, yellow, pink, lavender or blue; petals are checkered, dotted or striped. Blooms appear in clusters at the tops of erect stems at any time of year. Vandas produce many aerial roots that help to keep the plants supplied with moisture.

Selected species and varieties. *V. cristata* grows 3 feet tall. Leaves are oblong, narrow and 4 inches long. Flowers are 2 inches across and olive green or yellow; the lip is blotched in brownish purple. The petals are curled or drooping. Bloom is most abundant in spring. *V. × rothschildiana* grows 3 feet tall. Leaves are strap-shaped and 8 inches long. The flowers are flat, round, 3 to 6 inches across, and blue or purplish blue. Bloom is most abundant in fall and winter. *V. tricolor* has 18-inch leaves and fragrant, fleshy, 3-inch flowers that are yellow spotted with reddish brown. Vanda hybrids are the orchids used in Hawaiian leis. Flowers are flat, and primarily white or pink.

Growing conditions. Grow vanda at 4,000 to 8,000 footcandles. Night temperature should be 60° to 65° F. Grow in a special orchid-potting medium, or in soilless medium with extra fir or redwood bark added. Fertilize weekly with 10-10-10. Stop fertilizing if plants do not bloom at the expected time. Keep the medium evenly moist at all times. As the bark in the medium breaks down over time, plants should be repotted at least every two years in spring or summer. Plants in fresh bark medium will need watering more often than plants in older medium, which retains more moisture. Humidity should be 60 to 80 percent to prevent leaf burn. In summer, mist plants in the morning. Constant air circulation is a necessity. Vandas are best grown in wooden-slatted hanging baskets so their aerial roots will hang freely. They benefit from being placed outdoors during the summer and returned inside just before the first frost. Scales, slugs, snails and virus diseases may damage vandas.

Propagation. Propagate vanda by division, by air layering, by potting the offshoots or from seeds.

—

Venezuela treebine see *Cissus*
Venus flytrap see *Dionaea*

—

Vriesea (VREE-see-a)

Flowering plant in the bromeliad family that has strap-shaped, stiff leaves that appear in a dense basal rosette. The foliage is frequently banded or variegated in red or brown. Flowers bloom in flat spikes and are long-lasting.

Selected species and varieties. *V. carinata,* lobster claws, grows 12 inches high. Leaves are pale green and 8 inches long. The blooming spikes consist of overlapping, deep yellow bracts that have a red base, and yellow flowers. The plant blooms in summer.

Growing conditions. Grow lobster claws at 3,000 to 5,000 footcandles. Night temperature should be 60° to 65° F. Grow in well-drained, loose, soilless medium with extra bark chips, osmunda fiber or coarse perlite added. Keep the medium evenly moist, and keep the cup at the base of the plant filled with water. Fertilize monthly with half-strength 20-20-20, adding the fertilizer solution to the water in the cup. There are commercial products available to induce flowering. After the plant has flowered, it will die, but it is quickly replaced by offsets that form at the base of the original plant. Lobster claws is usually not bothered by insects or diseases, but it is susceptible to scales, mealybugs, mites and crown rot.

Propagation. Propagate lobster claws by removing and planting the offsets that grow at the base of the plant after it flowers.

—

Wandering Jew
see *Tradescantia; Zebrina*

Warty aloe see *Gasteria*

Wax vine see *Senecio*

Weeping fig see *Ficus*

White velvet plant
see *Tradescantia*

Windowleaf see *Monstera*

Wood sorrel see *Oxalis*

Yellow jessamine see *Gelsemium*

Yellow palm see *Chrysalidocarpus*

Yellow sage see *Lantana*

—

Zantedeschia
(zan-te-DES-kee-a)
Calla lily

Flowering plant in the arum family that grows from rhizomatous roots and has arrow-shaped leaves. Tiny flowers appear on a tail-like structure called a spadix. Encircling the spadix is a bract called a spathe. The spathe flares at the top, and the edges curve backward. Blooms appear in fall, winter and spring. Calla lily is grown as a potted plant and for cutting flowers.

Selected species and varieties. *Z. aethiopica,* florist's calla, grows 3 feet high and has leaves that are 18 inches long. The spathe is 5 to 10 inches long and white; the spadix has yellow, fragrant flowers. 'Childsiana' is similar but grows 18 inches high. *Z. elliottiana,* golden calla, grows 2 feet tall and has leaves that are 12 inches long. The foliage is spotted in white. The spathe is 6 inches long, bright yellow on the inside and greenish yellow on the outside. *Z. rehmannii,* pink calla, grows 2 feet high and has narrow, 12-inch leaves that are sometimes spotted in white. The spathe is 5 inches long and pink, rose or purple.

Growing conditions. Grow calla lily at 5,000 to 8,000 footcandles. In summer, place plants in a shaded part of the greenhouse so light intensity is not higher than 5,000 footcandles. Night temperature should be 55° F for florist's calla and 60° F for golden and pink calla. Grow in rich, well-drained, soilless medium that is kept constantly moist. Fertilize monthly with 20-20-20 after flowers appear. Some growers allow the plants to go dormant during the summer months, but there is no evidence that this is necessary. Calla lilies attract mealybugs, mites and thrips, and are susceptible to root rot.

Propagation. Propagate calla lily by division in late summer, by offsets or from seeds.

—

Zebrina (ze-BREE-na)

Vining, succulent plant in the spiderwort family. The base of the leaf surrounds the stem. Zebrina is grown in the greenhouse as a foliage plant, but occasionally produces single pink flowers.

Selected species and varieties. *Z. pendula,* wandering Jew, has stems that grow 12 to 24 inches long. Leaves are oval to oblong, pointed, 3 inches long, green striped in silvery white on the upper surfaces and reddish purple on the undersides.

Growing conditions. Grow wandering Jew at 3,000 to 6,000 footcandles. Night temperature should be 60° to 65° F. Grow in well-drained, soilless medium; during spring, summer and fall, keep the medium evenly moist. In winter, let the medium dry out slightly between waterings. Fertilize every two weeks during spring and summer with 20-20-20. Plants do best when humidity is 60 to 70 percent. Pinch growing tips to keep plants compact. Wandering Jew does best in a hanging basket. Wandering Jew attracts aphids and is susceptible to botrytis blight and root rot.

Propagation. Propagate wandering Jew by division, by stem cuttings or from seeds.

ZANTEDESCHIA AETHIOPICA

ZEBRINA PENDULA

149

PICTURE CREDITS

ACKNOWLEDGMENTS

The index for this book was prepared by Lee McKee.
The editors also wish to thank: Virginia Blakelock, Hobby Greenhouse Association, Bedford, Massachusetts; Sarah Brash, Alexandria, Virginia; Sarah Broley, Washington, D.C.; Daniel Chiplis, National Bonsai Collection, U.S. National Arboretum, Washington, D.C.; Louise Coleman, Eastchester, New York; Henry R. Fisher, Mifflin, Pennsylvania; Betsy Frankel, Alexandria, Virginia; Ralph Freeman, Suffolk County Cooperative Extension, Riverhead, New York; Leon E. Greene, Fairfax, Virginia; Kenneth Hancock, Annandale, Virginia; Peter Haring, Shreveport, Louisiana; Becky and Brent Heath, The Daffodil Mart, Glouster, Virginia; Kurt Hoppmann, Hoppmann Corporation, Chantilly, Virginia; Dr. Ken Horst, Department of Plant Pathology, Cornell University, Ithaca, New York; Gordon Jones, Planting Fields Arboretum, Oyster Bay, New York; Barbara Kaufman-Cate, New York, New York; Robert P. Kiener, Washington, D.C.; Carolyn Mack, Paul Ecke Poinsettias, Encinitas, California; David Maudlin, Washington, D.C.; Thanh Huu Nguyen, Alexandria, Virginia; Phil Normandy, Brookside Gardens, Wheaton, Maryland; Rodger Robb, Northrup King Company, Golden Valley, Minnesota; Ken Roberts, Solar Designs, Inc., Frederick, Maryland; Jayne E. Rohrich, Alexandria, Virginia; Joseph Savage, Nassau County Cooperative Extension, Plainview, New York; Bob Schober, Leola, Pennsylvania; Joyce Stephen, Sunroom Company, Leola, Pennsylvania; Harriet Sweeney, Washington, D.C.; Dr. Allen Weinstein, Silver Spring, Maryland; Vickie York, Kettler Brothers, Inc., Gaithersburg, Maryland.

FURTHER READING

Bailey, Liberty Hyde, and Ethel Zoe Bailey, *Hortus Third: A Concise Dictionary of Plants Cultivated in the United States and Canada.* New York: Macmillan, 1976.

Boodley, James W., *The Commercial Greenhouse.* Albany, New York: Delmar Publishers, 1981.

Bubel, Nancy, *The Seed-Starter's Handbook.* Emmaus, Pennsylvania: Rodale Press, 1978.

Bush-Brown, James, and Louise Bush-Brown, *America's Garden Book.* New York: Charles Scribner's Sons, 1980.

Langhans, Robert W., *Greenhouse Management.* Ithaca, New York: Halcyon Press of Ithaca, 1980.

McCullagh, James C., ed., *The Solar Greenhouse Book.* Emmaus, Pennsylvania: Rodale Press, 1978.

Nelson, Paul V., *Greenhouse Operations and Management.* Reston, Virginia: Reston Publishing, 1985.

Nicholls, Richard E., *Beginning Hydroponics.* Philadelphia: Running Press, 1977.

Organic Gardening magazine, *The Encyclopedia of Organic Gardening.* Emmaus, Pennsylvania: Rodale Press, 1978.

Seddon, George, and Andrew Bicknell, *The Complete Guide to Conservatory Gardening.* Manchester, New Hampshire: Salem House Publishers, 1986.

Sessler, Gloria Jean, *Orchids and How to Grow Them.* Englewood Cliffs, New Jersey: Prentice Hall, 1978.

Smith, Miranda, *Greenhouse Gardening.* Emmaus, Pennsylvania: Rodale Press, 1985.

Sutherland, Struan K., *Hydroponics for Everyone.* Melbourne, Victoria, Australia: Hyland House, 1986.

Toogood, Alan, *Conservatories.* London: Ward Lock, 1987.

Toogood, Alan, ed., *Simple Greenhouse Gardening.* London: Ward Lock, 1987.

Williams, T. J., *How to Build and Use Greenhouses.* San Francisco: Ortho Books/Chevron Chemical Company, 1978.

Wyman, Donald, *Wyman's Gardening Encyclopedia.* New York: Macmillan, 1986.

INDEX

REDEFINITION

Senior Editors	Anne Horan, Robert G. Mason
Design Director	Robert Barkin
Designer	Edwina Smith
Illustration	Nicholas Fasciano
Assistant Designers	Sue Pratt, Monique Strawderman
Picture Editor	Deborah Thornton
Production Editor	Anthony K. Pordes
Editorial Research	Gail Prensky (volume coordinator), Barbara B. Smith, Mary Yee, Elizabeth D. McLean
Picture Research	Caroline N. Tell
Text Editor	Sharon Cygan
Writers	Gerald Jonas, Ann Reilly, David S. Thomson
Administrative Assistant	Margaret M. Higgins
Business Manager	Catherine M. Chase
Finance Director	Vaughn A. Meglan
PRESIDENT	Edward Brash

Time-Life Books Inc.
is a wholly owned subsidiary of

TIME INCORPORATED

Editor-in-Chief	Jason McManus
Chairman and Chief Executive Officer	J. Richard Munro
President and Chief Operating Officer	N. J. Nicholas Jr.
Editorial Director	Richard B. Stolley

THE TIME INC. BOOK COMPANY

President and Chief Executive Officer	Kelso F. Sutton
President, Time Inc. Books Direct	Christopher T. Linen

TIME-LIFE BOOKS INC.

EDITOR	George Constable
Executive Editor	Ellen Phillips
Director of Design	Louis Klein
Director of Editorial Resources	Phyllis K. Wise
Editorial Board	Russell B. Adams Jr., Dale M. Brown, Roberta Conlan, Thomas H. Flaherty, Lee Hassig, Donia Ann Steele, Rosalind Stubenberg
Director of Photography and Research	John Conrad Weiser
Assistant Director of Editorial Resources	Elise Ritter Gibson
PRESIDENT	John M. Fahey Jr.
Senior Vice Presidents	Robert M. DeSena, James L. Mercer, Paul R. Stewart, Joseph J. Ward
Vice Presidents	Stephen L. Bair, Stephen L. Goldstein, Juanita T. James, Andrew P. Kaplan, Carol Kaplan, Susan J. Maruyama, Robert H. Smith
Supervisor of Quality Control	James King

Editorial Operations

Copy Chief	Diane Ullius
Production	Celia Beattie
Library	Louise D. Forstall
Correspondents	Elisabeth Kraemer-Singh (Bonn), Christina Lieberman (New York), Maria Vincenza Aloisi (Paris), Ann Natanson (Rome)
PUBLISHER	Joseph J. Ward

THE CONSULTANTS

C. Colston Burrell is the series consultant for The Time-Life Gardener's Guide. He is Curator of Plant Collections at the Minnesota Landscape Arboretum, part of the University of Minnesota.

Wayne Ambler, consultant for Greenhouse Gardening, is a teacher of horticulture. He is a member of the adjunct faculty at J. Sargeant Reynolds Community College in Richmond and teaches also at Patrick Henry High School in Ashland, Virginia.

Library of Congress Cataloging-in-Publication Data
Greenhouse gardening.
    p. cm.—(The Time-Life gardener's guide)
    Bibliograpy: p.
    Includes index.
    ISBN 0-8094-6640-6.—ISBN 0-8094-6641-4 (lib. bdg.)
    1. Greenhouse gardening.   2. Greenhouse plants.
I. Time-Life Books. II. Series.
SB415.G73 1989 635.9'823—dc19 89-4395 CIP